Privilege and Diversity

in the Academy

Frances A. Maher ◆ Mary Kay Thompson Tetreault

Routledge
Taylor & Francis Group
New York   London

Routledge is an imprint of the
Taylor & Francis Group, an informa business

Routledge
Taylor & Francis Group
270 Madison Avenue
New York, NY 10016

Routledge
Taylor & Francis Group
2 Park Square
Milton Park, Abingdon
Oxon OX14 4RN

© 2007 by Frances Maher and Mary Kay Thompson Tetreault
Routledge is an imprint of Taylor & Francis Group, an Informa business

Printed in the United States of America on acid-free paper
10 9 8 7 6 5 4 3 2 1

International Standard Book Number-10: 0-415-94665-4 (Softcover) 0-415-94664-6 (Hardcover)
International Standard Book Number-13: 978-0-415-94665-0 (Softcover) 978-0-415-94664-3 (Hardcover)

Library of Congress Cataloging-in-Publication Data

Maher, Frances A.
   Privilege and diversity in the American academy / Frances Maher and Mary Kay Thompson Tetreault.
      p. cm.
   Includes bibliographical references.
   ISBN 0-415-94664-6 (hardback) -- ISBN 0-415-94665-4 (pbk.)
   1. Discrimination in higher education--United States--Case studies. 2. Faculty integration--United States--Case studies. 3. Minority college teachers--United States--Case studies. I. Tetreault, Mary Kay Thompson. II. Title.

LC212.42.M34 2006
378.1'9820973--dc22   2006014065

Visit the Taylor & Francis Web site at
http://www.taylorandfrancis.com

and the Routledge Web site at
http://www.routledge-ny.com

Contents

Dedication

To John McDermot
Frinde Maher

To Jewel Plummer Cobb
Mary Kay Tetreault

Acknowledgments

Over the six-year period that we have been working on this book we have benefited from the information, advice, and support of countless numbers of people at the three campuses of Stanford, the University of Michigan, and Rutgers University–Newark. In the course of arranging for over 100 interviews, only one person declined to see us, and in the course of checking quotations with our informants, only one person refused to be quoted. Some people were interviewed more than once and some were contacted again and again for purposes of accuracy. Everyone we worked with was friendly, courteous, patient, interested in the project, and helpful to the best of their knowledge and experience.

We lack the space to acknowledge each participant by name. However, we would like to especially thank some people at each campus who contributed in different ways to our ongoing analysis, offered up in the forms of case studies and drafts of sections and chapters. First of all, our gatekeepers — Alan Sadovnik at Rutgers University–Newark (RU–N), Carolyn Lougee and Frederic Stout at Stanford, and Julie Ellison and Abigail Stewart at Michigan — helped us negotiate our entries, and figure out whom to interview and how best to gain access to a wide range of informants. At Michigan, we would especially like to thank Mark Chesler and Patricia Gurin; Renato Rosaldo, James Gibbs, and Paula Moya at Stanford; and Charles Russell, Lillian Robbins, and Steven Diner at RU–N. Archivists and librarians at all three campuses helped us track down needed documents, particularly unpublished sources that were hard to find and even harder to sort through. Special thanks to Margaret Kimball and Michelle Futornick at Stanford, Janice Freedman at RU–N, Thomas Frusciano and Erika Gorder at Rutgers University – New Brunswick, and Francis Blouin at the Bentley Historical Archive at Michigan.

There were many colleagues outside our three campuses with whom we spoke, shared drafts of material, and asked questions. We learned a great deal from them about ways to write about privilege and diversity in universities. They include Jill Tarule, Ellen Schrecker, Nancy Porter, James R. (Dick) Pratt, and the Portland (OR) Feminist Research Group. Catherine Bernard from Routledge and Judith Simon of Taylor & Francis provided helpful editorial suggestions.

For awarding her the Keiter Faculty Chair, a position she held from 2001–2006, Frinde Maher would like to especially thank Wheaton College. Support from the Chair included a financial stipend and course releases for the six-year period during which the book was researched and written, and it is impossible to imagine the completion of the project without it. She would also like to thank family, friends, and colleagues for their patience throughout this whole process. Vicki Bartolini and Mary Lee Griffin have shouldered far more than their share of departmental responsibilities in the Education Department at Wheaton College, always with enthusiasm and encouragement and without once complaining about her absences. Six years is a long time in terms of family as well, during which family deaths, weddings, and births of grandchildren have been important markers. Her sister Abby Record, daughter Sarah Maher and son-in-law Steve Dembitzer, and her son Matthew Maher not only provided welcome relief, support, and company at the times when she needed them, but patience, forbearance, and understanding during the times when they needed her. And Louisa and Alex Dembitzer, now ages 4 and 2, are sources of constant stimulation and delight.

Frinde owes her deepest thanks to her husband and life partner of 15 years, John McDermott. He does the grocery shopping and cooking and much of the household maintenance — a wood stove in the winter, a garden in the summer, a 200-yard driveway all year long. Much more importantly, his intellectual and emotional understanding and support have been crucial. A writer himself, he understands about plugging away day after day, and about all the ups and downs of the process of writing a book. Frinde is the constant beneficiary, in this project and in life, of his patience, his humor, his teasing, his encouragement, and his love. This book is dedicated to him.

Mary Kay Tetreault would like to thank the faculty members and administrators who taught her much of what she knows about the workings of universities, the "meaning making" within them, and the imperative of diversity during the 17 years she served as dean or chief academic officer at California State University, Fullerton, and Portland State University (PSU). The book's dedication to Jewel Plummer Cobb, who served as president of CSU, Fullerton, arises from all she taught her about enlightened administration and the workings of gender and race. Dr. Cobb, a biologist, an educational administrator, and an inspiration to many, personifies the value of linking excellence and diversity. Mary Kay is also indebted to the Office of Research and Sponsored Projects at PSU, and especially William Feyerherm, for support for her research as well as the Centre for Research and Teaching on Women at McGill University, where she spent the 2005-2006 academic year as a Visiting Scholar.

Mary Kay especially thanks her husband Marc and her daughter Chantal, who always conveyed that this work was worth doing as well as extending their love and support.

Finally, without our collaboration there would be no book. We have learned, first while working on *The Feminist Classroom* and now this book, of the importance of working through difficult ideas, being patiently committed to "getting it right," and sustaining one another's involvement at every point in this long process. When an interview did not quite go as planned, or someone says something outrageous, with whom does a solitary author have a laugh?

1

Frameworks of Analysis:
Histories and Theories of Privilege

I am a first-generation college person myself. My parents didn't go to college. So on one level I share feelings with some people from under-represented backgrounds who, the research shows, both feel the need to work incredibly hard to be successful but also wonder if their colleagues question their legitimacy. I have been successful as an academic but certainly have my days when I wonder when people will "find out" that I really don't belong here. I certainly don't mean to say that I have had the same experience as women and persons of color. The position and experience of a White male is very different. But the question of "belonging" has always been there for me.

Terrence McDonald—Dean of the College of Literature, Science, and Arts, University of Michigan[1]

It is something that is not supposed to matter because the university is a place of upward mobility. There is the fairness justification. To be fair, people with different racial and ethnic identifications should have a chance to be professors. People also understand the importance of role models—it is good for Latinas to see a Latina in the front of the class-room. But this other justification or rationale for diversity, the one that says that one's social and cultural contexts matter for one's perspectives on the world, is much less well understood, and still much more difficult to communicate. One's race, ethnicity, cultural background, religion, and gender can all be sources of different understandings and different questions about what is good, what is bad, what is real, what is right, what is beautiful, and what is just. These different perspectives are a source of knowledge and truth. This is a really hard idea and one that takes a great deal of expertise and experience to acknowledge. It is so much easier to imagine that our various frameworks are neutral or free from the commitments that accompany our social positions.

Hazel Markus—Codirector, Research Institute of Comparative Studies in Race and Ethnicity, Stanford University[2]

This book is about an unfinished journey. Beginning some 35 years ago, at universities across the country, students and faculty from underrepresented groups demanded entrance and full acceptance into the academy—as undergraduates and graduate students, as faculty, as scholars, and as institutional leaders. As the previous quotes suggest, the new consciousness that they brought to the whole enterprise of higher education challenged the prevailing notions of equity as a simple notion of fairness—"everybody should have a chance to be a professor"—and uncovered persistent patterns of a White, male, heterosexual, and middle-class domination of higher education. The newcomers' presence, in turn, would fuel long-term transformations in ideas about legitimate knowledge and where it comes from. What counts as knowledge—"what is good, what is bad, what is right, what is true, what is beautiful, what is just"—can all be different because of how you have been positioned.

Both McDonald and Markus speak of these transformations in terms of positionality, namely, the idea that it is individuals' social locations, their "set of contexts and perspectives," that enables their particular view of the world.[3] In our first book, *The Feminist Classroom,* we used this concept of positionality to analyze the shifts in classroom and curricular knowledge occasioned by the entrance of White women and people of color into the professoriat.[4] Puzzled, however, by the ongoing sense of marginality held by many of the newcomers, we decided in this book to turn to issues of institutional positionality. How are people's positionalities determined and changed by the institutional contexts they inhabit? When and how do newcomers' own agendas become levers for institutional transformation?

Much of the dominant literature on higher education today focuses on topics such as the growing role of corporate values over academic values, the supposed shift in higher education from a social institution to an industry, and the decline and irrelevance of the liberal arts in the face of scientific and technological dominance.[5] Frustrated by the abstractions and omissions of this negative national literature, especially how fleetingly it touches on demographic changes in the faculty, we decided to examine these changes and their implications for institutional structures and scholarship in several sites, touching only secondarily on changes in student bodies. Stanford University, Rutgers University–Newark (RU–N), and the University of Michigan, although vastly different from each other, have all experienced intense engagement with these issues: Stanford as the elite university most caught up in the "culture wars" of the late 1980s, RU–N as the *U.S. News and World Report*'s most diverse campus in the United States, and Michigan as the site of the recent successful defense of the principle of affirmative action in admissions in the two 2003 U.S. Supreme Court cases of *Grutter vs. Bollinger* and *Gratz vs. Bollinger.*

Through the lenses provided by the stories of these universities, we trace the evolution of more diverse faculties, from the period of the 1960s student sit-ins on campuses across the country to today's more diverse campus environments.

In the mid-1960s, according to one respondent, African American faculty could not fill a card table at Stanford, whereas today there are 45 African American faculty members. Female faculty in two of the institutions, RU–N and Michigan, filed class-action complaints in the 1970s against their institutions for sex discrimination; today, female administrators at Michigan and Stanford help grapple with how to integrate women's gender roles with their professional roles. And yet these individual and institutional stories are ones not only of progress but of the contradictions that remain.

To provide a frame for this book, we first present in this chapter our working definitions of privilege and diversity and our methodological approach. These are followed by an exploration of the larger historical and societal contexts that have shaped the responses of these universities to the challenges of diversity over the past several decades. These include the reconfiguring of hierarchies in the higher education system beginning with the Cold War, the GI Bill, and the creation of the 1950s suburbs. How did Stanford come to be associated with "Big Science," technology, and the Silicon Valley miracle of the 1990s? What do we need to understand about the growth and increasing segregation and separation of American cities and suburbs to understand Newark, New Jersey, and to situate RU–N today in this story? What has it meant for Michigan to be a top research university with public university commitments? How has the national bifurcation of universities into comprehensive and research universities following World War II shaped the experiences of people inside them? How does the current craze for institutional rankings differentially affect institutional and departmental cultures?

Comparing critical events and ongoing developments across three settings, we document how the institutions' histories and dominant academic cultures have shaped their projects of changing the representations of women and people of color on their faculties, building women's studies and ethnic studies programs, altering departmental and interdepartmental structures and policies, and transforming traditional standards of success and scholarly paradigms. We also look at the forces that have persistently operated to contain and marginalize these efforts over time.

Some Definitions

We have chosen the terms *privilege* and *diversity* as a framework for our work. For much of the past 30 years, discussions of these issues have taken the form of a rhetorical opposition between the supposed two poles of diversity and *excellence*, where excellence is a code word for commonly agreed-on high standards of academic performance—in other words, rigorous scholarship with universal applicability—and a deservedly high stature for those who meet these standards. Diversity has then meant a spreading out of, a dilution of, and a threat to those standards.

However, to us the use of the term excellence is employed not so much as a mark of quality as a mark of privilege—that is, the power of elites to control the norms of the scholarly enterprise in such a way as to keep new people, new topics, and new methodologies at bay. The operations of privilege, embedded in the structures, processes, and standards of the academy, are the barriers against and through which the newcomers must negotiate their way. Privilege—from the Latin *privus* (private) and *lex, legis* (law)—in its root meaning pertains to a law, in this case often silent and unseen, that works for or against individuals and groups.[6] In the case of the American academy, privilege has accrued mostly to a male elite that dominates hiring practices, scholarly norms, departmental and governance structures, and many other dimensions of university life.[7]

We have found it harder to write about privilege than diversity because, at an individual level, privilege is often unspoken, an unmarked category. It means rarely having to be conscious of your gender, race, class, or sexuality. A pervading emphasis in our culture on individual experience and achievements rather than the collective dimensions of group experiences represents a profound lack of consciousness about the social, cultural, and economic determinants of the position of the privileged and their relationship to others. We want to better understand these often invisible historical and structural contexts that operate to situate various groups of faculty differently within institutional power structures. We hope to contribute to a fresh understanding of how these "silent laws" have worked to define who gets to attend, who gets to teach, who gets to administrate, and what will be researched and studied in higher education today. Examining them reveals the persisting powers of the dominant voices to continue to "call the tune" and to marginalize women, men of color, first-generation college students, and gays and lesbians, among many others.

For both men of color and women, the operations of privilege have meant attempting to assimilate to these norms as a way of avoiding this marginalization. bell hooks held that "assimilation, touted as an answer to racial divisions, is dehumanizing; it requires eradication of one's blackness so that a white self can come into being."[8] Jane Roland Martin argued, "The academy charges an exorbitant admission fee to those women that wish to belong." She likened their position to that of immigrants in the 19th century, saying that "rather than thinking that the academy's mores might be enriched by women's presence, it is generally taken for granted that our belonging in the academy entails our conformity to the existing values of the host society."[9] In an article based on his recent book, Japanese American and law professor Kenji Yoshino argued that he and other gay academics have felt obliged to "keep our orientation from looming large. That was a desire to 'cover,' Erving Goffman's word for how individuals with known stigmatized traits mute them to make themselves more socially acceptable." He went on to assert that "covering" represents a new form of assimilation that gays can help other groups understand:

All outsider groups feel the bite of the covering demand. African Americans are told to "dress White" and abandon "street talk"; Asian Americans are told to avoid seeming "fresh off the boat"; women are told to "play like men" at work and make their child-care responsibilities invisible; gay people are told to be "straight acting" and not to "flaunt." … It used to be that individuals were excluded from the workplace … solely on the basis of race, sex, orientation, religion, or disability. Now individuals need not be straight White male able-bodied Protestants. They need only act like straight White male able-bodied Protestants. That, of course, is progress. But it is not equality.[10]

This book also employs the term diversity to analyze the challenges to institutional privilege brought about by the entrance of new groups into the academy. By diversity we mean people and ideas that are different from the assumed norm of White, heterosexual, middle-class, and college-educated men. Throughout our analysis, we assume that identities, whether of privilege or oppression, are not fixed or inherent but rather defined by their locations and definitions within shifting networks of relationships and institutional structures, arrangements that can be analyzed and changed. For example, we have seen how, in some institutional discourses of higher education, the term diversity has moved from being seen as the polar opposite of excellence to becoming one of its defining features. It is now said that you cannot have excellence without diversity. This shift may be seen as a subtle marker for how much progress has been made.

Methodological Frameworks

In this work we have created comparative, institution-wide analyses through these twin lenses of privilege and diversity, lenses through which we explore defining issues and critical events, institutional practices and structures, and the various influences of individuals as actors within each context. Our methodological approach may be defined as institutional ethnography, as described in the work of Canadian sociologist Dorothy E. Smith.[11] Its purpose is "to explicate the actual social relations in which people's lives are embedded and to make … the ruling relations themselves, including the social organization of knowledge," that shape everyday university life visible for investigation.[12]

Like all ethnographies, institutional ethnography provides a "thick description" of people's behaviors in particular settings, derived from comparisons among individual narratives, relevant documents, and other analyses of important events. Ethnography is driven by the search to discover "how it happens" in terms of the identification of an issue, critical event, or area of everyday practice. In our case these events concern the discourses around gender, race, ethnicity, and, to a certain extent, sexuality and class on these three campuses. We investigate how the university organizes and shapes the everyday world of faculty members' and administrators' experience of diversity issues. Beginning with people's own stories, we compare institutional accounts and language with their more informal narratives. Locating individuals working in different parts of institutional complexes of activity, we trace the points of connection among them, describing the social processes, namely, the operations of privilege and the challenges of diversity across each institution, that have generalizing effects about the institution's "ruling relations."[13]

Intent: How Postwar Government Policies Shaped Higher Education Contexts

In January 2000, during our first visit to Stanford, we met with Carolyn Lougee, a European historian and chair of the History Department, who has served as our primary gatekeeper there. We talked with her over lunch in the Business School dining room, surrounded by a sea of mostly young men whom we imagined to be in conversations about wildly successful start-up companies. We were vaguely aware of the high-tech revolution in the country, most noticeably taking place in the nearby Silicon Valley. When we told Lougee about our interest in privilege and diversity, she surprised us by saying that we might be interested in those issues as they applied to men of color and women, but what really mattered was the enormous influence of the technological boom on the university and the whole context of higher education. Later that day we interviewed Sylvia Yanagisako, a cultural anthropologist and chair of that department, and were similarly surprised at her unsolicited remarks about the predominance of engineering and technology at Stanford. She said that not only do humanists and social scientists feel marginalized but some scientists do as well.[14]

Encounters such as these led us to understand that we needed to take into account larger historical and national societal contexts for framing events in specific universities, particularly since the 1950s and the inception of the Cold War. The historical developments in which we are interested are as follows: (a) the Cold War buildup of Big Science, leading to the rise of the science-based research university and of a certain kind of social science practice as well; (b) the exponential growth of the suburbs and the sharp decline of the inner city, leading to increasing racial segregation encouraged by Whites-only mortgage policies; and (c) the expansion and democratization of higher education, mainly for White men, fueled, like the expansion of the suburbs, by the GI Bill. Together these postwar policies worked to advantage the research university and within it Big Science, to build up the suburbs at the expense of the inner cities, to constrain opportunities for women, and to further institutionalize the already long-standing racial privilege and discrimination in American neighborhoods, schools, and universities.

As noted by anthropologist Karen Brodkin:

Law, talk about it, making it, and enforcing it, is about making and enforcing categories and boundaries. ... From the Constitution itself ... to labor law, residential segregation, and urban renewal policies, the state has been a central force in defining races and genders and to assigning them their spatial, cultural, and socio-economic places in this society.[15]

All these developments can be traced to federal, state, and local government policies and choices. They created universities organized by specific patterns of White-male exclusivity that would prove difficult to challenge over the next half century. It is necessary, in other words, to be specific about the ways in which the dominance of American society by the privileged was embedded through explicit governmental policies into the structures, operations, and hierarchies of the academy. These policies simultaneously rewarded White men and disadvantaged women and people of color. It was the context created by these policies that members of these groups faced in the 1970s as they sought to enter and redefine the university. This dominance, although historically rooted and traditional, was not "natural." Hence the focus of this section: "Intent."[16]

The Cold War, Big Science, and the Rise of the Research University

The Cold War created a climate in which national defense and science were more important than ever. In the early 1950s the majority of funds for defense work went not to universities but to applied research taking place in military and industrial laboratories. Russia's launching of Sputnik in 1957 changed all of that. Shocked Americans set off a barrage of public criticism and began massive efforts to improve science education and research in the United States to compete with the Soviets. In the post-Sputnik world, basic research, graduate education, and the construction of university facilities were championed by the federal government. "National leaders saw scientific excellence as the key to winning the Cold War, and recognized research universities as the chief producers of scientific innovation and talent."[17]

Largely because of the impetus provided by Vannevar Bush, former MIT provost and a key national science policy advisor in the late 1940s, federal spending made the research university a key political and economic actor on the national stage. For the first time, the federal government began to allocate money directly to universities for science education and research. Through legislation such as the National Science Foundation (NSF), whose funding reached $136 million in 1959, the National Defense Education Act of 1958, and the Higher Education Facilities Act of 1963, universities received huge infusions of money to train and hire scientists and to build scientific research facilities. Grants from other agencies such as the National Institutes of Health (NIH) and the National Aeronautics and Space Administration (NASA) also gave substantial support for researchers, graduate students, and facilities. By 1960 universities had become increasingly publicly subsidized institutions—both agents for and partners with the federal government. The Cold War turned them into magnets for industrial investment as well.[18]

Aside from their giant scientific and technological impact on the society, the results of these policies for American higher education were profound. They rewarded some institutions at the expense of others. When the NSF was established in 1950, despite its efforts to erode institutional elitism through its peer-reviewed, meritocratic grant-making process, institutions that grew tended to have the size, program mix (including medical schools), and infrastructure to maintain their competitive advantage regardless of the drift in federal funding emphasis.[19] A small select group of "experts" controlled the allocation of research dollars and tended to award grants to a small and elite number of research universities year after year. Margaret O'Mara, in her study of the period, concluded:

> By continuing to award grants and contracts to the same set of institutions, the military's policy of locating their research projects in places of greatest expertise and resources became a self-fulfilling prophecy. The favored institutions reached higher and higher levels of excellence in science and engineering because federal grants allowed them to upgrade facilities, lure eminent faculty, and develop graduate programs. Such resources gave them a huge advantage in future federal grant competitions.[20]

This move toward organized research also had an impact on the institutional cultures of universities as a whole: a distortion of university research "away from the puzzles of disciplinary paradigms in order to pursue problems of their patrons' choosing," "the preponderance of federal research funds in the national sciences," and the emergence of "two classes of faculty on campus—those who had the advantage of being associated with organized research units, and those who did not."[21] Institutions that may have had concerns about these developments were forced to accede to them because of pressure to accommodate faculty research projects and the lure of being a part of this heady national effort. In addition, organized research added to a university's scientific cachet.[22] Some faculty members objected to the changes on their campuses, especially the displacement of undergraduate teaching and federal influence on departmental research agendas. However, to administrators such as Frederick Terman at Stanford, the opportunity to expand and advance their institutions through organized research was more than worth those risks.

The Stanford Advantage

Stanford was perfectly positioned to benefit from Cold War military spending. It had undeveloped and economically desirable land, entrepreneurial administrators, and a location near key defense facilities amid one of the fastest growing affluent suburban areas. Massive federal defense investments during the first two decades of the Cold War enabled Stanford to revitalize its engineering program through basic research and to vastly enlarge its academic scope and physical size, prompting an explosion of industrial research contracts and high-tech production.[23]

For universities, winning federal research and development (R&D) funds became a matter of not only intellectual merit, but access to political power. Stanford, lacking the prewar stature of Harvard and MIT, was one of the universities O'Mara characterized as needing to work a little harder, "establishing Washington offices, adjusting their academic missions, becoming more entrepreneurial and political in their approach."[24] Furthermore, California was well positioned to benefit from the flow of federal dollars because of its well-equipped companies, trained personnel, mild climate, and infrastructure such as new housing and highways. O'Mara concluded, "The combination of institutional favoritism in the R&D process and geographic favoritism in both military production and R&D allocations meant that scientific activity and scientific professions became concentrated in certain parts of the country." California institutions of higher education received 28.6% of the funding for federal research programs in 1963; the entire Midwest received only 13.9%.[25]

Michigan Gets Its Share: The Social Sciences

The story of the University of Michigan as it relates to the expenditures for the postwar university represents an interesting contrast to that of Stanford. Rather than becoming the center of one of O'Mara's technological and scientific "cities of knowledge," Michigan's orientation was shaped differently. Although always strong in the social sciences, Michigan became pre-eminent in this area during this period, a dominance that was created by federal, state, and foundation support. The major funding source for the social sciences was not the federal government but the large private foundations—Carnegie, Rockefeller, and Ford. And these foundations, like the federal government, tended to reward those institutions that were already pre-eminent in their fields. From 1946 to 1958, Michigan ranked number one among the public universities in the amount of foundation support for the social sciences and the number of social science PhDs obtained there. It placed number six in the social science national rankings.[26] Michigan's preeminence was solidified with the founding of the Institute for Social Research (ISR) in 1947, which we describe in detail later. As Roger Geiger put it:

> During the postwar decades Michigan was a major site of the entrepreneurial transformation of American academia; it was simultaneously an important site of the intellectual revolutions in American social science associated with behavioral perspectives and quantitative methods.

In both cases, [ISR] was a central factor. In 1945 the social sciences at Michigan did not amount to much, but by the 1960's, Michigan could claim one of the finest social science establishments in the world.[27]

Yet ultimately, compared with the programs at Stanford and other major universities, Michigan's sciences suffered in this period. Programs in the natural sciences and mathematics grew and generally prospered amid the enormous increases in federal dollars, but their attainments were modest by comparison to peer institutions. Michigan was not as formidable a science university in 1963, relative to its peers, as it had been before the war.

In one respect, Michigan's failure to compete in the realm of Big Science underscores the contrasting nature of Stanford's achievement, as Michigan at the end of World War II was a much bigger player in the national arena than was Stanford. However it was the Cold War policies toward the federal funding of universities that underlay the success of ISR as well. And it was arguably Cold War conservative ideologies that helped at the time to turn ISR and Michigan political science in a self-consciously apolitical and scientific direction. The department's focus on behaviorist methodologies occurred at the same time as the field embraced the " 'behaviorist revolution in political science,' [a move that] raised their national rankings decisively."[28]

Thus Cold War policies toward the university helped to decisively situate both Stanford and the University of Michigan in important places in the terrain of American higher education. At the same time, and even more salient for our study, they set up dynamics within each institution in terms of privileged departments and schools—patterns that some believe persist to this day. The absence of such places as RU–N from these hierarchies of institutional privilege has had a decisive impact on those institutions as well over the years. The belated introduction of PhD programs in the sciences in the 1960s suggests that RU–N was a latecomer to the table of federal support for the sciences. It was not a member of the circle of elite institutions that were favored by early NSF funding, and the 1967 image of Newark as a city set aflame by urban riots is the antithesis of the suburban Eden in which White scientists could work, live, play, and educate their children, as in sunny California.

Suburbs and Cities: Spatial Arrangements of Race and Gender

No other New Deal initiative had as great an impact on changing the country as the Selective Service Readjustment Act, [or] the GI Bill. With [its] help, millions bought homes, attended college, started business ventures, and found jobs. ... Through these opportunities, and by advancing the momentum towards suburban living, mass consumption, and the creation of wealth and economic security, this legislation created middle-class America. [However] the GI Bill was deliberately designed to accommodate Jim Crow. Its administration widened the country's racial gap. The prevailing experience for blacks was starkly differential treatment. … The effect was to produce a critical lag in the rate and conditions of Black assimilation into the wider currents of American life.[29]

The terrain of the 1950s was one of sharply increasing racial segregation and hierarchy nationwide.[30] An emerging geography of White suburbs and all-Black cities was the result of the federal government's complicity in promoting segregation in the social institutions critical to upward mobility in education, housing, and employment.[31] The GI Bill and the other postwar policies built the 20th-century American middle class, and although this group included a significant Black bourgeoisie, these policies condemned the majority of African Americans to entrenched second-class citizenship. Blacks had undergone many forms of discrimination in the armed services and had received a disproportionate share of dishonorable discharges, thus making many ineligible for benefits. Government agencies such as the Veterans Administration (VA) and the U.S. Employment Service also denied African American GIs access to specific benefits. In crucial respects, the enforcement and interpretation of its provisions were left to state and local enforcement agencies. These agencies, particularly in the South but also in the North, were free to interpret the law in this pre–civil rights era so as to exclude African Americans from many of its provisions.[32]

The GI Bill, along with federal housing agencies such as the Federal Housing Authority (FHA), also created the suburbs. This distinctive kind of community, flowing from and largely funded by federal housing policies during this period, reflected spatial arrangements shaped by gender and race.[33] As Ira Katznelson put it, "Residential ownership became the key foundation of economic security for the burgeoning and overwhelmingly White middle class. The social geography of the country altered dramatically. The encouragement given to homeownership helped spawn the suburban sprawl that would characterize postwar growth."[34] The GI Bill provided veterans with generous mortgages, thus making home ownership affordable for many Americans for the very first time.[35]

But most suburbs were for Whites only. FHA mortgages included "protective covenants" to maintain segregation. According to Brodkin, "A 1947 FHA guidebook for suburban development, *Planning Profitable Neighborhoods,* stated: 'Protective Covenants are essential to the sound development of proposed residential areas, since they regulate the use of land and provide a basis for the development of harmonious, attractive neighborhoods.' "[36] Developers who depended on the FHA to approve home loans for veterans were required to refuse to sell to African Americans in most neighborhoods. Banks refused to lend in "redlined" neighborhoods because the FHA would not insure mortgages there.[37] "Segregation kept African Americans out of the suburbs, and redlining made sure they could not buy or repair their homes in the neighborhoods in which they were allowed to live. The GI Bill and FHA and VA mortgages functioned as a set of racial privileges."[38] As Katznelson concluded:

> Even with the sharp upward trend toward better living standards, more urbanization, and greater economic growth, the racial gap widened. Just at the moment when the United States developed an increasingly suburban middle-class bulge, and Irish and Italian Catholics and Jews were advancing into mainstream White culture, African Americans remained stuck, in the main, in economically marginal class locations.[39]

The suburbanization of the country affected gender relations as well. As restrictions in employment increased for women following World War II, the suburbs afforded White middle-class women a setting to enjoy their unprecedented material prosperity. This resurgent domesticity, allied with a newfound consumerism, complemented employment restrictions that faced educated women and indeed was imposed on them by the ideology of the Cold War and the suburban dream. As Rosalyn Baxandall and Elizabeth Ewen explained:

> The middle-class ideal included the notion that wives were not supposed to work for wages. Raising children and managing a household was a mark of leisure-class status. With their husbands at work, women were the center of home life, but with a new imperative: to become modern housewives—that is, the new consumers. This ideal is based on the division of family life into public and private spheres. … The expansion of the postindustrial economy after World War II was supposed to make it possible for second-generation families to realize the dream: women at home, men at work, children in school. Suburbs in particular became synonymous with the achievement of this new status.[40]

In terms of the universities we are studying, the growth of the suburbs was inextricably linked to the emergence of the American research university as a result of the Cold War science imperatives. Stanford's ability to set up one of the first "cities of knowledge" was fostered by its location in California, one of the nation's most booming Cold War economies. California became a magic combination of military spending, middle-class suburbanization, and new private-sector wealth. The politics of the Cold War helped to normalize the idea that scientific and industrial activities should occur in the suburbs because of the fear that urban areas could be prime targets for a Soviet nuclear attack. Through this growing policy of "dispersion," the federal government encouraged business and industrial firms to move out of central cities. O'Mara described it this way:

> The story of Stanford and the San Francisco Peninsula provides a vivid example of how the concurrent forces of mass suburbanization and the

growth of the Cold War science complex interacted with each other to map out a low-density, decentralized geography of high-tech production. ... The presence of these select advanced scientific companies, combined with the ecological, infrastructural, and demographic conditions on the Peninsula, made the moment ripe for creating a whole new sort of economic base for the metropolitan region that would revolve around the scientific research programs at Stanford.[41]

Administrators at Stanford understood early on the way in which the right sorts of jobs and the right sorts of people added to the value of land, one of its major assets. They saw a unique opportunity to develop a community in which work, home, recreation, and cultural life were brought together with some degree of balance and integration. They had the right ingredients: "high-end housing that would be attractive to professional families, a large regional shopping center that would take advantage of local purchasing capacity, and—most importantly—an industrial park made up of business and manufacturers who desired the cachet and the technical support gained by a location very close to Stanford."[42] The centerpiece, the Stanford Industrial Park, aimed at strengthening Stanford's position as a top research university through the economic development of its surrounding region.[43] Research parks were for white-collar professionals rather than for blue-collar workers. Stanford's success was thus furthered by the racial and economic homogeneity of Palo Alto, by its Whiteness.[44]

The destruction and isolation of the city of Newark, New Jersey, provides a devastating portrait of the "other side" of suburban development, showing the effects of these self-same policies on another university community—RU–N.[45] Systematic decisions by politicians and policy makers during the second half of the 20th century condemned Newark and other American cities to economic, social, and educational neglect and racial isolation. According to both Brodkin and O'Mara, suburbanization and urban renewal made postwar cities particularly unattractive places to live. Urban renewal policies bulldozed some working-class neighborhoods to make way for freeways and created central business districts that replaced an older mix of manufacturing, commerce, and residential neighborhoods.[46]

With the industrialization of southern agriculture following World War II, poor southern Blacks facing unemployment and legal segregation migrated to northern cities in staggering numbers. Between 1940 and 1960, more than 92,000 Black Americans arrived in Newark. The percentage of the city's residents who were African American jumped from 10.7% in 1940 to 34.5% in 1960 and 54.2% in 1970. Newark's Central Ward, one of the only places where Blacks could find housing, was 63% Black in 1940 and 85% Black in 1959. Those who arrived in Newark in the 1950s found very few entry-level jobs; low- and midskill manufacturing jobs either had departed for the suburbs or were closed to Blacks because of racial discrimination. Federal policies gave tax credits for plants and equipment to new industries in the suburbs rather than to old industries in the cities. Although office and service jobs remained, these jobs typically required a high school education or clerical skills, which most southern migrants did not have.[47]

Newark, although it built some public housing in the late 1930s, used federal urban renewal dollars in the 1950s for institutional and corporate buildings in the downtown area. The highways built to revitalize downtown Newark destroyed residential neighborhoods; according to one RU–N informant, large Italian and Jewish communities were exiled because of the building of Route 280. Spending and educational quality plummeted in most city schools, which were filled with the rural Black poor after World War II.[48]

As the city became more and more Black and poor in the 1940s through the 1960s, RU–N remained a bastion of Whiteness. Like many of its kind, the university served students lacking the resources or the encouragement to go away to college because of their social class and/or gender. The university nonetheless was an important vehicle in the "middle-classing project" of the period.[49] As one administrator told us, the university was always multiethnic—because the city had been. Germans, Poles, Irish, Ukrainians, and other groups made up the population of both the city and the university until Blacks arrived from the South in the 1940s and later. At this point, however, although the population of the city changed, the population of the university did not. It took the civil rights movement to prompt the federal government to begin funding programs to benefit urban areas and to push the university to open itself up to the residents of its own community.

The University of Michigan was also profoundly affected by the racialized suburbanization of postwar America. Although Michigan is an overwhelmingly White state, Ann Arbor, the suburban location of the university, is only 40 miles from Detroit, one of the country's most racially segregated cities. Over 80 percent of Detroit's population is African American. Although the university, at 65% White enrollment, is the most "White" of all three of these campuses, it has a long history of engagement with racial issues, even though its relationship to Detroit is distant and elusive.[50]

Student Bodies: Affirmative Action for White Males Following World War II

Although up until World War II colleges and universities had been largely restricted to middle- and upper-class men (and women), the GI Bill changed all that, becoming one of the most extensive affirmative action programs in our nation's educational history. Benefits included tuition and living expenses for college or technical schools. Millions of returning GIs, many with working-class backgrounds, were able to go to college for the first time. According to historian John Thelin:

The 1944 bill guaranteed military personnel a year of education for 90 days' service, plus one month for each month of active duty, for a maximum of 48 months. Tuition, fees, books, and supplies up to $500 a year would be paid directly to the college or university (at a time when private universities charged about $300 a year tuition and state universities considerably less). Single veterans were to receive a subsistence allowance of $50 a month, married veterans $75 a month.

By the fall of 1945, eighty thousand veterans had applied and were accepted to participate. By 1946, GI Bill college enrollments surpassed one million, and total benefits paid out by the federal government as part of the act exceeded $5.5 billion, or $48 billion in 2000 dollars. By 1950, of the fourteen million eligible veterans, more than two million, or 16%, had opted to enroll in postsecondary education as a result of the GI Bill.[51]

However, as we have already seen, African Americans benefited much less than Whites from this generosity. Many not already judged ineligible for educational benefits faced discrimination as they sought admission to White colleges and universities. "Even outside the South, Black access to primarily White colleges and universities remained limited. De facto quotas, and in some cases, high selectivity closed these schools to the vast majority of Blacks qualified for higher education." But the historically Black colleges, which the majority of these veterans attended, were few and small, enrolling only 3% of American college students, so that there were often insufficient places to accommodate them. The result was that "White students had far more college places than Blacks."[52] There are also some data, however, on Latino students taking advantage of the GI Bill.[53]

Women who had served in the women's Army and Air Force units were also dealt out of the GI Bill, as their army units had been organized as auxiliaries and did not become part of the military until July 1943. Women's enrollment in colleges dropped to 32% in 1950. "One consequence of the GI Bill was to masculinize the postwar campus—both in terms of the sheer numbers of new male students matriculating and by intensifying the splits between the typically male fields of study and those appropriate for women."[54] In addition, the sciences, the professions, and the professoriate all grew exponentially during this period, and women (and people of color) were excluded from this expansion.

The GI Bill expanded the categories of mainly White men who came into the academy; it profoundly democratized the college-going population and led to a large increase in the number of first-generation college students. But enrollments were not a free-for-all. These first-generation college goers raised anxieties at elite schools such as Harvard and Stanford about a decline in "standards." Educational leaders, led by Harvard's James Bryant Conant and Henry Chauncey of Educational Testing Services, began to argue that the country could no longer afford to draw its leadership solely from the members of the upper class. The development of the SAT as a new standard for college admission heralded a shift, at least in rhetoric if not always in practice, from social-class elitism to meritocracy. This development was another feature of the rise of the professions and the sciences at the time, a shift not in the dominance of White men but toward the dominance of a different kind of White man across American institutional life.[55]

Student bodies became diversified by class, if not by race or by gender, and to some extent were chosen according to measures of academic ability. It took decades before women caught up, and before people of color were allowed to enter.

Scientific Gender Scripts: The White Male Scientist (and Social Scientist) as Hero

Another important result of Cold War federal funding policies was the boost they gave to the importance and image of the scientist—the researcher, the engineer, the doctor—in the academy and in society at large. The Cold War concern with scientific competition, the push for technological excellence, and the desire for significant economic growth all worked to privilege American scientists and the institutions and industries in which they worked. It was during this period that scientists acquired something of the reputation of the "Mathematician-Astronomer-Priests of the ancient Mayas."[56] As Daniel Bell observed in *The Coming of the Post-Industrial Society,* "The new men are the scientists, the mathematicians, the economists, and the engineers of the new intellectual technology."[57] A handmaiden of these "new men" in the period following World War II was the emergence of "meritocratic elitism," a ruling class based on talent, not birth. "Science became the domain of the elites."[58]

Women were increasingly unwelcome among these new "Mathematician-Astronomer-Priests." According to the historian of science Margaret Rossiter, even though there was a national shortage of faculty in the sciences and engineering after World War II and female scientists were available in record numbers, forces were at play that hastened women's marginalization, underutilization, and exit from universities. As a rising proportion of female scientists married in the 1950s and 1960s, universities enforced antinepotism rules. This practice kept many highly qualified women (if they found employment at all) working as research assistants, as nonfaculty personnel, or on other peoples' grants. Qualified older women without PhDs were also pushed out as more PhDs were hired, raising issues of ageism, sexism, and homophobia.[59]

As for African Americans, their numbers in the ranks of American scientists was astoundingly low, again because of American racial policies and practices. A study of Black scientists summed these up:

> Segregation produced isolation: Black PhD's in science were forced to teach in Black colleges and high schools, which were often unsympathetic

to the needs of a research scientist. ... The Black colleges had little money available for scientific equipment or laboratories. In the South, where most Black colleges were located, Black scholars were denied the use of public libraries and White university libraries and were barred from local chapters of learned societies. To this can be added Jim Crow laws designed to restrict the social and political actions of Blacks, the constant threat of violence, and the exclusion from the community of science in general.[60]

Diversifying Student Bodies and Faculties: The 1970s to the Present

This book would have been impossible to imagine had these legacies of the 1940s and 1950s not been challenged by the social movements of the 1960s and the civil rights legislative victories that followed. Empowered by these shifts in national consciousness and legal recourse, people of color and White women sought entry into all levels of the academy beginning in the late 1960s. In terms first of student enrollments, over the course of the decades of the 1960s and 1970s female students caught up and even surpassed men; they are the majority of undergraduates today. But it was much harder for students of color. Inspired by the civil rights and anti-Vietnam movements, excluded racial minorities, with support from their White allies, demanded access to the academy. At RU–N a student sit-in in 1969 forever altered the all-White composition of the student body. At the 25th anniversary of the "Conklin Hall takeover" in the spring of 2004, Newark Provost Steven Diner remarked, "The Conklin Hall takeover looms in my mind as the watershed event that transformed the campus to what it is today."[61] Similar events occurred at both Michigan and Stanford, after which these universities, as did many others, initiated measures to promote student racial diversity that continue to the present day.

Federal and state affirmative action legislation and Supreme Court decisions further shaped student admissions over the years. As a result of the 1978 *Bakke vs. UC Board of Regents* decision, race alone was deemed unallowable as grounds for admission to higher education. Thus the Michigan defense in the Supreme Court cases of 2003, as we shall see, argued that racial diversity constituted a benefit to all students, not just students of color.

More recently, interpretations of affirmative action policies have been challenged by the complex relationships between American Blacks, disadvantaged by the legacy of Jim Crow laws, "who were intended as the main beneficiaries of affirmative action in admissions," and the large numbers of immigrants arriving after the Immigration Act of 1965.[62] African Americans born in this country, and for that matter Puerto Rican Americans and Chicanos, vie for places in higher education with immigrants from the Caribbean Islands and Africa, from Mexico and South America, from Asia and Southeast Asia. Many of these newcomers come from better educated families and are in a better position than American Blacks to take advantage of civil rights legislation and the affirmative action policies of the 1970s and 1980s. James Jackson is the director of ISR at Michigan and the founder in 1976 of ISR's Program for Research on Black Americans, a large-scale national survey that looks at both racial and ethnic differences over time. He told us:

> Of course Caribbean Blacks were in a better position when it came to civil rights legislation. Compare an American man with a fifth-grade education, no job, and five kids who wants to be hired, trained, or educated with another one from a Caribbean island who comes to this country and already has a higher education degree and a lot of work experience from back home. Which Black man is going to get the job? [63]

Not only do immigrants enjoy educational and class advantages but nonimmigrant racial minorities suffer from a continual "downward construction" of their status through persistent patterns of institutional racism. Hazel Markus, Claude Steele, and Dorothy Steele described how these patterns operate:

> The failure to successfully include millions of nonimmigrant minorities in the mainstream of society stems in some large part from a pervasive downward social construction of these groups by the majority culture, not by individual racism. This tacit ... set of processes results in many African Americans, American Indians, and Latinos being persistently devalued and their prospects and opportunities limited or neglected.[64]

The question of whether nonimmigrant minorities are especially disadvantaged has led some to complain that "better prepared" immigrants are unfairly benefiting from affirmative action policies. These tensions engender difficult conversations about student admissions, inclusion, and retention at all three of the campuses we studied. They are felt most acutely at RU–N, where they plague discourses of recruitment for racial diversity. Whereas "excellence" is the term used to describe sought-after faculty members, the discourse of student diversity uses such terms as "qualifications" and "preparedness" and sometimes pits different racial–ethnic minorities against each other. Although some see Caribbean immigrants as indeed more "prepared," others see racism, and therefore the appropriateness of affirmative action policies, as necessary to help all peoples who can be categorized as Black and thus be dismissed as unprepared and unqualified.

Faculty transformations have been much slower than student ones. Ellen Messer-Davidow described the employment patterns of female faculty since the 1970s (and to a lesser extent, today). Women remain at 30% of the faculty in higher education overall. Men are clustered in the sciences, and women are in the helping fields. Men are predominant in the higher professorial ranks, in research universities, and in central administrative positions; women are lecturers, they predominate at 4-year and 2-year colleges, and they hold clerical and middle-management administrative positions, "These sex patterns, the status studies argued, correlated with the prestige accorded disciplines and institutions and with the power vested in jobs."[65]

How to explain these persisting gender differences among the faculty? Virginia Valian's book *Why So Slow? The Advancement of Women* provides a useful idea for understanding the difficulties women face in the academy. The gender schemas assigned to women do not fit the qualities valued in professional roles. She said:

> The schema for women is incompatible with the schema for a successful professional, resulting in lower expectations of a woman's potential achievement. ... The more she typifies the schema for a woman, the less she matches the schema for a successful professional. ... The more she typifies the schema for the successful professional, the less she matches the schema for a woman.[66]

Similar constraints have dogged the academic careers of faculty of color. Explanations for their low numbers include pipeline issues such as a small number of minority PhDs and "bidding wars" for those faculty available, disproportionate tenure rates, persistent institutional racism that restricts hiring and devalues scholarly work that focuses on race and ethnicity, and a climate that works against the success of faculty of color.[67] Some analysts go so far as to assert that "an apartheid of knowledge for faculty of color separates and devalues the type of research, teaching, and scholarship that they produce."[68] They hold that faculty of color are held to a double standard that affects their teaching, their advising, and their scholarship. They spend more time teaching and advising than their White counterparts. Although their research productivity is comparable, their scholarly interests are different and discriminated against.[69] Women of color experience multiple marginalities in which "the interlocking effects of gender and race compound the pressures of the workplace environment" and "hamper their success as faculty members." For example, they perceive that they are more likely to have their authority challenged by students than men or White women are.[70] We will see all of these issues at play in our institutional portraits.

Inside Higher Education Today: Bifurcation and Stratification

A final framework in our study is the stratification of the university system developed after World War II. Each of these three universities has a specific position in a powerful and long-standing national network of status and privilege that significantly affects the experiences and accomplishments of people within it. We can see these positions in several ways. First, there is the bifurcation of institutions into comprehensive and research universities. Second, there is the stratification among research universities, both created and affected by national rankings systems. Finally, there is the stratification of departments *within* universities, strongly related to but, as we shall see, not synonymous with the rankings of those departments nationally. It is within these dynamics that female faculty members and faculty of color have made their way, challenging departmental norms and policies, creating new structures, and slowly transforming the standards for scholarly research excellence.

Historians of American higher education emphasize two contrasting themes in the development of universities since World War II—the massive growth of the student body and the rise of the modern research university. Indeed, many writers have pointed out that unlike the German model, for example, the American university is unique in its simultaneous commitment to expanding the frontiers of knowledge and providing access for increasingly broader segments of the population.

The postwar growth of student enrollments, resulting in part from the GI Bill, meant that the country's universities moved significantly closer to providing mass access to higher education. Emphasizing its magnitude, Thelin wrote, "By 1945–50, total student enrollments had ballooned to almost 2.7 million—an increase of about 89% in one decade. This was no aberration, for the figure increased to about 3.6 million in 1960 and then doubled again over the next decade, reaching over 7.9 million in 1970."[71] The places for most of these students were provided by the newly established comprehensive institutions, those that provide a variety of undergraduate and masters programs with both liberal arts and vocational emphases. Today three out of four undergraduates attend such institutions. It was the comprehensive state universities' growth in enrollments and in masters programs that was actually responsible "for expanding if not creating an educated middle class."[72] Of our three institutions, only RU–N fits the profile of a comprehensive university.

The other half of the bifurcation in American higher education has been the precipitous rise of the research university. Colleges and universities showed increasing capacity to add advanced, academically selective programs, from the undergraduate level on up through professional schools and doctoral programs. This growth led to the ascendancy of a relatively few research universities going back, as O'Mara pointed out, to the Cold War funding patterns of the federal government.

The Big Science of the early Cold War was largely focused on the physical sciences and engineering. The 1950s honeymoon with these arrangements ended in the late 1960s and early 1970s, due both to concerns growing out of opposition to the Vietnam War about weapons work at "applied physics labs" at several major universities and congressional worries about whether self-interested university research was really supporting federal priorities.[73] The funding of research in the life sciences is more recent. The doubling of the NIH (and health) budget in terms of R&D spending came at the expense of the physical sciences and engineering. For instance, the NSF's current budget is $6 billion; the NIH's is $29 billion, although defense (Department of Defense and Department of Energy) is the top priority at $74 billion.[74] Despite changing federal priorities, universities need to maintain and increase the size and quality of their programs, and their national influence has led to deepening involvements with the federal government and industry. This reliance pushes them toward an entrepreneurial model of seeking funding because the institutional infrastructure now depends on it. Indeed, Richard Lewontin argued that the recognition of the societal benefits of intellectual work is here to stay, benefiting the conditions of scholarship as a whole, including the humanities. "It is part of a halo of legitimation surrounding the socialization of research costs that it [also] illuminates intellectual matters far from questions of international economic and military power."[75]

The push for commercialization has been fostered by recent government policies to make it possible for universities to engage directly with the private sector in the development and commercialization of new technologies. The Bayh–Dole Act, the 1980 Patent and Trademark Amendments (Public Law 96-517), allowed universities, nonprofit institutes, and small businesses to retain intellectual property rights to inventions developed with federal research support.[76] Commercialization is particularly intense in the life sciences, where major discoveries are being made and unimaginable profits hoped for. Powell and Owen-Smith interviewed a number of life scientists in various institutions and pointed out:

> The [old] separation between public and private science no longer holds in the life sciences. … Universities are much more engaged in transferring basic science into commercial development and garnering income in the process. … In the eyes of some university administrators, faculty, and members of state legislatures, university-based invention and discovery reverse the flow of influence and highlight the university as "an engine of economic development." … The commercialization of university-based knowledge signals the university's role as a driver of the economy.[77]

Based on these developments, the stratification of the university system originating after World War II has continued to increase. The concentration of resources in a few institutions has resulted in structurally accumulated advantage and disadvantage—the elites continue to receive disproportionate resources. However, the increasing attention to the development of intellectual property, the creation of products and start-up businesses, and the need for immediate payoffs have sharpened a pecking order in the sciences and engineering. Research in engineering, physics (especially materials), and chemistry (especially materials and pharmaceuticals) are advantaged over the descriptive research typical of the life and environmental sciences. Primarily in the past decade, the molecular biosciences have assumed pre-eminence, in part because of the Human Genome Project. All of this has widened the gap among institutions: those with a small research base struggle to find the resources for patent applications, whereas larger institutions have a whole staff of patent attorneys. As Jennifer Washburn wrote in *University, Inc.,* "The more catch-up institutions strive to attain national research stature—and emulate the high tech commercial success of MIT and Stanford—the more acute the competition becomes."[78]

In terms of these three institutions, Michigan and Stanford are at the top of the research pyramid, consistently sitting among the top ten. For example, in 2005 Michigan ranked third behind Johns Hopkins and UCLA in terms of total research expenditures; Stanford ranked eighth.[79] At Stanford and Michigan we were told frequently that being entrepreneurial was a key value of the institution. Although Michigan and Stanford are solidly positioned as "Research Ones," comprehensive universities such as RU–N must straddle this comprehensive–research bifurcation. To quote David Hosford, who was the dean of arts and sciences from 1982 to 1998, RU–N "has always had to ride two horses—a moral commitment to serve the student body coupled with a strong desire to compete in a larger arena."[80] Since Rutgers University became a member of the American Association of Universities in 1982, RU–N has looked to increase the level of external grant funding and number of PhDs awarded annually so that the Newark campus can move up the research pyramid. But competition for research funding is on a very different scale at RU–N than at the other two institutions, as we will see in subsequent chapters.

Rankings Exacerbate the Problem

Mark Chesler, a professor emeritus of sociology at the University of Michigan, told us about the discomfort of some senior men there with the suspected lowering of standards occasioned by the hiring of faculty newcomers. "When they look at the large number of women, the large number of people with non-traditional researcher interests, the increasing size of the faculty of color, some think this doesn't quite match the standards of a major research university."[81]

What is the significance of this comment about "the standards of a major research university"? Although attempts to measure the quality of American colleges and universities have been around since the late 19th century, it was not until 1957 that one of the eastern universities undertook an extensive study measuring and ranking the quality of graduate programs in 24 departments nationwide. Twenty-one of Michigan's departments were rated as being among the first ten. There were only three universities with more highly ranked programs: UC–Berkeley, Harvard, and Yale.[82] Today there are at least eight ranking systems for undergraduate programs, *U.S. News and World Report* being the most notorious. The National Research Council is the leading ranking organization for graduate programs. All these systems reflect the highly competitive behavior of American higher education institutions and, according to Patricia Gurin, professor emerita of psychology at the University of Michigan, speak to "our cultural history of individualism and competition."[83] Clara Lovett, the recent president of the American Association of Higher Education, wrote in the *Chronicle of Higher Education's* "Point of View" section that "the unintended consequence of the rankings craze is that it generates behavior totally at odds with our rhetoric about providing educational opportunity for all students, regardless of their backgrounds. Further, it devalues the hundreds of institutions that E. Alden Dunham described in 1969 as 'the colleges of the forgotten Americans.'"[84]

These patterns of stratification have a heavy impact on all three institutions. RU–N and Michigan are both public, but RU–N is a comprehensive university, focusing on an access mission for first-generation college students. Although, like Stanford, a top-ranked "Research One," Michigan's identity as a public university is a special aspect of its mission, in contrast to Stanford's elite private status. Administrators there speak of a long-standing commitment to student access, frequently drawing on the words of James Burrill Angell, president from 1871 to 1909, who characterized the university's mission as providing "an uncommon education for the common man."[85] According to former University of Michigan president James Duderstadt, although private institutions such as "the Harvards and the Yales certainly set the bar for quality, they don't produce the bulk of the professionals, the work force, the research, and so forth, that this country needs. Those are the missions of the great public universities."[86]

Nationally, the pecking order of rankings affects student college choices— even undergraduate students prefer the selectivity of the research university. In a recent study of college applicant choices, Roger Geiger pointed out that "super" students of high ability—defined as being the upper 5% of the applicant population whose SAT scores are higher than 1,400—are choosing top-tier institutions, both public and private—again, the top-ranked research universities.[87] Indeed, Robert Reich, writing in the *Chronicle of Higher Education,* used the examples of Stanford and Michigan, among others, to argue that selective colleges heighten inequality. Selectivity in admissions to the most prestigious institutions is rising steeply. For example, Stanford accepts only 13% of its applicants today; 20 years ago, it accepted 19%. At Michigan the rate of acceptance dropped from 72% to 59% over the same interval.[88]

Stanford's president John Hennessy believes Stanford's increasing selectivity is largely negative, part of the larger culture's excessive focus on rankings. "*U.S. News and World Report* has been damaging in an incredible number of ways, both to the young people and their families who think they are being served by this ridiculous ranking mechanism, as well as to the institutions, which have become, in many cases, simply beholden to it."[89] James Duderstadt concurs. He believes that more colleges and universities are needed with the capacity to produce graduates of the highest caliber.[90] There are many more qualified students available than there are places at the top:

Yet, in truth, not only do the majority of applicants rejected by these elite institutions have the academic ability to both succeed and benefit from their academic programs, but in many cases they have academic credentials comparable to or even better than those students who have been accepted (particularly when the latter are athletes, alumni legacies, or the relatives of influential donors). Put another way, selectivity in many institutions has reached the stage where admissions decisions are made more on the basis of subjective evaluations than empirical data.[91]

The rankings are also closely tied to the national reputations of faculty members, which are at bottom based on research productivity and, for example, the number of faculty members who are National Academy members and recipients of national faculty awards. Today Stanford is ranked behind Harvard with 223 members to Harvard's 267. Michigan, with 65, is behind the "reigning" public university (University of California–Berkeley), and Rutgers University, which makes no distinctions among its three campuses, has 30.[92]

Duderstadt's description of the damaging effects of selectivity on the composition of student bodies can be applied to faculty as well. Comprehensive universities and liberal arts colleges, institutions with few or any doctoral programs and fewer resources, struggle to create their own idea of a university and to maintain reasonable expectations for faculty publications and external funding. These struggles are most apparent in requirements for tenure and promotion, but the impact of the rankings exacts other psychological costs as well. Some faculty see themselves as doomed to work all of their careers in a second-rate place, working harder for fewer rewards. Indeed there may be no more profound example of the operations of privilege in higher education than these differences of status among institutions, differences all summed up in the national rankings. There are many more talented researchers than appointments for them at the most prestigious research universities. The rankings exacerbate the differences among universities because they put pressure on those outside the circle of research universities and doctoral granting institutions to compete for research funding and offer doctoral programs, which can distort the balance between teaching and research, affording teaching, particularly of undergraduates, a second-class status. To Thelin the problem is lack of clarity on crucial questions of institutional mission:

> Faculty with heavy teaching loads at institutions whose primary constituents were open admissions undergraduates were also required to publish books and articles and write successful grant applications—all without much in the way of institutional support. This was the widespread scenario that resulted when the excesses of the research university were mistaken as a model for all of American higher education.[93]

This lack of clarity about mission and constrained resources contributes to some faculty members' cynicism about institutional rhetoric. As one professor said, "You expect us to teach underprepared students, engage with the community, and publish like we were a Research One."

This mistaken ideal of the research university bears down on these three institutions, perhaps most obviously on RU–N, whose faculty members struggle with the demands of heavy teaching loads and the research expectations of a higher ranked institution.

Furthermore the national rivalries between institutions for star researchers create further inequalities within them. According to Randall Collins:

> The structural realities work against [equality]. Consider differentials in pay among departments. Well-known research professors are paid more than teachers, even at schools that attract academically elite students. The prestige of a department depends primarily on its biggest names and their research-based reputations; hence the competition among the many upper-tier universities today drives up the salaries of the star professors, and leaves proportionately less for the mass of teachers and lesser-known researchers. ... This is one basis for the increasing split between the elite research professors and everyone else, and the ... growth of an academic underclass of temporary employment at very low salaries.[94]

We saw the phenomenon of this competition at Michigan and Stanford. At Michigan we were told that the university invests decades to support young faculty members who are sometimes then recruited by other more wealthy universities (although Michigan does some raiding of its own).

The Hierarchies Among Academic Fields and the Promises of Change

Once women and people of color had a toehold in universities, faculty members and student groups mounted a series of long-term challenges to institutional status quos. They established Black studies, ethnic studies, and women's studies; initiated curriculum reform in general education and in the major; and transformed scholarship in the mainstream academic disciplines. Marilyn Boxer, herself one of its founders, wrote about women's studies that "this academic enterprise ... started with one program in 1970 that now numbers more than six hundred—plus thousands of practitioners and tens of thousands of courses."[95] Women's studies programs enroll more students than any other interdisciplinary field.[96]

Ethnic studies programs began to grow dramatically in the late 1960s and early 1970s. The earliest were primarily African American studies programs, although a few ethnic studies programs were founded in California. They all shared "a comparative focus on groups socially constructed as 'minorities' in U.S. society, a status that results from these groups' shared history of being racially constructed as distinct from European immigrants and their descendents."[97] From the start, then, these programs went against the grain of predominant ideas and practices in the academy. Their practitioners challenged the assumption that "Western civilization was superior ... and that its values and norms are applicable to all peoples at all times." They set out to expose and change other aspects of institutional racism, link academic excellence to social responsibility, and forge new epistemologies and bodies of knowledge by questioning established research paradigms and linking research to activist agendas in their communities. According to a recent history of African American studies programs, the movement that created them was multiracial and multipurpose. White students joined with Asian students, Latino students, American Indian students, and Black students in the struggle to found the field. The battle they waged was multiracial, seeing Black studies as the first stop in a wider ranging agenda for educational, economic, and social equality.[98]

The responses to their efforts represent powerful instances of institutional White and male privilege. Using arguments about Black studies' supposed ephemerality, political partisanship, and shaky scholarship, among others, administrators and faculty who were opposed to these new programs contained them in several ways. One was to fund curriculum integration projects rather than separate programs, so as to "make Black Studies intellectually and structurally dependent on the traditional disciplines."[99] Another was to erect structural and organizational barriers, the most significant of which was the creation of Black studies and ethnic studies as interdisciplinary programs rather than as freestanding academic departments. Without faculty of their own, programs were often dependent on departments for faculty and courses and were denied the departmental power to hire and tenure their colleagues. This practice, often applied to women's studies as well, resulted in few, if any, full-time faculty members and increasing numbers of part-time teachers, a practice that then seemed to lend support to the idea that these programs lacked intellectual rigor.[100]

Like women's studies, ethnic studies now numbers about 700 departments and programs. Yet some scholars of higher education contend that both disciplines are marginalized, victims of these structures of privilege going well beyond each campus. Indeed, much of the literature on women's studies, as well as Black and ethnic studies, presents the impact they have made on the academic disciplines as elusive. In some cases they have been "labeled as low-status programs catering only to members of underrepresented groups."[101] Marilyn Boxer asserted, "Women's studies should not be dismissed without a hearing by those who assume that because of its political goals it is only 'a cause to be advanced' rather than 'a domain to be studied.' ... Academic feminists must gain a place in the intellectual contests where serious attention is paid."[102] And the very success of ethnic studies has brought about a societal backlash, beginning in the 1990s with the so-called culture wars and continuing today.

Conservatives charge that multiculturalism "promotes ethnic particularism at the expense of national unity and a 'common culture.' "[103]

Yet the proliferation of women's and ethnic studies programs, coupled with pushes over the past several decades to diversify and mainstream the curriculum, is seen by some as a sign that their agendas have become institutionalized. These marks of success bring other worries. As Ellen Messer-Davidow put it, "As we worked in the academy to institutionalize feminist studies, the academy's institutional–disciplinary order worked on it by structuring our activities and shaping our knowledges."[104] Ethnic studies scholars worry that an inclusive multiculturalism will erase ethnic studies programs' concerns with structural racism and their connections to struggles outside the academy. For example, E. San Juan Jr. asserted:

> The "gradual academization" of ethnic studies would force it into the dominant European orthodoxy, which emphasizes ethnicity to the exclusion of race, and therefore systematically [erases] from the historical frame of reference any perception of race and racism as causal factors in the making of the political and economic structures of the United States. If race and racism should remain the analytical core of the ethnic studies project, then would not total retreat into the academy be a contradiction, for how could it separate itself from the ongoing, real-life struggles of peoples of color in the United States today?[105]

Noliwe Rooks pointed out that in spite of ethnic studies being a place for "broad discussions about the meaning of race and for crafting strategies to [deal with] racial inequality, few discuss African-American studies as central to meeting these goals."[106] The problems of enhancing the integrity and reach of ethnic studies and women's studies programs are exacerbated by nationally based structures of privilege that marginalize the scholarly fields associated with women and people of color and maintain the dominant positions of the others. Messer-Davidow summed up the situation in the 1990s from the perspective of mainstream defenses against feminist interventions into the academy: "What were mainstream academics trying to conserve? In national venues such as conferences and publications, they wanted to protect the intellectual orthodoxies of their disciplines, and on campuses they wanted to preserve the departmentalization that structured university decision making and resource allocation."[107]

It is generally agreed among the authors of the higher education literature that relationships with outside funding bodies and similar dynamics have not only advantaged some institutions at the expense of others but also privileged some departments *within* universities at the expense of others, an aspect of the operations of privilege that we will examine in detail in terms of these three institutions in the coming chapters. Patricia Gumport asserted, "The distribution of academic R&D across fields has essentially been the same over the past two decades: more than 80 percent of federal funds go to life sciences (54%), engineering (16%), and physical sciences (11%). Research allocations to the behavioral and social sciences ... account for only 6% of the total [for] that period."[108]

In terms of women's studies specifically, Sheila Slaughter examined the relative power of disciplines and disciplinary fields as a way of showing how curriculum formation and departmental status within a given institution are shaped by "direct linkages between curricula and powerful groups and organizations outside the university." In contrasting the fields of physics and women's studies, she shows how and why physics departments may command much more power inside any university than women's studies could and how the humanities and the social sciences, once again, are devalued inside the academy because they are devalued outside:

> The status of physics as a field is undoubtedly related to its organizational network, its ability to secure substantial funding, its ties to powerful corporations, its utility in economic development, the career paths it opens for its students, the international prizes and awards open to scholars, and the overhead funds it brings to universities. Physicists are not simply acted upon by external forces; they are part and parcel of governments and corporations. They have successfully connected their knowledge to a wide variety of power and funding sources that allow their field to thrive.

> In contrast to physics, women's studies is located in a relatively sparse network of organizations and it constructs itself very differently. NWSA [the National Womens Studies Association] sponsors few journals. It has no formal ties with corporations, and no ... ties with government funding agencies. *Its ties to government are to agencies that prohibit discrimination rather than agencies that provide funding.*[109] (italics ours)

However, institutional change holds different meanings at different institutions, depending on the specific weight of departments and disciplines within them, as well as their positions in the rankings hierarchies, as we shall see. For example, although some faculty we spoke to at all three places complained about the hegemony of science and technology, their unhappiness was not as acute as much of the discourse nationally. The campus narratives expressing the most concerns about the power of these disciplines were understandably at Stanford. At Michigan few complained about the hegemony of the sciences, and the preeminence of the social sciences is seen as a boon to the university as a whole. They are credited with promoting a campus-wide culture of interdisciplinarity and a wide range of research agendas in all fields, as well as providing the research underpinnings for the defense of the recent Supreme Court cases and the programs to support women in the sciences. At RU–N the administration built its research reputation through funding in the sciences. Today, the emphasis is more on bringing the basic sciences into partnerships with engineering and biomedical science at nearby universities such as the New Jersey Institute of Technology (NJIT) and the University Medical and Dental School of New Jersey (UMDNJ).

One of the themes we take up later in detail concerns the ways in which faculties and administrators at each place have worked within these complex situations, both within departments and across them, in interdisciplinary ways, to build structures to support their innovations in curriculum and scholarship. Carolyn Lougee, who was the dean of undergraduate studies at Stanford from 1982 to 1987, made a persuasive case for the intellectual grounds for curriculum reform during Stanford's core curriculum debates of the late 1980s. She now believes:

> Ethnicity and gender are much more in the mainstream now and the studying of cultures other than Western culture. It's all well understood now and better than earlier. ... I don't think people look at women's studies and race and ethnic studies anymore the way they did. People understand now why these are important for students to study and know.[110]

Sherri-Ann Butterfield is a sociologist of African Caribbean heritage recently hired at RU–N. She was brought to Newark as part of a new initiative to hire scholars who would study the city. Her description of her research in conjunction with RU–N's Institute on Ethnicity, Culture, and the Modern Experience is an example of the narratives we encountered again and again, narratives that linked hiring, departmental change, and "what will count as knowledge in the future."

> I'm a child of immigrants, as well as a sociologist, so I'm used to having this conversation about immigration, ethnicity, and race ... on a regular basis. I feel supported by the current provost because we are both urbanists and in a lot of ways I was exactly what he wanted in terms of my research agenda.[111]

The layered accounts given by our informants' partial perspectives, by which we build up our analyses later, will yield a fuller and more nuanced narrative of each institution's engagement with these issues. We now turn to an introductory examination of these three universities over the past 30 years—how have RU–N, Stanford, and the University of Michigan grown and changed over this period?

2
Portraits of Three Institutions

The major research universities of the United States are, in many respects, all alike, and they seem to have become more alike during this past half-century. For all their celebration of their own unique achievements and ethos, these universities—public or private, eastern or western, urban or suburban—are all subject by degree to the same political and economic forces.[1]

Burton Clark—*The Academic Profession: National, Disciplinary, and Institutional Settings*

This chapter seeks to show how the common social, political, and educational forces described in the first chapter have interacted with the specific cultures of each of these institutions over the past several decades. We found faculty and administrators we interviewed at each site to be engaged differently with issues that they nevertheless all have in common. What do our informants believe about privilege and diversity in their institutions, and how do their beliefs and practices interrupt the generic university evoked in much of the national literature?

The patterns of White privilege identified in the previous chapter are structural, demographic, and intellectual, as are the challenges mounted to them. Structurally, the bifurcation of the higher education system into research and comprehensive universities and the growing impact of the ranking systems have positioned Stanford, Michigan, and Rutgers University–Newark (RU–N) in different places in national hierarchies, with significant effects for life on each campus. Demographically, the transformations of the White male student bodies of the 1950s and earlier have created not only gender and racial/ethnic diversity but also new discourses about student and faculty identities and qualifications. At Michigan, the defense of affirmative action in the 2003 Supreme Court cases was couched in terms of the benefits for all students of widening the grounds for admission, in keeping with the university's tradition of democratic access. Stanford, in recruiting a racially and ethnically diverse national elite, struggled with modifying the curriculum in the 1980s to reflect new student and faculty voices. At RU–N, on the other hand, faculty and others, faced with the legacies of urban segregation and educational apartheid, are wrestling with how to ensure the admission of American-born African Americans and Puerto Ricans when better prepared immigrant populations of color apply. At all three places, the push for a faculty diversified by race and gender has meant numerical shifts that in turn have moved to alter, in different ways and to different degrees, significant aspects of campus cultures.

Faculty at each of our sites have also been involved intellectually in the national curriculum transformations beginning in the 1980s. Stanford faculty challenged the traditional Western civilization course in the famous core debates of the late 1980s; there are many courses at all three places that are diversified by gender, race, culture, and sexuality. Nevertheless various informants at all three institutions note that there is still no place in their curriculum for a full analysis of White privilege, which is still the "silent norm."

A persistent treatment of faculty accomplishments and research as a result of primarily individual efforts within traditional disciplines has been challenged by new scholarship and interdisciplinary efforts of different kinds—an emphasis on urban scholarship at RU–N, and the new kinds of knowledge enabled by the ties across the social sciences and humanities at Michigan. At Stanford, debates about the nature of the new scholarship have energized curricular reform, affected tenure cases, and caused a split in one academic department, as well as fostered interdisciplinary innovations.

Rutgers University–Newark

RU–N began as the University of Newark, an amalgamation of five local educational institutions that came together under that name in 1935. From its beginnings, according to a recent history, the university embodied values it holds today—providing "collegiate and professional education to diverse student populations ... premised on a single historic principle of American higher education: community service." As a 1934 faculty report stated, "Social Welfare ... depends on educating an enlightened citizenry conscious of social responsibility, acquainted with social problems, and prepared to deal with social relations according to well-considered social values."[2]

Although the city of Newark fell into decline in the 1930s and 1940s, the institutions that were to become part of Rutgers–Newark were evolving and growing. Dana College, the precursor to the Faculty of Arts and Sciences–Newark (FASN), first served as the liberal arts preparatory college for the New Jersey Law School. It was founded in 1927 and named in 1930 for John Cotton Dana, a renowned librarian committed to building libraries for the people, particularly the newly arrived immigrant populations. In 1946 Dana College merged with the New Jersey Law School (founded in 1908) and the Seth Boyden School of Business (founded in 1929) to become the University of Newark. The new university was one of New Jersey's largest higher education institutions and boasted the state's only law school. The postwar deluge of college-bound veterans led New Jersey's political leaders to begin a movement to streamline the state's higher education system. The University of Newark became Rutgers University–Newark on July 4, 1946, "thus adding a law and business school to the Rutgers system."[3]

Norman Samuels's reflections on his 20 years as provost (1982–2002) are a powerful representation of the tensions between the demands of the national ranking system for research excellence and the commitments to a diverse student body:

> I don't separate the ranking from *U.S. News and World Report*—at the top of their diversity category—from their ranking of us as one of the top 100 national research universities, *without* respect to diversity. The two go hand in hand. To me, to have lost the access and diversity dimension while achieving success on the academic side would not have been a victory. One without the other would have been less than half. But the two together, that's extraordinary.[4]

The story of RU–N can be seen as one of a gradual struggle to move away from the perception, as here, that aspiring to research excellence and student diversity pull the university in different directions, to the discovery of ways that they might become one and the same. Specifically, the "social welfare mission," always a part of the university, is being reconceived now as part of a scholarly agenda as well.

When we first got off the New Jersey Transit Train at Broad Street Station in Newark, just 20 minutes from Penn Station in New York, we walked down a steep flight of old-fashioned wooden stairs and out into a semideserted, industrial, urban landscape: empty parking lots with tufts of grass growing in them, abandoned buildings, and here and there a used-car lot or an auto parts dealership. From another angle, we could see several opulent art deco buildings built sometime between the turn of the past century and the 1920s, evidence of a former period of business vitality and affluence. We had the impression of a city that is designed to get cars in and out and not one that is pedestrian friendly. When we arrived at the edge of the campus on University Avenue, however, we saw signs of an urban-renewal life; the Newark Museum is off to the left in an expansive green park, and ahead we began to see the chrome and silver skyscrapers of a (newly) respectable urban skyline.

In between the run-down neighborhood along the railroad tracks and the revitalized city center is RU–N. The feeling of urban blight was somewhat mitigated once we got alongside the campus. It is quite small geographically, covering about 10 square city blocks and 37 acres, and containing 31 buildings. At one corner of University Avenue is the Student Admissions office, clearly an attempt to make students' access into the institution more welcoming. Following University Avenue into the center of the campus, we were surrounded by buildings typifying state university architecture from the 1960s: concrete, rectangular, and gray, relieved somewhat by several large open grassy areas.

As one publicity document described the current campus refurbishment program, "lawns, brick walkways, and benches are rapidly replacing concrete." The modest character of the campus is further brought home by glimpses of the Manhattan skyline, in all its grandeur, that is visible from some offices and classrooms.

Crossing one of these grassy quadrangles led us to the entrance of the Paul Robeson Campus Center.[5] The outdoor kiosks were covered with signs advertising the usual campus events, although these had a distinct multicultural flavor: Latino music, Black speakers, Portuguese writers, and the like. On one visit we saw a few students in the Campus Center quietly talking and studying, a visual reminder that RU–N is primarily an undergraduate commuter college.[6] They seemed diverse and mixed like a kaleidoscope: any lines among Blacks, Whites, Asians, and Hispanics seemed hard to draw. We saw an Asian woman and a Black man holding hands as they walked in. They came up to a table where a White male with a shaved head was sitting talking with a friend who may have been Puerto Rican. The four proceeded to have a lively conversation; they knew each other well. The scene did not seem remarkable in the context of the room. Samuels recalled sitting at graduation every year and watching the stream of faces coming toward him. "The faces are the map of Rutgers–Newark—people of all ages, races, men, women, disabled people."[7]

The student numbers reaffirm this "map of Rutgers–Newark." In the fall of 2004, undergraduate enrollment figures were as follows for RU–N: of the 6,706 undergraduates, 17.5% were African Americans, 20% were Asian Americans, 15% were Latinos, and about 35% were Whites.[8] The remaining 15% or so were primarily "ethnicity unknown," and 500 came from other countries.[9] Most RU-N undergraduates are from northern New Jersey, and more than half are first-generation college students. More than half are women.

Maggie Shiffrar, professor of psychology, spoke eloquently about what this institutional commitment to access means to her:

> I grew up in a working-class family and went through Head Start as a kid and thought that one of the most important things I could do was teach in an inner city. The kids here float my boat no matter what the struggles are. To take kids who are undergraduates in my class who are doing well but not getting recognized and set them up in somebody's lab into graduate school—now that's gratifying. I have taught at Stanford, and those kids don't need any help. You can see the fruits of your efforts here.[10]

The university includes several colleges and schools. The Faculty of Arts and Science–Newark (FASN) is the former Newark College of Arts and Sciences. University College–Newark is the adult undergraduate evening program. Also part of RU–N are the College of Nursing, the School of Criminal Justice, the School of Law–Newark, the Rutgers Business School–Newark and New Brunswick, and the graduate school. FASN offers 46 academic majors, the usual array available in comprehensive universities. The graduate school and the professional schools offer 21 master's programs and 13 doctoral programs, mainly in the sciences. One respondent, a former faculty member, said flatly that RU–N was not a "hot" research institution but an undergraduate college. The library, despite a few doctoral programs, is an undergraduate library. But some faculty and administrators sharply disagree, as we will see later.

According to Rutgers University President Richard McCormick, RU–N has not been a freestanding institution since the campuses at New Brunswick, Newark, and Camden "formally and officially and completely became the State University of New Jersey in 1956." Today the responsibility for RU–N is divided between the RU–N provost's office and the office of the president in New Brunswick. President McCormick, who said, "I am not a Newark expert," told us: "The provosts on those campuses not only are the chief academic officers but also preside over campus life and facilities, dorms, buildings, police departments, relations with the outside world, and so forth."[11]

From a faculty perspective, cross-campus relations do not appear so seamless. Since the 1960s the campus has been trying to get a larger share of the university's resources. Faculty wonder, "Who controls us? Do we control ourselves, or does New Brunswick control us?"[12] Control from New Brunswick appears to be relaxing under McCormick's leadership with a new budgeting process. Although the outcome is yet to be determined, Provost Steven Diner believes those in charge have "made a great effort to be fair, considering that the administration of the New Brunswick campus is also the central administration of a three-campus system." According to Diner, overhead recovery from external grants has moved from a low of 10% to 20% for RU–N, with the eventual goal of 50% recovery to all three campuses. In addition, admissions are increasingly decentralized.

A Gradually Diversifying Student Body

The central themes organizing our study of RU–N concern two dynamics that frame an ongoing tension over its identity and mission. The first is the changing nature of the student body as it has become increasingly diverse. Most of the new undergraduates after World War II were White men, here as elsewhere, as the college had long been home to first- and second-generation immigrant populations from Europe.[13] Richard P. McCormick Sr., a historian and father of the current president, described the Newark campus on the eve of the 1967 ghetto rebellion. With 2,500 undergraduates, only 62 were Black, and there were no Black faculty members. "Located in the heart of a decaying city with a Black majority, the overwhelmingly white campus was a vulnerable target. In July 1967 Newark was ravaged for five days by civil disorders of such alarming proportions that National Guard forces were brought in to restore order."[14]

The situation on campus changed radically, all of a sudden, in 1969. From being mainly concerned with maintaining its (White) student base and getting a larger share of the Rutgers financial pie, the university suddenly was faced with the challenge of opening itself up to African Americans. On February 24, a group of 25 Black students from the Black Organization of Students (BOS) took over the administration building, Conklin Hall. According to McCormick, they called for more Black students and faculty, a scholarship fund for Newark students, and a series of new initiatives to engage the university more with the city of Newark.[15]

Some demands were quickly acceded to, if not met, such as commitments to hiring more Blacks in admissions and counseling, increasing the number of Black faculty, giving more money for scholarships and remedial programs, and establishing a Black Studies program. The greatest immediate change was the transformation in admissions, funded by the statewide student scholarship program, the Equal Opportunity Fund (EOF) program of 1972, and its accompanying Academic Foundations Department (AFD) program.[16] By 1976 the EOF program enrolled more than 2,000 students, two thirds of them Black, on the three Rutgers campuses, funded by $16 million from the state of New Jersey. By 1979 Blacks were more than 10% of the undergraduate enrollment at RU–N in particular, numbering 634. "Only three other public universities—City University of New York, Wayne State, and Temple—had higher proportions."[17]

The actions originating with the takeover of Conklin Hall changed the university from a White enclave in a Black city to a vital multicultural and multiracial part of the city's life and prospects. Since the 1980s, however, there has been a slower but equally big change, namely, that the African American presence has been eroding in the face of growing numbers of immigrants from all over the world. Who are they? One informant told us that in one class her students, who spoke 16 different languages, came from the Caribbean, Africa, the Middle East, India and Pakistan, China and Japan, and Poland and Russia. Acela Laguna Diaz, chair of the Department of Classical and Modern Languages and Literature, described a great new influx from Portugal and Brazil into the Ironbound, an old ethnic neighborhood in downtown Newark named for the railroad tracks surrounding it.[18] Hispanic students are also drawn from Cuba, Peru, Argentina, Uruguay, Colombia, Mexico, and the Dominican Republic, but especially Puerto Rico. As Charles Russell from the English Department put it, "The fourth great immigration period in our history is occurring now, and it's happening in northern New Jersey. It's Africa, it's Eastern Europe, it's the Middle East, it's South Asia; there is no place on the globe where it's not."[19]

The university has long been caught between its commitments to the legacy of Conklin Hall and its longtime desire for "better students"; an Honors College was begun in the 1980s. Yet the infusion of new immigrants has profoundly altered this discourse. The campus has experienced an appreciable rise in average SAT scores during the past decade. In 2004 Diner convened a committee to ascertain whether this increase in more highly qualified students had resulted in a loss of ethnic, racial, and socio-economic diversity. According to Gary Roth, vice provost for Academic Programs and Services, who chaired the committee, student diversity has been maintained.[20]

How has this been possible? More than 20% of the Black students who select "African American" to describe themselves are international students or permanent residents. Immigrants and the children of immigrants are increasingly better prepared because they originate from the more privileged sectors of their home country populations. Echoing James Jackson, Roth explained:

> For many the process of immigration itself is one of downward mobility. Parents who were middle class in their native countries become working class in the United States because of barriers of language proficiency, racism, and differential standards for professional licensing between countries. Two decades ago, the overwhelming bulk of students attending Rutgers–Newark were first-generation college attendees. Now, close to 50% of the incoming students have one or more parents with some college experience and/or degrees.

The ramifications of this shift in student profiles take several forms at RU–N. Faculty frequently ask how they can remain true to the legacy of Conklin Hall and the commitment to educate African American students in the face of these better prepared immigrant students. Charles Russell asked, "This country may have responded well to multiculturalism and immigration and opening opportunities to many people, but has it really dealt with the legacy of slavery and American apartheid?"

Many faculty spoke about the complexity of students' affiliations and identities. Belinda Edmondson, an African Caribbean faculty member (and past chair of African American Studies), said that Black immigrants do not necessarily identify with African Americans. Echoing Hazel Markus's point about the "downward construction" of nonimmigrant minorities, she blamed the racialized caste system in the United States:[21]

> When White immigrants from Europe or Asians come, there's no real issue about not identifying with the people here who look like you, so if you're Irish or Italian or so forth, you come here and you become White and that's cool, assimilation is a good thing. But for Caribbean and African people to come here and assimilate to an African American identity is to essentially become a member of the caste system.
>
> For Caribbean immigrants ... the whole point is to move up, so American success depends on saying "I am NOT African American," because that would be bad. ... So that means that you always have to be the immigrant,

you always have to be different, you never get to be American, because to be American is to be Black. But because Blackness becomes like the invisible man, it becomes the big black hole—the distinctions are collapsed.

Edmondson said that on a political level, American-born and immigrant Black students often come together in student organizations such as BOS and in courses in African American studies. Clement Price, an African American historian and the director of the Institute on Ethnicity, Culture, and the Modern Experience, was not so sure. "Activism among Black students on this campus has declined. … There was a time when every self-respecting Black student on this campus was informally a member of BOS." He added, "Blackness has become complicated by immigration, so now there's a Haitian student organization, a Ghanaian student organization, so maybe BOS now really is for Black American students, born in the U.S."[22]

Yet African American students are still a powerful voice on campus. Edmondson said that they "have a heritage of struggle," whereas immigrants are more concerned with upward mobility. She described a recent student colloquium attended by Latinos, Asians, and Whites, as well as African Americans. "When it comes to the academy, some people can be very subservient, because you're trying to get in. African Americans have been very important in saying, 'No, you can challenge a state or an institution and win.' Other students are influenced by this idea. They look for some idea of how one goes about that, and that is a great legacy."

Acela Laguna Diaz confirmed the benefits of immigrant status also within the Puerto Rican community. "At times, we have done a better job of recruiting Puerto Ricans from the island than Puerto Ricans from Newark and the Newark area." According to Sherri-Ann Butterfield, East Coast Latinos face similar issues to those of Caribbean Blacks:

> Most people think Latinos are Puerto Rican since they are the largest community in this area. However, we have numerous groups from Central and South America and a lot of times they don't really know what it means to be Hispanic or a Latino American. They come here, these terms are thrown at them, they receive a certain kind of treatment, and they have no context for that.

Jamie Lew from the Department of Urban Education concluded that a simplistic Black and White discourse really does not fit many RU–N students: "I think that really speaks to engaging with how the meaning of race and ethnicity is changing in our society."[23] She wants to contextualize and historicize these issues:

> The point is to build interethnic alliances that include African Americans. Which means looking at their history, and all the issues concerning divide and conquer. And for people to really see themselves as not necessarily

separate from African Americans, or to see them as different from the rest, but to see their histories in a larger connected way.

Lew was the only one of our informants to imply that the racial position of White privilege—as in "divide and conquer"—should be a concern for Whites as well as for people of color. Largely absent from the discussions about student diversity is any attention to the relations of diversity that include White students as well, both immigrants and native born. Diversity is treated as a matter for students of color alone to deal with and represent, even though, as Belinda Edmondson said, the debates about immigrants are implicitly organized around a Black–White caste system they must continually negotiate.

The narratives at RU–N about native-born minorities and immigrants are resoundingly silent about the dominant position of Whiteness that marginalizes them all, at Newark and elsewhere.

A Complex Research Agenda: Faculty in the Middle

If the changing nature of the student body marks one side of the tension at the heart of RU–N's mission, the other side is RU–N's membership in the American Association of Universities (AAU)—a feature of its being one of the three campuses of Rutgers University. In 1977 President Edward J. Blaustein decided to make Rutgers a major research university by joining the AAU, a step humorously labeled the "Great Leap Forward" by RU–N faculty members. A 1980 mission statement for Rutgers University as a whole focused on achieving national and international distinction in as many program areas as possible. Norman Samuels described this new direction for his campus as a conscious integration of access and excellence:

> If all you have is access then you've got a nice community college. The challenge was how to institutionalize both, not merely as a matter of expectation so that you can recruit a first-rate faculty inspired by being at a first-rate research university but also that they will translate the values of a research university into a first-rate undergraduate education.

The AAU tenure standards reward scholarship and visibility in one's discipline over teaching and service. The wrenching change this represented for individual faculty members at RU–N can be seen in Charles Russell's case. Most faculty members went up for tenure in their fifth year; if they received a negative decision, they reapplied the next year. When Russell applied in 1982, the criteria had changed. He recalled, "Everybody was rejected without warning. The messages to the faculty were that the normal time to tenure was in the sixth year and that serious scholarship reflected in substantial publications was now required."

Russell remembers his anger and mortification at what he had gone through—"rage toward the system and feeling that life is unfair. I felt not only the rejection of the tenure committee but the avoidance of some of my colleagues." When he applied a year later, with essentially the same record of two books, he was tenured and promoted. In retrospect, Russell sees in the AAU membership costs not only to individual faculty but to the campus as well. Many decline to participate in program development related to undergraduate education—the use of computers, for example—because it is not rewarded.

Since that time, the tension of being evaluated under Rutgers University tenure standards is a constant preoccupation of the faculty. Some believe they favor faculty at New Brunswick, who have better prepared students, lighter teaching loads, and more doctoral programs. In contrast, Provost Diner, who sits on the Rutgers University Promotion and Review Committee, asserted that the FASN faculty members hold up as well throughout the process as do colleagues from the other two campuses.[24]

Once RU–N was under the AAU umbrella, Samuels saw the path to excellence as the traditional one—a faculty with external funding and strong publication records. Although graduate programs were added in the sciences, management, and criminal justice, he understood that the sciences provided the quickest route to signaling RU–N as a research university:

> Our emphasis was in the sciences for a number of reasons. You can make an impact faster than in the social sciences or humanities, you can bring in more federal dollars, and you can have a visual impact because of the buildings and the labs and equipment. When you walk legislators and potential donors through them, they see students mixing mysterious potions. It is a research university in its most primitive and basic way. The society and the government value it.

Samuels convened science faculty leaders for advice, including psychologists from the Psychology Department's Institute of Animal Behavior. When they came back with proposals to enhance their own disciplines through additional labs and equipment, he recalled saying, "That will get us nowhere. We're not going that way. We're going to build something big and new." After extensive consultation with major national figures and a lengthy nationwide recruiting effort, Samuels brought in Paula Tallal and her former husband, Ian Creese, from UC–San Diego in 1986 to found the Center for Molecular and Behavioral Neuroscience, a leader in the field ever since.

The result of investing in the sciences has been a point of great pride for RU–N over the past 20 years. However, this emphasis has reflected and perpetuated patterns of White male dominance in the science faculty. Samuels told us flatly that to get the best scientists for his program, he had to make diversity issues in faculty hiring take a back seat. As we will see, however, although there have been few White women in the sciences as well, the women scientists at RU–N claim having an easier time there than at other institutions.

The scientific emphasis during Samuels's tenure as provost has changed under the current provost, Steven Diner. Diner sees RU–N as an urban university having multiple research missions. In an April 2004 message, he said, "We must advance the frontiers of knowledge, pursuing research for its own sake as well as for its potential to improve society and human life. And we must connect our university much more deeply to … the people of New Jersey."[25]

But Diner also has a new version of an urban university. He bristles at the stereotypical construction of urban universities as academically inferior and for low-income students, seeing RU–N as "a place where students born without privilege can get a first-rate education." He told us that the university's urban mission was not new. The Law School started the country's first clinical legal education programs in the 1960s, and the Office of Newark Studies was established during Mayor Kenneth Gibson's administration in the 1970s. Both Diner and Samuels told us that Samuels was very committed to Newark. However, under Diner there has been a new effort to reconceptualize the nature of research at RU–N, consciously linking research excellence with diversity issues by emphasizing the urban mission as a scholarly one. He has hired faculty in broad cross-disciplinary areas—urbanization, ethnicity, and globalization—and envisions the university as a major player in the fortunes of the city. For him, cities such as Newark should be primary centers of teaching and research, and the university should know how to take advantage of "what sits at its borders." He envisions RU–N as representing a new paradigm of the "engaged university."

RU–N today, as we shall see, has two programs engaged with this mission—the Institute on the Study of Ethnicity, Culture, and the Modern Experience and the Cornwall Center for Metropolitan Studies. With Diner's support, the university is newly invested in urban research agendas that challenge traditional models of what counts as important knowledge. In this way faculty members at RU–N are resisting the very basis of the tension they live under. Why should there be a distinction between knowledge, expertise, and status on one hand and scholarly involvement with a city on the other?

Stanford University

Stanford President John Hennessy, as numerous administrators before him, drew inspiration from Stanford's founders for his inauguration speech in 2000. He reminded those assembled of the unique place and culture that make Stanford what it is today:

> Stanford University was born with a Western pioneering spirit, an entrepreneurial drive, and a willingness to be bold and take risks. Jane and Leland Stanford clearly possessed this spirit. … David Starr Jordan [the founding president] made this point with eloquence and simplicity: "Our university is hallowed by no traditions. It is hampered by none. Its finger posts all point forward."[26]

If one drives to Stanford from either of the two airports that serve the university—San Francisco or San Jose—one sees firsthand the "decentralized geography of high-tech production," which today ensures that rush-hour traffic often is bumper to bumper in all directions. The congestion and visually jarring quality of eight lanes of traffic ease once one comes to the shaded and affluent streets of Palo Alto. We entered the Stanford campus via Palm Drive, the mile-long entrance lined with the trees for which it is named. At its end is Memorial Church, an imposing structure set off by the foothills in the distance. The red tile roofs on the surrounding buildings are spread out as in an Impressionist painting. The university's promotion materials boast of 25,000 trees on campus, mainly palms, redwoods, and eucalyptuses.

Once on campus we were struck by the privilege of place: the northern California light, the mild temperature, the expansiveness of the grounds. Two thirds of the 8,180-acre campus is open space. In our numerous trips to Stanford, the campus seemed sparsely populated. There are sizeable groups of students on the patios at Tresidder Union at meal times, but perhaps the most common sign of life is students bicycling hurriedly from one place to another. The campus is highly residential, home to 91% of the undergraduates.

The university encompasses seven schools: the Graduate School of Business, and the Schools of Earth Sciences, Education, Engineering, Humanities and Sciences, Law, and Medicine. The architectural center of the campus, the Main Quad, was built between 1887 and 1891 and features archways built of sandstone that provide relief from the sun and peaceful places to walk. Beyond the Main Quad in every direction are buildings from the 20th century, a number of which are under renovation or construction. One new complex is the James H. Clark Center, which houses the Bio-X program. Another planned complex, more than 116 years after Frederick Law Olmsted mapped out a major science and engineering quad west of the Main Quad, is SEQ2, a project that calls for the construction of an environment and energy building and a new School of Engineering center, among others. The project is expected to cost between $375 and $420 million.[27]

History: Stanford Tech, "Steeples of Excellence," and Science and Engineering

The founding grant for Stanford embodies values claimed since its founding in 1891: commitments to coeducation, a broad range of academic disciplines, and the discovery and dissemination of knowledge "for the benefit of all." The grant stated the following as its purpose:

> To promote the public welfare by founding, endowing, and having maintained upon our estate known as the Palo Alto Farm ... a University for both sexes, with Colleges, Schools, Seminaries of Learning, Mechanical Institutes, Museums, Galleries of Art, and all other things necessary and appropriate to a University of high degree.[28]

Historians of Stanford generally agree that whatever the founders envisioned, it had only a West Coast regional reputation for most of its history. Even though it joined the AAU in 1900, it did not begin to emerge as a prestigious institution of national preeminence until the 1960s. It was J. E. Wallace Sterling, president from 1949 to 1968, who announced his ambition for Stanford "to become the Harvard of the West."[29] However, Richard Lyman, who was president in the 1970s, remembers that Stanford had a distinct inferiority complex when he arrived in the late 1950s. The phrase "the Harvard of the West" was partly ironic. He recalled, "It wasn't until around 1980 that it began to be commonplace to see Stanford used as a metaphor for a top university in the country."[30] Since the 1990s, in both popular magazines and rankings, Stanford has been continually placed in the top five institutions nationally.[31]

The university's postwar growth was orchestrated by means of partnerships with institutions outside the university, due largely to the efforts of Frederick Terman, who became the dean of the School of Engineering in 1943, then provost in 1954, under Sterling. Terman ensured that the School of Engineering and the sciences became pre-eminent as the most successful and highly esteemed departments in the university, both in terms of their reputations and the external dollars they generated and came to rely on. His strategy for securing a national reputation was to build "high but narrow steeples of academic excellence rather than … coverage of more modest height extending solidly over a broad discipline. Each steeple is formed by a small faculty group of experts in a narrow area of knowledge, and what counts is that the steeples be high for all to see and that they relate to something important."[32]

The "steeples of excellence" were built by identifying important scientific and engineering niches within departments that would focus on some subfields and research topics at the expense of others, such as biochemistry and biomedicine over naturalist biology, or laboratory experiments over fieldwork. In the case of the sciences and engineering, it sometimes meant shaping departments to respond to defense needs over faculty interests.

Terman and other administrators imposed a faculty culture that according to Rebecca Lowen, a historian of the period, created and celebrated a new academic type, "a professor devoted to research and strongly connected to the world outside the university, an entrepreneur in search of research funds upon which his career, and the university's financial well-being and reputation, depended."[33] Needless to say, this type, Stanford's version of the scientist as hero, was paradigmatically White and male.

Indeed, the recruitment of women faculty was not a part of Terman's equation. In this period of invisibility for women scientists as a whole, the number of female faculty at Stanford in the science and engineering departments was even lower than at similar institutions. In 1960, for example, there was only one woman each in engineering, anatomy, genetics, physics, and geology. Stanford also ranked 19th in the awarding of science doctorates to women between 1947 and 1963, essentially Terman's years, well behind Columbia, Harvard, Chicago, and Cornell.[34]

Terman also restructured departments in the School of Humanities and Sciences and the School of Mineral Sciences.[35] In the 15 years following the war, the social sciences, for example psychology, were built and reshaped to emphasize the values of neutrality, behaviorism, and consensus history with an increasing emphasis on quantifiable, "objective," and scientific approaches to societal questions. In the political science department, a retiring political theorist was replaced by a behaviorist specializing in voter behavior. Lowen characterized these new empiricists as having "a passion for quantifying and rationalizing behavior and processes, a belief in expertise, and a vision of social and economic organizations in which independent experts guide and serve the needs of private corporations and advise those agencies of the federal government that promote and assist private enterprise."[36] There was a deep cleavage at the time between social scientists committed to humanistic and interpretive approaches to studying politics and society and those favoring a more scientifically empirical approach. As was true also at Michigan, more qualitative, theoretical, and historical approaches became suspect because they were possibly too politically inflected.

Donald Kennedy joined the Biological Sciences faculty in 1960, one year before Terman stepped down as provost, and was president of Stanford from 1980 to 1992. He disputed Lowen's account. Rather than engineering, he said it was the "NIH [National Institutes of Health] and medicine that funded most of the rapid development in organized research at Stanford. ... It wasn't defense. It was medicine, all the way."[37] But he agreed that government support was key. President Emeritus Richard Lyman also credited Terman for supporting the humanities; when Terman was provost, "the Department of History suddenly grew to be one of the top two or three in the country."

Terman also established the Stanford Research Institute, which conducted defense-related research and assisted West Coast businesses, and the Stanford Industrial Park, which, as we have already seen, has been a major source of income for the university, further reinforcing the cooperation between the university and electronics firms in the area.[38] Terman's legacy is also widely apparent today. James Plummer is the Frederick Emmons Terman Dean of the School of Engineering in the Terman School of Engineering. Echoing Hennessy's inauguration remarks, he attributed much of Stanford's rise to national preeminence to the atmosphere that Terman and others fostered. "What Terman did back in the '50s and '60s laid a lot of the foundation for the entrepreneurial culture of this place."[39]

The importance of engineering and technology in the history of Stanford brings us back to the questions that our conversations with Carolyn Lougee and Sylvia Yanagisako in 2000 provoked. The world of technological advances is composed mostly of men, as the sea of mostly young men in the Business School dining room showed us. The number of women receiving degrees in engineering and physical and computer sciences was below 20% nationally in 1996.[40] Nevertheless, women receive almost half of the undergraduate and 45% of the graduate degrees in the life sciences—and many say that the next scientific frontier is in the life sciences. Certainly some of our informants in those areas would agree, as we will see later.

Stanford's long-term emphasis on scientific "steeples of excellence" has created complex contexts for the new challenges of building a gender-balanced and multicultural faculty community. Scientifically based definitions of excellence and the prevalence of an entrepreneurial, scientific, and engineering ethos throughout the university enforced a culture favoring White, male, scientific elites. Yet Terman's university is also being transformed today by a gender-balanced administrative team, a more diverse faculty, and new research paradigms. For example, Pamela Matson, dean of the School of Earth Sciences, underscored the university's new commitments to teaching as helping to reverse the concentration on the research agendas of the Terman years: "As long as I've been here people have talked about returning to more of what we were before the Terman era. There's really been a major focus on undergraduate teaching, valuing the faculty for their teaching contributions, incorporating education and research into the same package."[41]

The Best Possible Students

President Sterling had a simple formula, on the surface at least, for reaching his goal of national preeminence: "Simply find the best possible faculty and students, give them all possible support, and then see what results."[42] What are the results, after nearly a half century, of seeking the best possible students and faculty?

Jane and Leland Stanford originally founded the university for "the children of California."[43] Stanford was one of the first private universities to be coeducational from its inception. Although it is unlikely the Stanfords could have imagined how diverse the population of California would become, Provost John Etchemendy found in the founders' intentions a rationale for the idea that world-class universities must be multiracial, multiethnic, and pluralistic. "By being co-educational and nondenominational from the very start, this young school at the turn of the century made a statement about the value of diversity, not just as a social good, but (also) as a critical part of a first-class education."[44]

The student body has broadened over the years beyond White, middle-, and upper-class students. As James Gibbs put it, "Stanford used to educate the California *social* elite. Under Sterling and Terman, it began to educate the California, and national, *intellectual* elite."[45] Stanford now boasts a majority minority student body. In 1968, responding to protests led by the Black Student Union and supported by many White students and faculty, the university made the decision to select students on a need-blind basis.[46]

The historian Albert (Al) Camarillo told us that this policy "undermines ... economic privilege because it allows someone who can't afford to pay an opportunity to come here regardless of her ethnicity, or race, or economic background. You are talking about the redefinition of privilege."[47] These changes led the anthropologist Renato Rosaldo to say, "One of the amazing things about Stanford is its scholarship program, so that you'll work with undergraduate students who are the children of farm workers."[48]

How do the 6,705 undergraduates at Stanford today reflect the population of the most diverse state in the union? The student body is 2% American Indian, 24% Asian American and Pacific Islanders, 10% African American, 11% Mexican American or other Hispanic, and 41% White, with 6% international students and 5% unidentified.[49] The minority group that has come to predominate at Stanford as elsewhere is Asian Americans. This change occurred only after charges of discrimination against Asian Americans in the admissions process were brought against Stanford in 1985.[50] Mexican Americans, California's largest minority group, are underrepresented at only 8%.

However, Stanford is committed to providing increased access only to those seen as meriting an elite education. Having been at Stanford for almost a half century (he came as an associate professor of history in 1958), former president Richard Lyman explained:

> There has always been the tension between doing something for the most disadvantaged and maintaining the standards of an institution that is highly selective. And we were accused from the get-go by the Black students we brought here of favoring Black students who were as nearly White as possible: the sons of Pasadena doctors rather than people from Oakland. ... We're being accused of making silk purses out of silk. Well, I don't think it makes any sense not to have selective institutions. You need higher education of a variety of kinds for a variety of people, and for Stanford to try to act as if it were a community college would be a waste of resources. ... Stanford remains an elite institution with all the attitudes you would expect from that.

Hazel Markus came to Stanford from Michigan. She described to us some of the attitudes one would expect from this elite institution:

> Undergraduate education is of absolute first and foremost importance. People talk about their teaching all the time. You should have a signature course that is you and your perspective. Of course, it is important to be funded, to publish, to produce graduate students, but somehow this undergraduate piece is very significant. As a faculty member, you are a part of making a very special, high-quality experience for a precious, highly select group of students. Because it is such an ordeal for

students to get into Stanford in the first place, students are almost too awestruck about the professors and the institution.

This majority minority student body at Stanford today, moreover, does not produce the fully diverse campus environment one might expect. Campus barriers of race, ethnicity, social class, and intellectual interests separate students from each other. One student told us that the student body was divided into "techies" and "fuzzies," with mutual feelings of distrust across the scientific–humanities gulf. Maria Cotera, currently a Michigan faculty member, who received her PhD in modern thought and literature from Stanford in 2001, observed a Balkanization of students by ethnicity and social class:

> There was an implicit understanding that nobody talked about, that if you are brown, you must be there as the result of a fellowship, and if you are White, you must be there because of privilege. That never really got discussed. There is a tremendous amount of class antagonism at Stanford. It gets mapped onto racial antagonism. It is very racially polarized, but in fact I thought what was also going on was class antagonism. You see White students who are working class, there are a few there, and they really fall through the cracks. ... They don't have the community. The thing that is alienating about Stanford is the class stratification.[51]

This association of only White students with privilege masks class differences as racial ones and thus marginalizes working-class Whites as well. The psychologist Claude Steele spoke about group racial privileges and assumptions that still threaten African Americans' aspirations and impede their progress at Stanford (and elsewhere):

> I don't see quite the level of pain among students at Stanford that you can see on other campuses. On the other hand, I do see these segregations that occur, and I think that's in part an adaptation to that. You can go through here and be an Econ major, and make a million dollars on Wall Street, buy a big house on Long Island, and never have any contact whatsoever. And also the curriculum is very segregated, so a lot of the minority kids go to CCSRE [the Center for Comparative Studies in Race and Ethnicity] and the White guys go to the Econ department, and you get higher education in the United States being a very segregated kind of experience.
>
> We're getting kids, Black kids, who have credentials that are really, really, very, very high. And they're not fulfilling their aspirations, for example, in the sense of going to med school, to the same degree that they would if they went to a historically Black school, who are getting kids with lesser credentials, but who are meeting their goals. So there are these kinds of identity threats and pressures in an environment like

this that are exacerbated by being such an elite school, making this a pressured place.

> I'm increasingly convinced that these segregations are a response to that. I think White kids ... are afraid that if they make a mistake, they're going to be seen as racist or something, and so they segregate, and pursue a course through here that minimizes that kind of strain. And just as the minority kids, in reaction to their identity pressure are segregating and pursuing a course that makes them comfortable. So I think the identity dynamics have a lot to do with these phenomena we're seeing.[52]

But class issues have been around for a long time at Stanford. John Bravman, presently the vice provost for undergraduate education, came to Stanford in 1975 from Long Island. His story illustrates both the power and the challenges of Stanford's philosophy of access and need-blind admissions 30 years ago. Bravman recalled what it was like to be from a family that was not formally educated:

> Stanford was the only private school my parents could afford because of its commitment to access and financial aid. ... I really had no notion of what I was getting into. I was a "techie," as the students say; I knew I was going to be some kind of engineer from the beginning. Stanford provided the access to me that I've been eternally grateful for. But you immediately are confronted with freshmen driving Mercedes and Porsches and everywhere in between. ... I was a hasher; I worked in the food service kitchen for 4 years, so I ended up becoming friends with the chefs.[53]

The Best Possible Faculty

Stanford faculty members are national leaders in terms of their numbers of Nobel laureates (15), MacArthur fellows (23), members of the National Academy of Sciences (134), and other measures of academic status.[54] Although Hennessy is quite critical of the *U.S. News and World Report* admissions rankings, he sees the national rankings from disciplinary associations differently:

> We do look at the way our peers regard us. We absolutely look at it. So many of the things that we use for evaluation [are based on] peer opinion and reputation. I do tend to try to look at that in more detail. We expect and hope that some of our departments will be considered among the best, but again, that ranking is somewhat arbitrary. What I really want is the opinion of my peers, not the opinion of *U.S. News and World Report.*

During our time at Stanford, we explored what administrators and faculty members are doing to mediate issues of privilege with diversity. How do groups of faculty, particularly White women and people of color, experience this push to be the best? The specific ways in which these standards of excellence have militated against a widening of the definitions of the "best possible faculty" can be seen in university documents and records of conversations over the years. In a 1987 University Committee on Minority Issues Report, the authors partially attributed the slow pace of recruitment and retention of minority faculty members at Stanford to the university's "clinging to a single 'Stanford style,' " a dominant way of learning and working.[55] The "Stanford style" represents normatively cultural expectations in terms of patterns of interaction and intellectual styles that women and minority members of the community have struggled to meet, adopting, as we shall see, tactics of both assimilation and resistance over time.

Today the recruitment of women and minorities to the faculty is an administrative and institution-wide priority. The present administration and many of the faculty seem enthusiastically committed to figuring out these issues, not putting them off the table as previous administrations had done.

The University of Michigan–Ann Arbor

President [J. B.] Angell, one of the early presidents of the university, spoke so eloquently about the force of a great public university in building a democracy, and how these universities had to be open and accessible to everyone. President Henry Tappan brought in the notion of graduate education and faced a lot of opposition in the 19th century from those who believed a midwestern university should just be educating people to go out and train for jobs? He countered: No, no, we were going to educate people to discover new knowledge. We were going to be the force. We would have no equal. You see that dialogue and that sort of assertion almost from the beginning of time at the university.[56]

As University of Michigan President Mary Sue Coleman has noted here, her institution began with the goals of becoming not only pre-eminent in research but also a leader in opening higher education to new groups of students, an institutional stance that resists the common assumption that a research mission is an opposite mission to a democratizing one. Ann Arbor, the flagship campus of the University of Michigan, has more than 37,000 students in its undergraduate and graduate programs and 20,000 faculty and staff.[57] There are nearly as many students in the entering freshman class—5,553 in 2004— as in all four classes at RU–N or Stanford.

Nancy Cantor, provost from 1997 to 2002, ascribed Michigan's public-spirited ethos at least partly to its location. "I think Michigan has been an institution heavily influenced by the ups and downs of the civil rights movement in Detroit, and the effects of White flight on Detroit, and the historical context of a labor state. I think all of that fed into the legacy at Michigan."[58]

Like Newark, Detroit is an example of policies leading to the economic, social, and educational decimation of American cities. As Joan Manning Thomas, professor of urban and regional planning at Michigan State University, said, "Fifty years of emptying out Detroit. How do you turn that around?"[59] Mary Sue Coleman and others at Michigan are demonstrating their commitment to "turn that around" by taking a long-term lease on a building in a prominent location downtown to consolidate all of their programs there. Coleman told us, "It took us almost a year to find a space that we thought was the right kind for what we wanted to do, but we have now completed that. It will open sometime this summer."

Nearly everyone we met at the University of Michigan mentioned the city in one way or another, often as a prelude to discussing student diversity or talking about the recent Supreme Court cases. However, when one first arrives at the Detroit airport, it is not apparent that nearby Detroit and its surrounding suburbs constitute one of the most racially segregated areas in the country. Unlike RU–N, the university remains comfortably secluded from the city. The drive to Ann Arbor put us immediately on a freeway that is midwestern in character—on mostly flat, open, rural land. Once we exited the freeway, we traveled along a road that showed some of the remnants of rural poverty—isolated farmhouses and auto repair shops. Inside the city limits, some very substantial homes with beautiful grounds—albeit some of them fraternity houses—come into view. The overall impression is that of a medium-sized midwestern town, similar to Lawrence, Kansas, or Bloomington, Indiana, that encompasses a university larger than it is.

There are several lively commercial areas in the town: those closest to campus feature mostly bookstores, sandwich places, and coffee shops, including the Café Royale, which is crowded with students working in study groups or alone on their computers. Other neighborhoods feature high-end clothing stores, art galleries, and upscale restaurants. One of our informants remarked to us that as Detroit became a Black majority city, Ann Arbor became a destination for (White) people to shop, see a movie, or have dinner.

Once on the main campus, we were struck by the size and scale of the university—huge buildings and expansive quadrangles with well-tended grounds. In places we felt as though we had walked back into the 19th century. However, the memorable buildings on such a grand scale—the Michigan Union (1919), the Law Quadrangle (1924), Hill Auditorium (1913), and the Michigan League (1929)—were all built in the early part of the 20th century. The Law Quadrangle is a prime example of Tudor Gothic architecture. When we first saw it, we mistook the massive Law School building for a cathedral. We needed to allow considerable time to walk from one appointment to another on the main campus; to go to the North Campus, where engineering, medicine, and the arts are housed, we needed to catch a bus.

An undergraduate at Michigan has more than 200 majors to choose from. The Web site for prospective students boasts, "If you've thought about it, we probably have it."[60] There are 19 schools and colleges, 11 of which offer undergraduate areas of study: Literature, Science, and the Arts (LSA); Architecture and Urban Planning; Art and Design; Business; Education; Engineering; Kinesiology; Music; Natural Resources and Environment; and Nursing and Pharmacy. There are a School of Graduate Study and professional education schools such as Dentistry, Law, Medicine, Public Health, Public Policy, and Social Work. The annual budget is approximately $3 billion, with an additional $3 billion of investment assets. The university is also a major R&D laboratory, conducting more than $500 million a year of research supported primarily by federal contracts and grants. Michigan is often the public university with the largest research expenditures.[61] As in many places, the erosion of public support for the university has been dramatic. In the 1960s state support was approximately 60% of the total budget; in 2005 it was 15.3%.[62]

History: The Growth of a National Public University

The origins of Michigan's commitment to be the first "truly public university in America" stem from the Northwest Ordinances (1785 and 1787), the Morrill Act of 1862, and other land-grant acts, with their emphasis on educating broad segments of the society and admitting the people into institutions of higher education. From its beginnings the university had a secular orientation and embraced this popular role; early programs were launched in applied areas such as agriculture, engineering, and medicine. When Michigan joined the Union in 1857, constitutional autonomy was granted to the university with the requirement that the governing board of the state university be popularly elected as a coordinate branch of the state government instead of being subordinate to the legislature.[63] That legislation gave the university much greater autonomy and stability than afforded to most public universities and set it on its path to becoming a pre-eminent state and national institution.

The commitment to "discovering new knowledge" took root during the presidency of Henry Tappan (1852–1863). Tappan foresaw a great American university, one modeled on the scholarly ideal of German universities that would also be central in the life of the state. He envisioned the university sending graduates into the public schools to improve the whole system of education in Michigan, becoming a powerful force against the excessive commercial spirit of the age, and demonstrating to a skeptical public what true scholarship was. He said, "We shall have no more acute distinctions drawn between scholastic and practical education; for, it will be seen that all true education is practical, and that practice without education is of little worth; and then there will be dignity, grace, and a resistless charm about scholarship and the scholar."[64] In the 1850s Tappan brought scholars to Ann Arbor who were associated with the new scientific ideas of the times.[65] However, Michigan in the 1850s was too much of a frontier setting for these European ideas, and Tappan was forced out by a hostile board of regents in 1863.[66]

The twin themes of access and excellence again became prominent during the presidency of James Burrill Angell (1871–1909). He too believed that the university should be not a bulwark of orthodox theology but a means to promote a better society. He further emphasized the research focus of Michigan, believing that scholarship should be pursued for its own sake.[67] Angell also became a spokesman for increasing access to higher education; he is the president who characterized the university's mission as providing "an uncommon education for the common man."[68]

Increasing Student Diversity

Michigan has long had a national student body. By 1860 nearly half, or 46%, of the students came from states other than Michigan and foreign countries. The first African American students arrived in 1868.[69] According to former president James Duderstadt, because the university was founded by an act of Congress in 1817, it has "long used the argument that we were as much a national as a state institution." The proportion of in-state and out-of-state students has varied over the years—during the period of the GI Bill, for example, in-state men were favored, and women and out-of-state students were turned away. If Michigan paralleled the national statistics, the enrollment of women, 64% of wartime enrollments, most likely dropped to between 25% and 35% and remained there until the late 1950s.[70] Not only were women excluded from campus housing but they were told to "wait or to attend other institutions—the teachers colleges and the smaller liberal arts schools, which the veterans were bypassing for more prestigious institutions."[71]

Since the 1980s the regents have followed the policy decision made during Harold Shapiro's presidency that declining state funds would have to be supplemented by increasing out-of-state enrollments, because out-of-state students pay nearly three times the tuition of residents. Now, according to Duderstadt, "we operate as a private institution for students from out of state." Another aspect of Michigan's national reach was that it never had a Jewish quota, so that Jewish students excluded from many selective institutions in the East found that Michigan would admit them. This worked to increase the number of out-of-state students regardless of ethnic background and, according to LSA dean Terrence (Terry) McDonald, "set off a very beneficial chain migration from the East that has extended across generations."

Another theme across generations, particularly for in-state students, is that of increasing access by social class. We were told several times that Michigan has "more alumni than any other school." Philip Deloria, chair of American Culture, made the following points about the continuing meaning associated with a Michigan degree in the lives of alumni—first-generation college students and then their own offspring:

You go to the Michigan football games and you see a whole generation of older fans decked out in maize and blue. It's easy to think that
they look a little ridiculous. But you talk to them and you realize they
are dressed like this because they love the institution so much. If you
trace back in their histories, you realize that Michigan represented the
chance for these folks to come out of a working-class context, go to a
great internationally renowned university, and get a great degree. It is
a turning point, not just in their lives but in the lives of everyone they
dragged along with them. It can mean their moms, dads, all of their
kids, their brothers, and their cousins.[72]

Michigan also has been a beacon for student activism. Terry McDonald told us:

I think there has always been this sense—and I don't quite know when
it began—of Michigan as being a socially concerned, socially conscious
kind of radical place. It is true that one of the first teach-ins against
the Vietnam War was held here and Students for a Democratic Society
was founded here, but this image certainly goes back before that. I once
asked students in a course I was teaching why they chose Michigan. One
said, "Because it was the place that my parents were the most afraid of."
Some LSA parents told me that a conservative guide to college and universities says that at Michigan political correctness "falls like acid rain."
That's not true, but I think that is part of the Michigan image.

Duderstadt said he used to complain that there was a group of activists that
would summer at Columbia, winter at Berkeley, and spend the fall and spring
in Ann Arbor. The protests of the 1960s are the quintessential examples of
alliances between Michigan resident students and national activists drawn to
Ann Arbor.

As at Stanford, RU–N, and at universities throughout the country in the
early 1960s, there was growing concern over the small number of African
American students at Michigan, even though African Americans had been
there since 1868. Within a student population of 25,000, they numbered fewer
than 200. Despite efforts such as the university's Opportunity Awards, their
numbers had increased to only 1,000, or 3%, by 1969. Frustrated by this slow
growth, various student groups organized the first Black Action Movement
(BAM) in 1970, using tactics identical to those at Conklin Hall and common
to student activists around the country—calling a student strike, boycotting
classes, and occupying the central administration building. Eight days later,
the university approved essential BAM demands to increase minority aid, services, and staff and to work toward a goal of 10% African American enrollment by 1973.[73]

African American enrollment peaked in 1973 at 7.3%, but it began to
decline after that. As a result of the activism of BAM II in 1975, the university

strengthened minority recruiting, put more money into minority scholarships, and increased student support services to improve retention. A series of racist incidents on campus in 1985 and 1986 led to the formation of the United Coalition Against Racism, all of which led to BAM III.[74] By the end of the 1980s, Michigan had come to espouse the goals of creating not only a diversified student body and faculty but also a transformed campus culture.

It was these many years of promoting greater access by race and ethnicity that lay behind the recent Supreme Court cases challenging Michigan's affirmative action policies. The plaintiffs in the two 2003 Supreme Court cases—*Grutter vs. Bollinger* and *Gratz vs. Bollinger*—picked in many ways the wrong enemy. No institution could have been more prepared to defend the advantages of diversity for college student bodies and the society as a whole. Earl Lewis, as of 2004 the vice provost and dean of the Rackham Center for Graduate Studies, wrote that the cases arose from the failure of opponents of affirmative action to get anywhere with the state legislature:

> In 1997 the conservative legal advocacy group the Center for Individual Rights, CIR, backed by a few Michigan state legislators, and financed by what appears to be an interlocking group of foundations opposed to affirmative action, launched a campaign directed at the University of Michigan. Soon after Lee Bollinger was named president three Republican legislators placed ads in newspapers statewide [to recruit disappointed White applicants]. ... More than five hundred replied. CIR settled on three individuals, in two separate cases. Jennifer Gratz and Patrick Hamacher complained that the undergraduate admission process unfairly discriminated against them. Barbara Grutter [sued] the university's law school, which had an entirely different admission process. She too alleged that the use of race in the admission process discriminated against her and favored Blacks, American Indians, and Latinos.[75]

After a series of earlier decisions in lower courts, summarized in a *Chronicle of Higher Education* article from July 2003, the Supreme Court agreed to hear both cases in December 2002. In July 2003 the Court's decision upheld the use of the principle of affirmative action in both cases. In *Grutter,* by a 5 to 4 decision, "the judges upheld the Michigan law school's admissions policies ... with the majority strongly endorsing the idea that the Law School had a compelling interest in enrolling a racially and ethnically diverse student body because of the educational benefits that such diversity provides." In *Gratz* the undergraduate admissions policy was overturned by a vote of 6 to 3, not because of its general commitment to affirmative action but because of its point system, a system not in use by the Law School. For example, the undergraduate admissions policy in LSA awarded Black, Hispanic, and American Indian applicants 20 points on a 150-point scale (The difference, for example between what a 4.0 average would receive as compared to a 3.0). The Law

School relied on a more "holistic review," one in the words of the majority opinion that is "flexible enough to ensure that each applicant is evaluated as an individual and not in a way that makes race or ethnicity the defining feature of the application."[76]

The key concept ensured by the outcomes of these two cases is the idea, as articulated by Sandra Day O'Connor in her majority opinion, that the majority in the Michigan Law School case "endorses Justice Powell's view that student body diversity is a compelling state interest in the context of university admissions." The allusion to Justice Lewis F. Powell, Jr., is a reference to the 1978 *Bakke* decision, the last time that the Supreme Court had tackled the issue of admissions. "In that case," according to the *Chronicle,* "the court struck down the use of quotas in college admissions. But an opinion written by [Justice Powell] and joined in part by a majority of the justices, held that colleges could give some consideration to race in an effort to attain a diverse student body." In other words, as a result of *Grutter* and *Gratz* and in the words of an affirmative action opponent, "the thin reed of Justice Powell's *Bakke* opinion has now been turned into a sturdy limb."[77]

With the help of other members of the Psychology Department and a team of outside experts, Patricia Gurin fashioned the social science case for the university. According to her chapter in their book on the case, *Defending Diversity,* the extensive social psychology and social science expertise of Gurin and her colleagues enabled them to employ three kinds of existing data. First, they used a multi-institutional national study of diversity effects for college students in 184 different institutions nationwide, titled the Cooperative Institutional Research Program study. Beginning in 1984, students were tested as freshmen, as seniors, and 5 years after college. Second, they used the Michigan Student Study, a detailed study of a cohort of University of Michigan students from 1990 to 1994 who were asked in extensive questionnaires about their experiences with diversity at the university.[78] Last, they used a study of the effects on students of the Program on Intergroup Relations, which explores issues of civic values and commitments. This program, offered primarily to first-year students, "explicitly incorporates the conditions … important for diversity to have positive educational benefits: the presence of diverse peers, discontinuity from the precollege background, equality among peers, discussion under rules of civic discourse, and negotiation of conflict."[79]

This availability of multiple sources of data is attributable not only to Michigan's programs and policies but also to the university's strength in the social sciences and to the collegiality across departments that allowed faculty in different disciplines to work together. Nancy Cantor underscored the importance of both the campus's previous diversity initiatives and its social science expertise: "Michigan had much scholarly firepower, cultivated during fifty years of eminence in social science research, and diversity was ingrained as a primary value. ... The opponents of affirmative action did not take note of the university's historic commitment to diversity."[80]

The original reaction to the decisions was overwhelmingly positive on the part of defenders of affirmative action across the country. Nancy Cantor spoke for many when she said, "The Supreme Court's decisions upholding affirmative action at the University of Michigan are a victory for justice and a vindication for all who believe that racial and ethnic diversity are essential to higher education in a multiracial society."[81]

Recently, however, there have been increasing concerns. The opponents of affirmative action policies, taking advantage of the right-wing turn in the country as a whole, have persisted. According to some people, there has been an unwillingness on the part of some universities to hold to affirmative action goals and thus a kind of backsliding.

Meanwhile, since the decision was handed down, Michigan has initiated new admissions policies that no longer rely on the old point system. Lester Monts, senior vice provost for academic affairs, was heavily involved in the Supreme Court cases and in retooling admissions policies after 2003. "We basically adopted and modified the process for undergraduates so that it is very similar to the Law School. We have students provide us more information on socioeconomic status. And write more detailed essays so we can find out more about their backgrounds ... and what they have contributed beyond the classroom."[82] Forty more admissions counselors have been hired.

However, today Michigan students are still markedly more White (66.9%) than anything else, with other percentages as follows: Asian American (12.8%), African American (7.6%), Hispanic American (5.0%), Native American (7.1%), and other or unknown (8.2%). Women slightly outnumber men, 50.6% to 49.4%.[83]

And many faculty members, particularly faculty of color, worry about the climate for students of color on campus and its implications for retention. Because of residential and school segregation, most Michigan students encounter members of other races for the first time in college. Several people mentioned that they and their minority students were facing demeaning treatment by White students, particularly in required "diversity courses" that many students take only to get the requirement over with. We wondered if their concerns about their students of color were a veiled way to reveal some of their own pain in the institution. In the 2001 class, only 45.7% of African Americans graduated within 4 years compared to 73.7% of Whites.[84] President Coleman mentioned that problems with minority retention were not about academics but about these complex and often new racial dynamics:

> Our minority students don't graduate at the same rate that our majority students do. It is almost never related to academics. Only 3 to 5% of students leave the university, whether they are minority or majority, due to academic issues. It is always about something else. It is about whether or

not I felt like I could be comfortable in this environment, whether or not I had financial problems, whether things were happening at home, that I just needed to be closer to home. We have a lot of work to do to figure out how can we make the environment more supportive.

The patterns of upward mobility admired by Philip Deloria are still enjoyed primarily by White students.

Diversifying the Faculty at a Top-Ranked Research University

Many we spoke to stressed Michigan's research accomplishments. Recently Terrence McDonald typically boasted, "From the time of Tappan's presidency, the eyes of much of American higher education have looked to Michigan with a single question: Can a public university also become a great university? The answer has proven to be an emphatic yes."[85]

Although there has been an ongoing institution-wide engagement in diversifying the faculty by both race and gender for a long time, the push for more faculty diversity has not seemed to pose as much of a threat to Michigan's standards of excellence as it has at Stanford. The faculty at Michigan is well-known for the intellectual pluralism within its many academic units. David Hollinger, a historian formerly at Michigan and now at Berkeley, characterized the Michigan faculty culture as "more democratic than exclusive, more egalitarian than hierarchical; it is a mystique more of pluralism than of uniqueness of any sort."[86] Jean O'Barr, the longtime director of women's studies at Duke, described the critical component of Michigan as horizontality, a lowness of the boundaries between disciplines.[87] Duderstadt sees the culture as having a high degree of faculty and unit freedom and autonomy, animated by a highly competitive and entrepreneurial spirit.[88] We too found an ease and openness among the faculty members and administrators we met.

Hazel Markus characterized Michigan as a huge public university that stands in contrast to Stanford, where the primary focus is on educating an undergraduate elite. At Michigan, she said, standards of excellence were more pluralistic and people could "breathe easier" as a result:

Oh, they breathe easier, absolutely, because there is a larger and more diverse group of people who understand the need for diversity and who are committed to diversity in teaching and in scholarship. People don't have to spend as much time justifying or defending their actions. At Michigan it became clear, I think from the late '70s and early '80s, that we had to pluralize everything. There are many metrics. There are many standards. There are many models of excellence. Diversity and excellence are together part of the same phenomenon.

And yet Michigan's easier structures have also been home to ongoing patterns of privilege, as we shall see. Intellectual pluralism and departmental autonomy have meant that although some departments have embraced diversity agendas, others have not. Abigail Stewart of the Psychology Department said that pluralism masks hierarchies of privilege and lets some off the hook:

> The funny thing is the hierarchies are relatively invisible here, more invisible than other places, and ... they evade challenge this way. Psychology hasn't hired a single feminist psychologist deliberately in the time I have been here, and yet we started the joint program in women's studies. You'd think that might have led us to think we ought to hire somebody. You don't have to confront the mainstream but it also means that you are not changing them.[89]

The Preeminence of the Social Sciences

The emphasis on the social sciences as the pre-eminent disciplines at Michigan has led to a different model of scholarship as well, stressing social agendas over scientific ones. Nancy Cantor summed up this Michigan gestalt as follows: "I think that more than most institutions, the social sciences had a very powerful position at the University of Michigan. ... They were Michigan's jewel in the crown, so that helped to make the argument that the substantive nature of the problems that Michigan's greatest scholars were working on were very much the center of a whole action research agenda."

In 1947 the statistician Rensis Likert brought his research operation from the federal government to Michigan and started the Institute for Survey Research (ISR). Michigan was chosen because it was already well-known for its strength in the social sciences, an emphasis going back to the era of John Dewey, Robert Cooley, and others:

> By 1946, the University of Michigan was strong in the social and behavioral sciences and had a long tradition of interdisciplinary dialogue. Social scientists in the 1940s were searching for a "methodology," a unifying program for building and funding for social science research. Combined with the sense of urgency of social scientists to assist with finding solutions to problems left by a world war, the timing was right to establish a strong social science research institution at the university.[90]

According to many, Michigan's current social science preeminence can be traced to the power and influence of the ISR, now a major interdisciplinary unit of the university. Duderstadt said:

> ISR is probably the key to the power of the social sciences. After the war years, some of the most creative social scientists involved in the war came to Michigan. They explored Harvard and MIT, but ended up in Ann Arbor, and our ISR was key to that. The possibility of joint appointments in a research organization and in academic departments was particularly

attractive. So the social sciences are exceptionally strong, and a source of considerable pride.

Although the University of Michigan was at first no better than many other institutions in terms of diversifying its faculty and student body,[91] university leaders understood early on that accommodations to these new challenges could not be piecemeal—the institution, rather than the newcomers, would have to change. Patterns of change in the student bodies and the faculty have been accompanied by innovations in university structures, particularly in interdisciplinary links between departments and programs that favor new forms and topics of scholarship and new faculty members. The research, especially in the social sciences, that is enabled by these structures in turn affects institutional demographics and the programs that support them. It is indeed sometimes difficult to separate out the different strands of these developments over time.

It has been the continued growth of the social sciences specifically that has provided the important intellectual underpinnings for two of the most significant efforts mounted by the university in the past 10 years—the defense of the Supreme Court cases against the affirmative action admissions policies of the undergraduate college and the Law School, and the evolution of the ADVANCE program, a program funded by the National Science Foundation to pair excellence and diversity in the sciences and engineering by increasing the number of women faculty in both. The importance of the social science expertise of Michigan faculty in the success of these projects, is a prime example of Tappan's belief that "all true education is practical, and that practice without education is of little worth ... [thus reflecting the] resistless charm about scholarship and the scholar."[92]

Commonalities and Differences

Before we turn to the thematic chapters of the book, we think it is useful to mark some key commonalities in these universities and to speculate on the differences that make their narratives distinct. They inhabit different locations on the same national terrain—the push to increase monies for research, particularly in the sciences; the pre-occupation with rankings; and the nature of the challenges to diversify faculties and student bodies. Historically, as well, events of the 1950s, 1960s, and beyond related to students affected all three in similar ways—from the GI Bill in the 1940s to the sit-ins and civil rights legislation of the 1960s, from the 1970s push to include women faculty and faculty of color to various engagements with diversity issues today.

By now all three institutions have programs devoted to the pursuit of the new scholarship on women and people of color. RU–N boasts the Center on the Study of Ethnicity, Culture, and the Modern Experience and the Cornwall Center for Metropolitan Studies. At Stanford the Research Institute of

Comparative Studies in Race and Ethnicity and the Institute for Research on Women and Gender provide support for faculty and graduate students across different disciplines who deal with issues of race and gender in their work. Michigan also has a Center for African American Studies, an American Culture Program, and an Institute for Research on Women and Gender.

The differences among our sites are equally important. RU–N's students come from a significantly different social stratum than those of Michigan and Stanford, even though all three campuses have more racially and ethnically diverse student bodies than ever before in their histories. It is no accident that the persistent downward construction of nonimmigrant minority students and the resulting implications for immigrant students of color are most keenly felt at RU–N, whereas at Stanford the focus on admitting national elite alters the nature of race and class antagonisms without in the least doing away with them. For Michigan, the defense of affirmative action policies before the Supreme Court has been the most recent example of the responsibility of being a public university "for the common man," although a more diverse student body has experienced new tensions as a result.

Although all three institutions have dealt with issues of hiring a diverse faculty, it has been at Stanford that there has been the most discussion of maintaining standards and academic excellence—of staying at the top. Michigan, also a top-tier university but with a more egalitarian ethos, has less concern about this issue. And although all three institutions are members of the AAU, it is not surprising that it is only at RU–N that AAU-derived tenure standards are sometimes seen as a problem. Although both Stanford and Michigan have incentive funds for hiring minority faculty, RU–N is just now beginning such a program. Yet the effects of these funds at Stanford and Michigan are also very different, as we shall see.

The presence of women and people of color has broadened and transformed departmental and scholarly emphases at all three places as well—but with very different effects. At all three institutions the social sciences and humanities are invested in issues of race, class, gender, and sexuality. Interdisciplinary forays and reconfigurations are also going on. We turn to our explorations of these themes next, illuminated by critical incidents and turning points at all three institutions. How have new faculties, structural changes, and new models of scholarship operated to reveal and challenge the operations of privilege?

3
Diversifying the Faculty

When I came in the fall of 1966, there were two other Black faculty, neither of whom was tenured. I became the first tenured African American faculty member at Stanford. I am happy to be part of that bit of history. There were three of us and we couldn't even fill up a card table! Ultimately, as we pushed, gradually more people came. Now there are 45 of us.

James Gibbs—Professor Emeritus, Stanford University[1]

There are over four times as many men as women [faculty] in our college. The ratios between numbers of men and women increase steadily as the ranks go up. ... For all women—especially for the small handful who eventually do reach the tenured ranks—salaries are so much, and so systematically, lower, that it is [clear] that women work under a system of systematically disadvantageous conditions.

Letter cosigned by eight female full professors in economics, psychology, physics, zoology, romance languages, and microbiology Rutgers University–Newark, 1971[2]

It was threatening to people ... to see women and minorities telling you that you had to do things differently after you had just let them on to your faculty a decade earlier—with great trepidation—and they had behaved themselves down to this point.

Carolyn Lougee—Chair, History Department, Stanford University

This chapter is concerned with how faculty members of color, White women, and their White male allies challenged the rigidity of the 1950s norms of the professoriat in the 20 years between the 1960s and the 1980s, a period ranging from the academy's early grudging acceptance of these newcomers to the beginnings of their challenges to university norms and practices.[3] By telling the stories of each university, we explore the structures, processes, and dynamics of privilege, often subtle and unwritten, of institutional faculty cultures that stacked the deck against them. But we also show how they began to challenge beliefs about the distinctive marks of faculty members in each institution.

Reflecting the attributes associated with the "Stanford style," Stanford always adhered to the tradition of hiring primarily Ivy League candidates with research records that made them among the top faculty in their respective fields in the world. According to some, these standards reproduced the profiles of existing faculty members and rarely turned up women and minority candidates for positions.[4]

Several White male administrators we interviewed failed to see how and why the "Stanford style" might be problematic for the "other." One said, "I find it hard to see how it would make one ethnic group feel less comfortable than another." Another said he did not understand "how measuring up to the Stanford Style was an issue for minorities." For one female professor, however, it was not puzzling at all:

> There are some groups of men … tied by personal friendship and professional collaboration, with no women in their networks, who scratch each other's backs and put each other up for things and it works. They understand each other, they share interests, and they bond. They don't even notice how highly gendered this is.

Basic to this style is a profound public silence around the idea that White males belong to, or benefit from, any kind of group membership or that standards of accomplishment as articulated by that group may be culturally based and biased. President Hennessy told us that success at Stanford is based on entrepreneurship and individual merit, ignoring how such individualistic assumptions might benefit members of some groups over others.

The Rutgers University–Newark (RU–N) faculty members' constructions of themselves are shaped by the ongoing tensions between their responsibilities to a changing student body and the demanding tenure standards of the American Association of Universities (AAU). We heard numerous times of faculty members' love of teaching, their engagement with students, and their passion for their own research. Yet the difficulties of balancing all of these demands are exacerbated by limited resources.

The acute ethnic group consciousness at RU–N, discussed in Chapter 2, is shared by faculty members as well; faculty members of color sometimes have sought to increase the representation of their own group to serve particular student constituencies. As for gender issues, many women think that it is easier to be a woman at RU–N, because there is less pressure to get grants and have doctoral students. Women are active members of faculty governance. But RU–N has never had a woman in a senior leadership position as president, provost, or dean. Few women are "Professor 2s," a designation beyond full professor for highly productive scholars. All the top administrators are White men.

As for the University of Michigan, faculty members often describe themselves as dedicated to the idea of a research university with a public mission. Some also spoke of the "Michigan attitude," which, in contrast to the hierarchical nature of the "Stanford style" and the tensions that define RU–N's status, is characterized by the consistent horizontality and democratic pluralism described previously. There are many models of excellence, widespread acceptance of new ideas across the institution, and low boundaries between departments. As we shall see, programs from the 1980s such as the Michigan Mandate for racial and ethnic diversity and the Michigan Agenda for Women have put these standards of pluralism into institutional policy, in some ways testing the limits of what diversifying the faculty might mean to an institution.

As a way to capture the phases that institutions go through as they diversify the faculty, we borrow from the stages of integration suggested by feminist phase theory. This classification system initially charted the evolution of thought about the incorporation of women's traditions, history, and experiences into selected academic disciplines.[5] Our use of phases here relates to evolving and fluid patterns of institutional responses to faculty transformations in each place. The language of this schema, particularly the word phase, suggests that universities move in a linear fashion and that one phase supplants another. Instead we have found that institutions may be working on issues related to several phases at once. Thus it is important to envision these phases as a series of intersecting circles, patches on a quilt, or threads in a tapestry that interact and undergo changes in response to one another. We chart the movements in each university from accepting "exceptional" women and faculty of color on male terms to profound changes in the dynamics of privilege in each setting. These changes transformed professional identities, institutional structures, and ideas about legitimate knowledge in the academic disciplines. "Critical incidents" at each place signaled these shifts, sometimes dramatically.[6]

Phase One: A White Male Professoriat

As a result of the Cold War, the position of academics began to change in the larger culture. Colleges and universities became more a part of the mainstream of American life, as the gap narrowed between the "ivory tower" of academe and the "real" worlds of business, science, and government. Faculty members in elite universities came to think of themselves as men of affairs—engaged with society rather than part of a "remote alternative culture."[7] The pressures of these changes are well captured in the 1960s academic novel, *The Department*. According to the protagonist, an English professor, the homogeneous White male faculty at his Boston-area university felt insecure and marginalized:

> We all live in a condition of pressure, not so much because we must "publish" to hold our jobs and better our rank as because we think we must justify our professional existence. Other men, the young men, come along and perform scholarly wonders, and are seen to be a new breed of genius, with new visions and new truths. The rest of us slip back, fade away, are delegated finally to insignificance and oblivion. ...

Scholars ... compete in a very big league. They measure themselves not only against each other but against Aristotle and Lucretius and Johnson and Kant and all the other immortals.

Nearing retirement, the narrator concluded that most "have not done, or been able to do, that which they ought to have done. Many feel like imposters."[8] Perhaps the academy was more than ready for a change.

Women and members of minority groups were still a tiny fraction of the professoriat. People of color were excluded because of the pervasive majority culture belief that few if any of them were qualified. With a PhD from Harvard (1941) and numerous publications, the African American historian John Hope Franklin did not work in a majority White university until Brooklyn College hired him as chair in 1956.[9] The dominant postwar gender ideology rigidified constructions of the ideal professor as male, White, heterosexual, Protestant, and middle class, with a terminal degree from a top-ranked university. Women's life course and family responsibilities were seen as incompatible with the career path of a successful professional. For example, at Michigan it took 33 years (1924–1957) to fill the Alice Freeman Palmer Chair in History—"the holder of which shall always be a woman ... appointed on the same grounds as a man would be, with the same privileges, duties, and salary as a male professor."[10]

Michigan had not observed its nepotism rules in the 1930s. Yet when qualified women did show up after World War II, usually as spouses, the university issued a new regulation in the 1949–1950 academic year that barred related persons from employment in the same department, except in emergencies and then for only a term or two. There were enlightened exceptions such as the Psychology Department, which hired seven junior women, one associate, and one full professor in 1951. Later they recruited Elizabeth Douvan from the Survey Research Center and appointed Helen Peak to an endowed chair in 1955.

As the faculty grew at an unprecedented rate in the 1950s and 1960s, women became roughly 6% of the faculty at Michigan. Stanford did not keep statistics on the status of female faculty until the late 1960s, suggesting little consciousness of gender among the faculty. There were eight tenured women on the faculty in 1967–1968, only 1.6% of the faculty. As the quote that opened this chapter suggests, RU–N had eight female full professors in a variety of disciplines. At all three campuses there were a tiny number of faculty members of color, although the Michigan regents in 1962 adopted a nondiscrimination policy that "formally welcomed members of all races and religions as students and faculty members."[11]

**Phase Two: Ending Race and Sex Discrimination and
Becoming "Just Like Them"**

The first significant calls to racially diversify university faculties nationwide
came on the heels of the civil rights movement, as students demanded more
minority faculty. At RU–N, David Hosford told us that, as a result of the Conklin Hall takeover, Black and Hispanic faculty were hired in a number of disciplines. Although there was intense competition because the pool of candidates
was small, RU–N had two advantages: people wanted to live in New York, and
they wanted to pay back the system for the education they received. He said
that "some came to grief over the tenure process," but others stayed. Clement
Price arrived in 1971, joining the faculty initially as an instructor, and was later
appointed as an assistant professor of history. Later other faculty of color came
in with senior appointments, for example, John Williams in English, Earl Shaw
in physics, and Hilda Hidalgo in social work and public administration.

Stanford recruited its first tenure-track Black faculty member, James Gibbs,
in 1966 because the Anthropology Department was looking for an African-
ist. He came recommended by a former Cornell professor, Robert Textor,
then at Stanford, who knew him as an undergraduate.[12] At the time Stanford
was expanding in international studies; their new strength in African Studies coincided with pressure from the Black Student Union to add courses in
African American Studies as well. The Committee on African Studies, a student–faculty committee chaired by Gibbs, then came up with the idea for an
African and African American Studies program. Concluding that St. Clair
Drake, who spent winters in Palo Alto pursuing his writing, would be the
ideal founding director, Gibbs and his wife invited the Drakes to dinner and
put the following question to him: "Would you be interested in directing our
program?" Gibbs told us that after Drake said yes, "I went immediately to the
dean and the provost and for once Stanford really moved."

During the 1970s, Stanford expanded its "best possible faculty" approach
and began the practice of providing funds to recruit minority faculty. President Emeritus Richard Lyman said:

> There was a fund for departments to appoint a minority person, even
> though that person didn't have a needed specialty and wouldn't have
> been next in their list of priorities. Also we had let departments frame
> job descriptions too narrowly. If we just pushed them to broaden them,
> so instead of saying we need a Byzantine historian, we will take a medi-
> evalist who's done some work in Byzantine history.

Michigan in the 1960s was a national center of student activism. Ann
Arbor was the birthplace of Students for a Democratic Society and the Vietnam teach-ins. Tom Hayden remembers how a generation "bred in at least
modest comfort, housed now in universities, uncomfortable with the world we

inherit" called for more than "muddling through"—for participatory democracy and economic and social policies that would link various movements for civil rights, peace, labor, and student interests. They saw the university as "a potential base and agency in the movement for social change."[13]

Despite students' calls to diversify the student body and the faculty, minority faculty membership remained tiny throughout the university. The Psychology Department was again way ahead of most. Patricia Gurin, chair from 1991 to 1998, told us what happened when five Black graduate students presented their demands at a meeting at the house of the then chair, Wilbert (Bill) McKeechie:

> I'll never forget the sense of indignation on the part of these men in power—that they should be asked to respond to these ruffians. But McKeechie just kept the conversation going. He was very open to hiring African American faculty. For the longest time there were just five faculty of color, and they were all African American, so it took a bit longer to get a much more diversified department, but he was critical.

The resistance to hiring faculty of color on a par with White faculty is illustrated by Michigan's decision to recruit Harold Cruz, the prominent African American cultural critic and expert on Black nationalism, as the first director of the Center for African and African-American Studies. We were told that the university settled on him rather than on the other candidate, a highly creditable African American historian, because it was thought he would be less independent and easier to discharge if African American studies turned out to be only a passing fad.

Thus although Stanford was the first of our three institutions to earmark special funds for minority faculty recruitment, all three places ended the 1970s with footholds having been established for individual (male) African American faculty.

In 1971 women at both RU–N and Michigan filed sex discrimination complaints with the U.S. Department of Health, Education, and Welfare (HEW), revealing widespread gender discrimination. This was possible because Title VII of the Civil Rights Act and a presidential executive order both prohibited workplace sex discrimination.[14] The RU–N complaint that opened this chapter provided these details:

1. Men outnumber women about 2–1 among instructors, 3–1 among assistant professors, 11–1 among associate professors, and 13–1 among the professors.
2. Nine departments have no women at all; of the remaining 15 all have more men than women; 13 of these have women concentrated in the lower ranks.

3. Men are more likely to earn tenure. Only 8 of the 54 women at RU–N have tenure.
4. Criteria for tenure are more stringently applied to women than to men.
5. There are pronounced salary differences at all ranks.[15]

One of the complainants, Dorothy Dinnerstein, was the only female full professor in Psychology at RU–N. Her salary was $18,384, compared to male faculty salaries between $22,214 and $27,030.[16] Another costly practice started women out as instructors and only much later put them on the tenure track, a policy proving disastrous for those who did not successfully make the transition. Lillian Robbins told us that women would be renewed but they would not get tenure: "When they were let go they were 10 years post-PhDs. They were essentially unemployable within and outside the university at that point. Whereas the men in the department who weren't going to make it, were out within 2 years so they were still young PhDs." Stanford also took notice of the need to hire more women; they may have been trying to avoid their own discrimination suit.

Yet if we look inside each institution we find similar narratives of this early period, shaped by pain, marginalization, and persistent feelings of inferiority. Members of the first generation often felt the isolation and pressure of being the only one in their group. The idea that newcomers should become "just like them" was particularly true at Stanford, perhaps because of the pressures of measuring up to the standard of the "best possible faculty." Renato Rosaldo, who came to Stanford in 1970, recalled that "there was a sense of debasing the coinage with the hiring of highly educated women." Myra Strober was hired in 1972 as the first woman to teach in the Business School. "It was 90 men on the faculty and me. There were five women students in the class, who made a slideshow called, 'What's a Nice Girl Like You Doing in a Place Like This?' " Strober, who later founded the Center for Research on Women at Stanford, was denied tenure, recalling that "they were not ready to let me into their club."[17]

Carolyn Lougee, who came in 1973, was the first woman hired in the History Department—to do French Renaissance history, a geographical, chronological field. By then women made up 4% of the Stanford faculty. She recalled fighting to maintain legitimacy with her male colleagues by repressing the differences between them—"covering," to use Kenji Yoshino's term. "Everybody knew I had kids, but I never talked about it, I never missed a day of work because of it, and I had to prove that I could be just like them." Female faculty members were often virtually alone, and many faculty of color were isolated in ethnic studies departments.

To sum up the results of this early period, through student sit-ins (in the case of faculty of color) and sex discrimination complaints (in the case of women), long-standing patterns of discrimination were revealed and a first generation arrived. The HEW suits, inspired by the women's movement, helped women see themselves as a "class." The data in those early cases provided powerful evidence on the federal level and opened up sex and race discrimination as objects of institutional analysis. However, as compelling as the data were, there was deep resistance to bringing these newcomers into the professoriat. Each university's available resources also shaped hiring practices. Stanford was able to attract nationally recognized senior faculty members, as in the case of both Gibbs and Drake. RU–N hired some professors of color. Clement Price, now a distinguished service professor, became one of two long-standing Black members of the History Department. Remembering the early days, he said, "When I was an assistant professor, it was a pretty lonely place, and that has to do with the fact that I was a Black person in a White environment."

In the second phase of responding to the calls for faculty diversification, it is clear that policies and practices revolved around a discourse of ending past discrimination and removing these barriers, after which there would be little else to do; exceptionally qualified White women and people of color would be allowed into the academy. Universities developed affirmative action policies and provided incentives for hiring a few newcomers, but resistance to more than a token presence remained deep in academic departments. For example, the suit at RU–N seems to have generated not an active program of recruiting women but a backlash. We were told that some men did not talk to Dinnerstein for several years after she filed the HEW suit. A 1976 "Affirmative Action Work Force Analysis" said, "Although there has been a 7 percent increase in the Rutgers University work force since 1972–1973, the proportion of women and men in the work force as a whole, and in the Faculty and Staff sectors of it, has remained the same."[18] Yet there were a number of full professors among the women at RU–N who signed the sex discrimination complaint, confirming Messer-Davidow's assertion that women had more of a chance at lower status institutions.

At Michigan the efforts of central administrators to urge departments to set goals for diversifying the faculty were met with resistance. Despite the HEW complaint and President Robert Wright Fleming's support, progress continued to be slow through the 1970s. By 1979, nearly a decade after the sex discrimination complaint, only 16% of the tenure-related faculty members were women, and most of them were in junior and untenured positions. The numbers were even lower in the College of Literature, Science, and Arts (LSA), which was seen as the most resistant by the university's Office of Affirmative Action. Only 11% of the faculty members were women, and they were usually lecturers or assistant professors. During the 1973–1974 academic year, 12 LSA departments had not met their goals for adding women to the faculty, and 11 departments had not even set goals.[19]

Federal pressure to diversify the faculty by race and gender did not eliminate entrenched patterns of privilege, and this pressure did not continue with the same intensity into the 1980s and 1990s. As the next phase shows, as the newcomers tackled both scholarship and the curriculum, their place in the academy became more secure, no longer because of the threat of discrimination complaints but because some of their White male allies began to see the value of diversity for both research and teaching. Throughout this phase, assumptions of middle-class backgrounds and normative heterosexuality were also unspoken discourses.

Phase Three: Challenges to University Standards, Norms, and Cultures

The women and people of color who joined the university early did not accept for long the idea that they must simply adapt to the university as they found it, assimilating themselves to dominant institutional norms. After being tenured and gradually joined by others, they began to demand changes at every level of the university. They took on issues of curriculum content and unfair tenure decisions. The 1980s and 1990s saw both gradual and sudden shifts by which departmental and institutional practices and cultures adapted to these challenges. The most important theme from this phase is the struggle over the idea articulated by Carolyn Lougee in this chapter's introduction, namely, that it was threatening for many established White men to see women and minorities telling them that they had to do things differently. How did people at each institution grapple with these challenges to their ideas of excellence and their ideal of the professoriat?

RU–N: Pushed Back to Traditional Notions of Excellence

We have seen the pervasive effects of the AAU membership on RU–N's mission in the 1980s, as the university added graduate programs, particularly in the sciences, and increased the scholarly requirements for tenure and promotion. These new standards were particularly challenging for the Academic Foundations Department (AFD), whose faculty, although all on the tenure track since the early 1970s, had extra summer and student advisement responsibilities and had been evaluated more on their teaching than on their research. According to Charles Russell, between 1987 and 2003 no person in the AFD got tenure, and nobody was actually renewed beyond three years into a second contractual term because no one was doing scholarship meeting the AAU standards. The AFD increasingly became composed of an aging senior faculty tied to the original vision of Academic Foundations and a number of junior faculty failing to get tenure who were increasingly being replaced by part-time people.[20] (Today the AFD is part of the Urban Education Department.)

Arthur B. Powell, an African American mathematician who had extensive experience in mathematics education but only a master's degree, received tenure in 1987 under the old system but was denied promotion to full professor in 2004. (He got his PhD in education from RU–New Brunswick in 2003.) He explained that the AFD's African American profile had always hurt them in the eyes of the White faculty:

We made a very conscious decision that we had to hire White professors because we were just not being successful in getting professors of color tenured. We understood we could not have a department composed entirely of Black and Latino professors, because of the policies of the university as we perceived them. A department without White members would be looked upon as even less than second class, so we needed someone to represent us to the faculty and the administration, someone who would not be looked upon as someone less than they were.[21]

The AFD story is one of misplaced good intentions, in that an effort was made to reduce the marginalization of faculty in an important program for student success. But poorly prepared faculty members (those with master's degrees who lacked the training in original research that most PhD programs provide) lost their footing as the scholarship requirements were tightened. The issue of security in a job geared primarily for student success in a newly research-based tenure culture became racialized and gendered because most of the faculty members were people of color or White women. What does it say about White privilege that "a department without White members would be looked upon as even less than second class"? AFD was perhaps also marginalized because some of the faculty were women, and the program engaged in a kind of teaching commonly associated with women's roles, namely remediation, caregiving, and emotional support.

During this period RU–N showed a lack of any plans or systemic thinking to push for a faculty as diverse as its student body. The research aspirations they took on with the AAU membership helped to entrench the traditional pattern of White male dominance seen across most other research universities. The campus managed to hire a few Black and Hispanic faculty in the 1970s and 1980s, and the percentage of women also increased, but there was neither an overall plan nor any significant reflection about how the institution needed to change.

Michigan: Student Activism and the Six-Point Plan

In spite of two decades of activism at Michigan, diversity issues were not solved by the 1970s, nor had the campus become a harmonious place for people of color. Again students were in the forefront of demanding that Michigan stay true to its commitment to racial equality. A series of racist incidents on campus in 1985 and 1986 led to the formation of the United Coalition Against Racism, "and BAM III [Black Action Movement] was underway."

The upshot of this period of student activism was a great deal of negative national attention. Jesse Jackson came to mediate between the students and President Harold Shapiro, and out of this whole process came the Six-Point Plan. "The Six-Point Plan included the appointment of a vice provost for minority affairs; the creation of a standing advisory committee on minority affairs and new grievance procedures; the creation of the Baker–Mandela

Center for Anti-Racist Education; and a greater commitment to attract and retain African-American students and faculty."[22] As we will see later, the main significance of the Six-Point Plan was that it set the stage for the Michigan Mandate of the 1980s.

Stanford: Diversity as a Challenge to Traditional Notions of Excellence

Our main examples in Phase Three come from Stanford. Unlike the two other institutions, Stanford was roiled at the beginning and the end of the 1980s by two critical events marking the challenges posed by faculty newcomers to traditional norms of excellence. They also illustrate how the conversation about diversity was to shift from affirmative action and threats of suits and discrimination complaints to debates about the legitimacy of feminist and multicultural scholarship represented by women faculty and faculty of color. Educated in graduate schools and by colleagues about the new scholarship on race and gender, they now made up a big enough cohort to support one another and to begin to work collectively for institutional change.

A Contentious Tenure Case

The story of Estelle Freedman's tenure case at Stanford shows how the "Stanford style" influenced scholarly judgments; it became a groundbreaking victory for the legitimacy of feminist scholarship. Freedman represents a new breed of feminist professors who were in graduate school in the early days of the women's movement. She recalled how she "had come to Stanford very committed to doing women's history as a new field, and committed to interdisciplinary women's studies, which was becoming feminist scholarship." Freedman thought she was doing fine because her first book had won a prize, and her teaching had won two major university awards.[23]

Denied tenure at the university level after her department recommended her for promotion with tenure in 1982, Freedman filed an internal grievance charging that the decision was based on discrimination against her as a woman and particularly against her research on women. Dean Norman Wessells sent Freedman's file out for external review again, and again he turned her down. In a 1982 letter in the *Campus Report*, Wessells argued that "affirmative action" was distorting scholarly goals: "The report of the Committee on the Stanford Professorate concluded that basic standards in scholarship and teaching should not be bent in order to achieve the goals of affirmative action." According to Freedman, Wessells raised the question of whether women's studies could be seen as academically legitimate. Feminist studies might be popular now, but if Freedman got tenure, she could still be here in the year 2020, when this subject might no longer be of interest. It was a passing fad, political, and not as important as "real history." Furthermore, another historian in the department wrote a memo to the deans questioning Freedman's work by stating that she had "other loyalties."

Speaking to the Committee on Women Historians of the American Historical Association in 1983, Freedman responded:

> This characterization of feminist academics is both dangerous and ... accurate. It is dangerous in that it presupposes that there is one set of loyalties that academics must share—loyalties to the traditional patterns of academic life, patterns that we well know have excluded women and minorities from full access to that life. To attempt to transform those patterns is to risk being labeled, essentially, a subversive. But [it] is at the same time accurate, for I do want to subvert traditional academic life to encourage both the advancement and the study of women within it. I believe that the only resolution of this seeming dilemma is to recognize the *legitimacy* of our loyalties to other women, and to women's studies, so we are appreciated rather than penalized for our work in these fields.[24]

In the course of her tenure decision, Freedman learned that there had been a ruling in 1981 in the Ninth Federal Appeals Court, *Lynn vs. Regents of the University of California,* that held that discrimination against the subject matter of women is tantamount to discrimination against women. Freedman consulted a labor lawyer, Marsha Berson, who now sits on the Ninth Circuit U.S. Court of Appeals, and filed an internal grievance to the dean and then a formal appeal to the provost. In response to the appeal, she was finally promoted with tenure in September 1983. From the security of an endowed chair, she feels personally vindicated today but says that at the time the legitimacy issue was most important for graduate students. "There were a lot of graduate students who had a passion for doing ... feminist scholarship of some kind. If their key person, who is working in feminist studies, is being told this work is illegitimate, what hope do they have in the profession?"

Freedman's victory was a dramatic example, a critical incident in the accommodation by the university to challenges posed by women and people of color. But there were also important changes going on in the sciences at Stanford at the time—important not least because of the centrality of the sciences in Stanford's culture. We take up the issue of women in the sciences in the next chapter.

The Core Debates: Challenging Beliefs About What Every Educated Person Should Know

The 1980s were concluded at Stanford by a second critical event marking the institutional impact of new members of the faculty and the increasing influence of the new scholarship on women and people of color, namely the faculty deliberations between the years 1986 and 1988 on the question of Stanford's Western Culture requirement, also known as the "Core." Our primary concern here is not the specific curricular changes at issue but what the debates revealed about the power relations among the faculty. How did the social positions among the faculty and their identities as members of specific gender and racial/ethnic groups come into play? What were the institutional implications of the perspectives of the newcomers and their allies as opposed to those of the traditionalists? Throughout the faculty deliberations run narratives of entitlement and marginalization, as participants did (and did not) verbalize their own and others' positionalities and investments. The challenges to the traditional curriculum began when Carolyn Lougee was appointed dean of undergraduate studies (1982–1987), only nine years after being hired at Stanford. Lougee recalled in an interview that she gave a report to the trustees on general education in the early 1980s. Impressed with her presentation, the provost, James Rosse, arranged for her to give it to the Faculty Senate as well. She convened the Western Culture Subcommittee on Gender and Minorities in 1984 but recalled they did little more than offer supplementary materials to faculty. It was not until she had the ear of the provost and President Donald Kennedy, who "understood when I talked about the shift in scholarship," that change began to occur.[25] Lougee's grasp of her position as a woman with the ear of powerful male allies enabled her to take these dangerous first steps.

In a report to the Faculty Senate in the spring of 1986, Lougee first called for a redefinition of academic goals for the Western Culture program because of the powerful critique it was receiving from students and concerned faculty.[26] She later characterized this as "very real feelings of frustration" among at least three groups on campus—minority students, regular minority faculty, and Western Culture teaching staff.

The explosion of scholarship among feminist, African American, and other ethnic scholars in the previous two decades gave the proponents of change intellectual support for their arguments. As Lougee said later in 1988:

We have seen the humanities and social sciences discover meanings of culture that stretch beyond the concept of "great works" as well as knowledge of, tools for studying, and respect for the experience and cultures of women and minorities. ... [The old model is not] adequate to the new political exigencies, the new social realities, and new scholarly understandings.[27]

The Committee on Undergraduate Studies Report complained that works on the core list were almost all by White men and that women and minority groups were not adequately represented.[28] Responding to these critiques, the provost, at the request of the Committee on Undergraduate Studies, appointed a task force on September 29, 1986, to undertake a comprehensive review of the program. The task force sought information and input from the faculty and interested student groups, prepared and circulated draft proposals, modified them, and held numerous public forums.

In the fall of 1987, the task force submitted a report to the committee that renamed the program Cultures, Ideas, and Values (CIV), a tongue-in-cheek reference to the pre-1980 Western CIV program but also, according to Carolyn Lougee, "exactly what we were talking about: cultures, ideas, and values." The committee asked for the inclusion of non-European cultures in all tracks of the required course and recommended less reliance on the core list. According to Lougee, they also stipulated that each course "shall confront issues relating to class, ethnicity, race, religion, gender, and sexual orientation" and "include the study of works by women, minorities, and persons of color." The authors of the report sought to present a balanced perspective—objectives of the proposed legislation "could be met by additions and reorganizations of existing courses—a process of evolution and not revolution." They were trying to refocus "the valued goal of a common intellectual experience for all freshmen from a common list of books to be read to a common quest to understand the origins of the American culture we now share."[29]

A photograph appeared in the January 27, 1988, issue of the *Campus Report* showing John Perry and Ronald Rebholz, professors of philosophy and English, respectively, with a caption that read, "They are expressing the differing views that indicate the depth of faculty division over the issue of the Western culture requirement at Stanford."[30] To have revealed the depths of the division, the photograph should have included some of the newcomers, both White women and faculty of color, who were not only "different" but younger and more junior in rank than their White male counterparts. Throughout the debates we have the sense of faculty cultures talking past one another: an older generation ignoring a younger one, White men talking past men of color, the tradition of great books talking past feminist interpretations, the discourse of a common culture deaf to the diversity of the American experience.

Faculty agreed that one of the purposes of the core reading list, an idea central to the CIV proposal, was a better understanding of American culture. However, the disagreements began as soon as the question arose as to whether this understanding was tied to non-Western as well as Western roots. The Pulitzer Prize-winning senior historian Carl Degler stood firm on his belief in the patrimony of the West. He laid out the chief arguments against a more inclusive framework by asserting that American culture is derived primarily from Europe:

> Few historians of the United States believe that the culture of this country has been seriously influenced by ideas from Africa, China, Japan, or indigenous North America, to name the most prominent non-Western sources of the present population of the United States. ... We are a part of the West, not because this country received Italians, Scots, Germans, Greeks, Irish, Poles, and Scandinavians within its borders, but because

the language, religions, institutions, laws, custom, literature and yes, the prejudices of this country were overwhelmingly from Europe.[31]

Degler's argument rested on the assumption of American culture as uniform, common, and public. His argument, echoed by others, mainly White men, revealed both an identification with a centuries-old dominant cultural formation and a denial of any claims to a personal stake, while accusing the others of grounding their challenges to the core in just such claims. He seems to have been oblivious as to how, in the name of consensus and assimilation, societal power relations position Americans differently.

But the consensus paradigm organizing Degler's world was no longer working for many. As Renato Rosaldo, a leader in the fight for the new requirements, noted in his testimony to the Faculty Senate, the new identifications of American roots were more complex:

> The character of U.S. society is changing. More and more North Americans insist on affirming the specificity of their class, ethnicity, gender, region, race, or sexual orientation rather than melting into the homogenizing pot. ... There are those of us who wish the opportunity to give students tools for understanding the dialogues between cultures. We cannot teach all world histories or cultures any more than we can teach all the great works. We can give students ways of reading and thinking critically about diverse and independent worlds in past and present.[32]

Three of the younger faculty (two men of color and a White female feminist)—namely Renato Rosaldo in anthropology, Gregson Davis in classics and comparative literature, and Mary Louise Pratt in Spanish and Portuguese—circulated a petition endorsing the CIV proposal. Signed by 70 scholars, it argued that other cultures should be "on a fully equal basis with that of Europe and courses that fully recognize the multicultural character of the United States. Until now such tracks have been excluded from the program." A Committee on African Studies endorsed their petition and went on to make their own position statement regarding the place of Africa in the study of Western and non-Western cultures.[33]

The crisis assumed national proportions when Secretary of Education William Bennett accused the reformers of "policy by intimidation."[34] Why did the debate about the core represent an intellectual, political, and psychological crisis for Stanford faculty members? In his book *Cultural Capital,* John Guillory argued that an important function of the university is the formation, identification, and distribution of cultural capital, that is, the preferred knowledge by which the elites who possess it can be distinguished from others who lack it. In literature, cultural capital is organized through the process of canon formation, the "canon" being the body of knowledge considered most valued and central. The canon is "an imaginary totality of works" that is the "repository of cultural values," such that the selection of these works in a syllabus becomes the selection of those values.[35]

Opponents of the CIV proposal were precisely worried about what these proposed changes meant for the redistribution of cultural capital. They argued that eliminating the core list "will in a few years gut the common intellectual experience of the course and sap any intellectual coherence … the requirements and its tracks might have." The core list reminded faculty members and students "that they are indeed engaged in some kind of a common intellectual experience."[36] William Chace was "afraid of losing the spine" of the program by giving up the core. New historical methods that treated other cultures as fully equal to European culture "worry me very much."[37] Opponents also saw the proposed program's looser guidelines as a lowering of standards. Albert Gelpi, then chair of the English Department, and others labeled the new task force guidelines as "vague and open to many interpretations [making way for] an endless, ill-tempered, politically charged struggle over the meaning and implementation of the new … legislation."[38]

Similarly, Kenneth Arrow, Nobel laureate in economics, felt "people were confusing real and vital social problems with the evolution of ideas. In every culture there has been an elite representation. It's important to recognize dominance as well as the right and values of the suppressed. I don't think personal and genetic pride is necessarily an important subject matter of the course."[39]

The testimony of Degler, Chace, and Arrow illustrates the ways some White men failed to engage with the concerns of the women and men of color. They gave no indication of a sense of their own position of privilege. The high culture they espoused, predominately male culture in the public sphere, was assumed to be timeless and universal and to carry no overt identity or viewpoint. When those who were seen to have a gender—women—and a race—people of color—spoke from their perspectives, it was called parochialism or special pleading. Yet as Gregson Davis in classics noted, drawing on his Caribbean upbringing:

> For me, Eurocentrism is not a facile slogan, but a distortion of history that is deeply pernicious … endemic among Western intellectuals for a long time. … I suspect that even an uncritical user of the term "Western Culture" must sometimes be dimly aware that such a concept contains within it a latent assumption about the nature of some opposed "other." … The very word Culture, when written with a capital C, is shot through with preconceptions about hierarchy and inherent supremacy.[40]

It was precisely this uncritical use of "Western Culture" that frustrated the advocates for change. During the first Faculty Senate debate, John Perry said that the core, once viewed as a flexible pragmatic document, "has now been widely perceived as the unshakable Stanford canon … exerting an enormous conservative influence over the entire program. … [The new proposal maintains] that each track ought to provide some recognition that there are roots other than the dominating one." Furthermore, echoing Guillory, Perry and others remarked on the inherently constructed and arbitrary nature of the core list. "The particular core list cannot reasonably be regarded as anything but one selection among many possible ones of [worthwhile] works. Modern work on interpretive theory canon formation ... has shown that a whole list of great works ... is suspect."[41]

In the spring of 1988, the CIV requirement was passed as a compromise that included some components of the great books and also some new components, namely, that each of the year-long nine tracks or courses would give substantial attention to issues of race, gender, and class during each academic quarter, with at least one of these issues to be addressed explicitly in at least one major reading each quarter. Courses were meant to include the historical and social context so that works did not simply stand on their own. As Rosaldo, who favored the changes, said, "What we had was a classic compromise. What we got was some space to allow people to do 'new things.' "[42]

As summarized by Mary Louise Pratt in a later article about the controversy, the changes inaugurated a different instructional context, "a space for much greater change by those who desire it. Tracks constructed around other understandings of culture and broader perspectives on the West are now possible,"[43] even though the idea of a core and many of the core readings remained. The idea of putting these readings in context could now be explored in some of the tracks. Students' attention could be drawn to the process of the construction of valued knowledge rather than only to its appreciation.

In the years following 1988, although CIV had many defenders, it also was criticized by many groups, including faculty, students, and alumni. In a survey of 1992 seniors, the first group to take CIV as freshmen, more than 60% of those who answered the survey rated the requirement as having "only slight to moderate value." The program was attacked by alumni primarily for paying attention to gender. As signaled by letters to the editor in the Campus Report—for example, one queried, "Do most women believe changes are warranted?"—it was clear that some alumni did not support the changes CIV represented at Stanford.[44]

The critics of CIV saw an opening to promote their perspective with the appointment to the Stanford presidency of Gerhard Casper (1992–2000), who was recruited from the University of Chicago. He was widely perceived as being brought in to restore the reputation of the university, damaged after the national furor over the core debates and a storm over the indirect costs claimed by the university.[45] Responding to critiques of CIV from faculty, students, and alumni, Casper appointed a Commission on Undergraduate Education in October 1993 to examine the CIV requirement. Chaired by Robert Polhemus, an early opponent, it also included Casper's provost Condoleezza Rice, ex officio. The committee proposed a three-quarter-long course called

Introduction to the Humanities, which broadly defined the humanities as the study of human identity, thought, values, beliefs, creativity, and culture. There would be no common themes across quarters and no common texts. Nowhere was it mandated that all three courses address issues of race, class, and gender. In the spring of 1997, the Faculty Senate approved the proposal to be in place for ten years. Meanwhile, Casper launched another initiative to improve undergraduate education, a program of introductory seminars for freshmen and sophomores that is thriving today.[46]

We attribute this change as deriving from the replacement of a provost and president who "understood the shift in scholarship," in Lougee's formulation, to a president and provost who had other values. Casper was highly critical of what he saw as the rigidity and polarization of the debates. He viewed the discussion of race, gender, and class as ideological on the part of many participants and called the controversy "a superficial treatment of the issues." To him, the culture wars were fought "by missionaries on both sides as religious wars."[47] Aside from his reversal of CIV, the impact of Casper's presidency was also strongly felt in his responses to previous efforts to diversify the faculty. According to many, both women and minorities suffered setbacks during this period. The Report of the 1987 University Committee on Minority Issues and the 1993 "Report on the Recruitment and Retention of Women Faculty," discussed next, received scant attention from Casper or Rice. Renato Rosaldo felt that changing the legislation on the CIV program had subtle impacts beyond the classroom: "All the reactionary White males got the message that this is our place. We can do what we want. The others are marginalized."

This message reflects Casper's deeply held belief about the power of rational and reasoned argument, with universities as custodians of the rational process. His speeches emphasized how each member of the university community is an autonomous individual positioned in a "republic of learning" that values "nondiscrimination" and where there is equality of opportunity. "[Each] individual member of the community is a contributor to the search to know. ... Your first question ... must never be 'Does she belong to the right group?' Instead, the only criterion is 'Does she have a valid argument?' An argument must not be judged on whether the speaker is male or female, black or white, American or foreign."[48]

He sees the university as a place where "the search to know is carried out by critical analysis, according to standards of evidence that themselves are subject to examination and reexamination."[49] Although Casper was publicly against discrimination and a supporter of affirmative action, he never seemed to acknowledge or even perhaps understand that group identities matter and that some positionalities are more powerful than others.[50] Like many others, he seemed unaware of his own position of privilege—as White, heterosexual, and male.

So who won and who lost the core debates? Lougee's perspective on the question is informative:

> In a way we won and in a way we lost. Ethnicity and gender are much more in the mainstream now [as is] the studying of cultures other than Western culture. It's all well understood now and better than earlier. ... I don't think people look at women's studies and race and ethnic studies anymore the way they did. I think people understand now why these are important for students to study and know.

The curricular debates of the late 1980s were a key moment when the profound implications of the demographic shifts in the student body and the faculty, as well as the changing nature of scholarship, became apparent to faculty members on both sides of the debates and, arguably, to a national audience as well. As Lougee observed, after having been let into the academy with great trepidation a decade earlier, women and minorities were telling their White male colleagues, mostly from an earlier generation, that they had to do things differently.

And yet Lougee also feels that "in a way we lost" because there is now no mandate regarding the content or topics of the required freshman course, Introduction to the Humanities, or for that matter the freshmen seminars. There is no agreement among the faculty that core courses will take up issues relating to class, ethnicity, race, religion, gender, and sexual orientation or include the study of work by women and minorities. In terms of the legislated content of the core curriculum, Stanford may have returned to the regressive past. But a more diverse faculty has made their own changes. Hennessy's and Etchemendy's current commitments on hiring may be more important than who wins the curricular battles. They would agree with Renato Rosaldo's point, that "basically faculty hiring is the number one priority, and this is mainly because we feel that it has the greatest ripple effect."

In that regard, perhaps a more long-lasting legacy of this period in Stanford's history may turn out to be the beginnings of institutional engagement with hiring and retention issues for women and people of color. By the early 1990s, Stanford had not only received negative publicity for denying women tenure but also lagged behind its peer institutions with respect to the recruitment and retention of women. Women in 1992–1993 made up 15.8% of the faculty; tenured women composed 11.0%. Stanford ranked third from the bottom for all faculty; only two technical universities—MIT and Cal Tech—were lower. The distribution of female faculty across schools and department was uneven; 30 departments (43%) had no tenured women on their faculties. Most of these departments, but not all, were in the sciences and mathematics. During the preceding five years, in departments with new faculty, almost 40% had hired no women.

A 1992 committee was appointed to address this lag, chaired by Myra Strober. After conducting surveys and focus groups, they summarized their work in the 1993 "Report of the Provost's Committee on the Recruitment and Retention of Women Faculty." "Because most women have had life experiences different from men's, faculty women often bring a diversity of ideas, viewpoints, and outside networks to the universities in which they work. Stanford is missing out on … that diversity. … We have created a vicious circle. Because some departments at Stanford are known as places that have few women, many women … choose not to come here. … To be able to hire the best talent we can in all fields, we will have to make Stanford a welcoming place for women faculty. Stanford can do better."

Drawing on early successes in Biological Sciences, discussed in Chapter 4, the committee recommended increasing the number and percentage of female faculty, promoting salary equity, using benefits to enhance recruitment and retention, assisting faculty to combine work and family, and instituting sexual harassment programs. They also asserted that a factor against women in the humanities and social sciences was the narrow definition of scholarly merit used by some search committees in fields where paradigmatic shifts are in process, a topic reflecting Freedman's tenure case. Finally they called for an annual report to the Faculty Senate on the numbers and status of women at Stanford.[51]

Departments were advised to provide help with research, reduce teaching loads and service, and grant appropriate credit for directing doctoral dissertations. Department chairs and deans were responsible for maintaining a climate of trust and support in their units. Overall the discourse of this report emphasized that women's value to the university lies in their having had "life experiences that are different from men's; [thus they] often bring a diversity of ideas, viewpoints, and outside networks to the universities where they work."

If Phase Three represents challenges to traditional norms of excellence, then we can see at Stanford, in Estelle Freedman's tenure case, the core debates, and the 1993 report on female faculty, the beginnings of an institutional understanding of the values of such a "diversity of viewpoints."

Partner Benefits: Challenging Heterosexuality as Inscribed Policy

The narratives about the progress of women and minorities overall obscure the heterosexual privilege that the majority of women and men enjoy. It is during this phase of challenges to established norms and cultures that heterosexual privilege first came to light—but not as early as race and gender issues. It took until the 1990s for partner benefits to be won at Stanford. Estelle Freedman told us how heterosexual privilege operated:

During my tenure case in the early '80s, heterosexuality was very much inscribed in policy. There were people who felt that this "too narrowly focused on women" was a code for lesbian. Because even though I wasn't publicly [or] politically "out," anybody who knew me, knew I was a lesbian. ... This gets back to institutional loyalty and what it means to be in the academy. My lifestyle was different. I moved to San Francisco; I was not exactly the young couple doing dinner parties with faculty. People don't necessarily live that way any more. But at the time there still was an older genteel tradition here and so, yes, I think that heterosexuality as an institution definitely helped define what it meant to be in the academy. When I came I was the only out lesbian on the faculty.

This began to change as gay and lesbian faculty advocated for domestic partner benefits. Freedman described the discussion in the Faculty Senate around the final victory in the early 1990s:

People said, "But those people's relationships are evanescent." And I'm sitting with a [gay] colleague who has been in a relationship for 35 years. Here are all these heterosexuals with their divorces, and their alimonies. ... In any case it passed. We have domestic partner legislation. It makes a huge difference. It's affected me, certainly, economically, and for gay and lesbian couples to be able to get graduate housing is a financial issue. Lesbian partners, spouses, do not have the advantage in the labor market that men do. ... Heterosexual privilege still exists. But it is muted by formal and informal changes, like domestic partner benefits, the Lesbian, Gay, Bisexual, Transgender Community Center, and the large number of people who are out. So there's a lot less bias.

According to Maggie Shiffrar at RU–N, domestic partner benefits were key in her decision to join the faculty. "Rutgers has a nondiscrimination policy and at that time Yale didn't. Actually they were discriminating anyway, but that has changed in the last year since the state of New Jersey started domestic partner benefits."

In terms of faculty hiring, only a few people spoke to us about gay and lesbian faculty; the general wisdom is that no one actually gets hired *as* a gay or lesbian professor or because of their pursuit of such topics—they turn to the field of gay and lesbian studies later on. According to Michigan's David Halperin, who was hired in an endowed chair in literature and languages because of his work in the history of sexuality and therefore might be an exception to this rule, "Women's studies was gaining respectability and universities were making a big push to recruit women and Blacks in that period. But [because of homophobia] lesbian and gay studies was produced not because universities went out to hire people but because people they had already tenured for other reasons decided that they wanted to do it and the universities couldn't stop them."[52]

Conclusions

In Phase Three, newcomers and their allies mounted challenges to campus cultures for the first time. Through critical incidents such as the Freedman case and the core debates at Stanford and persistent student activism at Michigan, the scholarly grounds for tenure were widened, the curriculum was transformed, and student bodies continued to be diversified. However, universities sought to deal with institution-wide issues of race and gender by essentially automating them—starting offices of affirmative action and developing equal opportunity policies but leaving the central business of the university alone, a period that James Duderstadt characterized as being "asleep at the wheel ... not paying attention to very real legitimate concerns." In some cases, institutional needs to measure up to traditional standards of excellence or external pressures delayed efforts for faculty diversification—at RU–N, AAU membership meant a neglect of affirmative action policies in this period. Gays and lesbians also began to challenge the ways heterosexuality was inscribed in policy, particularly through advocating for changes in partner benefits.

The national cultural wars of the 1980s were fought out at Stanford in ways that we did not see at the two other campuses. The alarm that William Bennett sounded, even before the core debates began, shows how changes in a top-tier institution threatened members of a growing national conservative movement. But the university's persisting emphasis on attracting the "best talent" reinforced the prevailing idea that diversifying the faculty puts standards of excellence at risk. The ethnic, gendered, and cultural backgrounds of the newcomers had given them the perspectives with which to transform ideas of scholarly and curricular knowledge. But Gerhard Casper's argument for the preeminence of the uncomplicated "rational man" shows a commonly held misunderstanding of the nature of privilege in expecting the newcomers to "cover" and "be like them."

It is also in this stage that the differences in the discourses of resistance to hiring women and minorities began to become clear. Women's lifestyle is seen as holding them back because of family obligations, geographical constraints, and gender socialization. Myra Strober, who has written extensively about gender and work, suggested that Lougee's instincts to hide her family life were right: "Men of my generation and older still don't get it. There are still a lot of issues about women who become mothers." Women's presence threatens male colleagues' sense of their own status—what will happen to the role of "professor" if people who represent "the other," the inferior social role, join it? "I think in some of the disciplines that are mostly men, there is a fear that the status of the occupation will fall if more women come in. My own work suggests that as the university at large becomes more and more female, the status and the pay decline."

If male privilege continued to define the discourses about gender, how did White privilege work within the context of diversifying the faculty by race and ethnicity? The tension between the call for excellence and the need to expand the definitions of what constitutes excellence can be seen most clearly in the discourses around minority recruitment. Whereas "life experiences" might be the code phrase for anxieties around narratives of gender, excellence, as the obverse of diversity, seems to be the code word for anxieties around narratives of race and ethnicity. The resistance of the White male majority suggests a nervousness about their role and future in the academy, according to Judith Ramaley: "Beneath the surface of scholarly identity are deeper and less coherent elements of core human identity itself—who am I, where do I belong, what does change mean to my deeper sense of self?"[53]

We discern a parallel here between diversifying the faculty and the rationale for upholding affirmative action in admissions at Michigan, which built its 2003 Supreme Court case defense on the "compelling state interest" of the educational benefits of diversity for all students. In all their manifestations, these early phases illustrate the compelling benefits to universities of diversifying their faculties; curricula and scholarship opened up to include new voices and views of the world just as student bodies had. A major line of argument running through the core debates was that the student body had been transformed. "It is only necessary to look at our own students in order to recognize that we come from diverse cultures and societies."[54] But it would take the next phases to change the institutional structures and processes that would begin to alter dynamics of privilege. Diversifying the faculty had to be seen to benefit not only the rising numbers of newcomers but also the institutions.

4
Linking Diversity to Excellence and Deconstructing Privilege

We believed that achieving our goals for a diverse campus would require a very major change in the institution itself. ... The first vital step was to link excellence and diversity as the two most compelling goals for the institution, recognizing that these goals were not only complementary but would be tightly linked in the multicultural society characterizing our nation and the world in the future.

James Duderstadt—University of Michigan, 1987[1]

It is imperative that an institution like Stanford reflects the multiracial, multi-ethnic society and pluralistic democracy that serve as a foundation to the University. Otherwise, we cannot call ourselves world class. ... Diversity allows for new shapes, textures, and imaginings of knowledge; it encourages the kind of innovation and insight that is essential to the creation of knowledge. The fact is that a diverse community of scholars asks diverse questions and has diverse insights, and so pushes the forefront of knowledge further, faster.

John Etchemendy—Stanford University, 2003[2]

To think that just bringing in people who are different would fix everything seamlessly seems ridiculous. I do feel like we are on the frontlines here, and that that is a special opportunity for comradeship and to do things that aren't being done anyplace else and to not be alone. It is hard work. Maybe it would be easier to be someplace else, because it would just be my problem and it would be easier to just sort of opt out and just do my work. It is hard to escape being in the fray here.

Elizabeth Cole—Center for African and African-American Studies and Women's Studies, University of Michigan, 2005[3]

The challenges mounted to institutional cultures and practices that we saw in the last phase, most particularly at Stanford, paved the way for administrators and faculty in each of these institutions to envision some deeper implications of bringing White women and people of color into the academy. They began to understand that the paradigms of excellence, heretofore linked to the accomplishments of one group, were too narrow—that diversity is needed "to push the forefront of knowledge further, faster." The encouragement of such new approaches revealed that institutional practices and cultures, rather than individual newcomers, must adapt and change. Excellence and diversity were linked in institutional missions, not assumed to be in opposition to each other. Phase Four is about this major shift.

As we will see in this chapter, however, a stance of linking excellence and diversity may still not be enough to end the marginalization of new groups in the academy. Persisting structures of White and male privilege will need to be named and, ultimately, transformed to make the academy a place where new knowledge from all quarters may thrive. If Phase Four links excellence and diversity, then Phase Five begins to dismantle privilege. And although we have seen evidence of Phase Four approaches at all three campuses, it is mainly at Michigan that we have seen instances of Phase Five practices and discourses emerging, not only in the social sciences and the humanities but in the sciences as well.

Phase Four: Linking Diversity and Excellence

The University of Michigan

The University of Michigan was the first of these three universities to make the shift into Phase Four. Although Harold Shapiro's Six-Point Plan was a harbinger of change, diversity had not been a central concern of the Michigan administration in the early 1980s. James Duderstadt recalled:

> The priority my administration gave diversity was, quite frankly, a bit of a surprise to me. I had been actively involved in trying to better engage and empower our underrepresented minority populations, especially in engineering. … I really didn't understand some of the building concerns among minority students, faculty, and staff …
>
> African American enrollments had declined from a high of 8% during the late '70s to 4%—it was clear that the university was trying to deal with these things by essentially automating them. Building organizations such as offices of affirmative action and equal opportunity and policies, reporting processes and then saying, we've assigned these, delegated these responsibilities, and let's get on to other things. So I was increasingly educated by students, by faculty, by many people, that this was a key strategic issue. It would require a very significant change in the nature of our university.

Duderstadt appointed a group of experts on organizational change—people from the Business School, the School of Social Work, and organization studies. He launched hundreds of discussions in 1987–1988 about diversity—with faculty, students, and staff and also with alumni and state and civic leaders. The outcome was the Michigan Mandate: A Strategic Linking of Academic Excellence and Social Diversity. Its goals were as follows:

1. to recognize that diversity and excellence are complementary and compelling goals for the university and to make a firm commitment to their achievement;
2. to commit to the recruitment, support, and success of members of historically underrepresented groups among students, faculty, staff, and leadership; and
3. to build on campus an environment that sustains diversity and pluralism and that values and respects the dignity and worth of every individual.

A Target of Opportunity Program was established to increase the number of minority faculty in all ranks. The central administration told academic units:

Be vigorous and creative in identifying minority teachers/scholars who can enrich the activities of your unit. Do not be [concerned about] narrow specialization; do not be concerned about the availability of a faculty slot within the unit. The principal criterion for the recruitment of a minority faculty member should be whether the individual can enhance the quality of the department. If so, resources will be made available by the central administration to recruit that person to the University of Michigan.[4]

Chairs were urged to look for talented individuals who would get either complete or partial support. This approach was extraordinary in that not only were there no new resources to fund the Target of Opportunity Program but the university faced a 10% cut in faculty hires. But this helped. Pat Gurin told us about developments in Psychology:

Duderstadt is an unsung hero. He figured out that the way to foster diverse faculty [hiring] was to make some kind of central incentives available. I could say, as department chair, there are no positions available. But if you're interested in hiring, find talented people who are of color or senior women, which was part of the Women's Agenda. So when I started as chair, there were five faculty of color; they happened to all be African American. And when I left, I think there were 32.[5]

Lester Monts is an African American attracted to Michigan because of the promise of the Michigan Mandate. Like others, Monts credits Duderstadt with embedding these issues in institutional practices and culture:

> In 1993, my last year in the University of California, there were 151 Afri-
> can Americans in the entire system, including San Francisco Medical.
> Here there were 139 African Americans tenured on this single campus.
> A lot of it came from the Michigan Mandate when Duderstadt created
> several programs. Duderstadt is sort of my hero. The kinds of resources,
> the availability to resources that I have here far exceeds that of most vice
> presidents. ... Two years ago, we made nine appointments. ... One of
> the big success stories is the minority faculty on this campus gain tenure
> at about an 89% level.

James Jackson told us that Duderstadt's major contribution was to expose as
subterfuge arguments about affirmative action on the basis of "quality": "People asked, 'What are the qualities of the people? We shouldn't bring people in
just because they are Black or just because they are Hispanic, or just because
they are women.' That argument has been around for a very long time."

Duderstadt also led the way in gender issues. Although female staff and faculty had made progress in the 1970s, in the late 1980s it became clear that more
was needed.[6] When Julie Ellison was hired in English Language and Literature
in 1980, she said the response of colleagues around the country was, "Oh, is
Michigan hiring women now?" because a former longtime chair was known
for his resistance.[7] In 1988 Duderstadt created the President's Advisory Commission on Women's Issues to develop a strategic plan for guidance.[8]

Duderstadt recalled that engaging with racial diversity had not initially
helped him with gender: "After the successful Michigan Mandate, I felt that
while I understood how far we had to go in achieving racial diversity, I did not
understand the challenges that women faced in many parts of the university."
What does this say about privilege? The civil rights movement and the wom-
en's movement had begun more than two decades before. Perhaps as a White
male engineer, a member of an elite, he had been protected. In the Michigan
Agenda's final version he described his evolution:

> I am fortunate to be a husband, a father, a friend, and a colleague of
> many talented, wise, energetic, and determined women. Through these
> relationships, I have come to see and understand some of the barriers—
> large and small—that continue to prevent women from achieving their
> full potential and contributing their great talents and leadership, not
> just to this University, but to society at large. And I have learned that at
> times my male-biased view of the world was just plain wrong!

In the 1993–1994 academic year, building on the work of several task forces,
President Duderstadt officially launched the Michigan Agenda for Women:
Leadership for a New Century. The implicit assumption in universities
throughout the country had been that the doors were open to newcomers—
women and people of color—if they assimilated to established institutional

norms. By contrast the Agenda writers argued that the university would have to change "if it is to remain faithful to its heritage—restated in contemporary terms—to provide 'an uncommon education for all with the ability to succeed and the will to lead.' " The Agenda also stands out in asserting that women "have already become the predominant gender in our nation and in our institutions." The challenge required a "much more sophisticated effort targeting different parts of the institution."

The Agenda called for Michigan to increase the presence and participation of female faculty and staff at all ranks, ensure that women of color are full beneficiaries of all components of the Agenda, restructure faculty tenure and promotion policies, appoint and retain ten new senior female faculty, adopt a university-wide policy encouraging flexibility in managing the intersection of work and family responsibilities, and become "the leader among American universities in promoting and achieving the success of women as faculty, students, and staff." It asked for "university resources [for] women and in women's programming, and advocated accountability throughout the institution."

As for women administrators, Duderstadt said, "When Edie Goldenberg became dean of LSA [College of Literature, Science, and the Arts], I don't think we had a single woman chair out of 50 departments." Goldenberg said that she appointed "the first female director of the honors program, the first female chair of political science, the first female chair of psychology, and on and on":

> I wanted us to get to the point where we could have a variety of styles of women chairs and we wouldn't be constantly thinking about, "we tried one and it didn't work." … Some male faculty stereotyped women as chairs by assuming that they would be unable to make tough decisions. And because I was female, some of the male chairs assumed that I would be watching them on the subject of gender, even more than I was.[9]

In 1991 the SHARE program (Special Hiring and Recruitment Effort for Senior Women) was initiated, in the recognition that institutional change at research universities relies on highly respected senior scholars. The program provides strong incentives for recruiting senior female faculty into underrepresented academic units. Now, nearly a decade and a half after the program was instituted (along with the Provost Faculty Initiatives Program or PFIP), a number of senior women have been hired through these programs.[10] Most of the early SHARE appointments in LSA were in the social sciences and humanities; now senior women in the sciences and engineering include Martha Pollock, chair of Computer Science and Engineering, and Deborah Goldberg, chair of Ecology and Environmental Biology. LSA also has a spousal policy that several chairs told us was instrumental in making diverse hires.

Building on the practice in women's studies to make joint appointments with other departments, Abby Stewart, then coordinator of Women's Studies, joined Earl Lewis, chair of the Center for African and African-American Studies (CAAS), to ask the College Executive Committee for a senior feminist of color scholar to be shared by the two units:

> We were told we could do it if we found a full professor and we couldn't find one. At one point they went on and on about how people in Women's Studies and in CAAS would be voting on tenure. And I said, Earl and I both have the vote in our own department. And there was this stunned silence. Who were these unruly people they were so worried about? They already were people that had voted on tenure cases. I thought, isn't it fascinating that a woman and an African American man show up at the EC and they talk about voting on tenure!!

She went on, "Eventually we did talk them into allowing us to do joint appointments at the junior level and we now are fully able to do that." Joint hiring practices among women's studies, other ethnic studies programs, and other departments has since proved to be a major way of hiring women and faculty of color at all levels.

The Michigan Agenda for Women also called for the establishment of a presidential commission to evaluate and restructure faculty tenure and promotion policies to better reflect the challenges of teaching, research, and service. The results were a modified duties policy, which enables women and men who are new parents to take a salaried term off from formal teaching responsibilities, and a "nurturing leave" policy, offered for all faculty in their fourth year, allowing one semester off from teaching and service responsibilities to concentrate on research. Conrad Kottak, chair of Anthropology, said the nurturing leave emerged from the increased requirements for tenure and the recognition of changed gender roles. Like many others, this policy turned out to be good for men as well as women.[11]

Another arena reflecting Michigan's attitudes toward newcomers has to do with issues of sexuality. Much as it had done earlier in relation to the intersections between gender and race, in the mid-1990s the Women's Studies program added several senior faculty members working on intersections of gender and sexuality, building on the work of Anne Herrmann and Martha Vicinus, who had been at Michigan for some time. At the time of our interview with Valerie Traub, currently the director of Women's Studies, there were more than 40 faculty engaged in lesbian, gay, bisexual, transgender (LGBT), and sexuality studies across the campus. Traub told us:

> This is the first place I've ever been where the encouragement for LGBT/ sexuality studies was coming from above as well as from below. And it was this amazing synergy. There was some resistance, but people generally just felt like they were benefiting from this infusion of young faculty. ... Michigan is a very high-powered rigorous intellectual place,

but it's not a heavily ideologically fractured place. We have one of the best, biggest groups of gay/lesbian and sexuality studies scholars in the country. [12]

The Women's Studies Program now provides an intellectual home for LGBT and sexuality studies. Traub and David Halperin also founded the Lesbian/ Gay/Queer Research Initiative as a program area in the Institute for Research on Women and Gender (IRWG).

Yet Nadine Hubbs pointed out that gender differences still privilege gay men over lesbians:

> I admire my male colleagues who are out, who are willing to risk their gender privilege and put it to good use. [But] for various purposes in this world, a White man is a White man. ... We don't see a lot of heroes of stage and screen who are butch women. There is a certain phenomenon of ascribing gay, including gender-queer, men with a weird kind of "shaman" status—fetishized and commodified, and problematic, to be sure. Queer identities always play out as gendered identities, which stand unequal in relation to privilege. It's true in the larger culture, and so in the academy.[13]

What does the perspective of two decades of linking and funding excellence and diversity initiatives at Michigan illustrate? The Michigan Mandate confirmed that exemplary faculty of color could be found who would bring new perspectives to departments and programs. Edie Goldenberg believes Duderstadt empowered people to diversify the faculty without sacrificing quality but improving it. According to a former chair of English, Robert Weisbuch, it made their lives "100 times better: We have a much more high-powered faculty, we're encouraged to read new texts, try new approaches. Everyone has been involved in efforts to attract women and minorities."[14] When Homer Neal, the accomplished African American physicist, became chair of Physics, he saw not animosity toward hiring women or men of color so much as complacency. "The department had been as it had been for decades. What could possibly be wrong with us?" By recruiting 20 to 25 physicists, including women and people of color, Neal moved the department up in the rankings.[15] Finally, alliances between women and men of color, exemplified by Stewart and Lewis, solidified a culture of collaboration that would influence departmental structures, scholarship, and university policies, paving the way for new practices to emerge.

In 1995 Duderstadt claimed progress for the Michigan Mandate, as the minority representation for students, faculty, and staff had more than doubled. Furthermore, "as the campus became more racially and ethnically diverse, the quality of the students, faculty, and academic programs increased to their highest level in history, [showing that] the aspirations of diversity and excellence were not only compatible but, in fact, highly correlated."[16]

But the Senate Assembly's Committee for a Multicultural University's 1995 survey on faculty attitudes indicated challenges for the future. Female faculty members of color were those most disaffected. Black and Hispanic women were most critical of the university's and their departments' efforts in recruitment: 63% of the Black women and 60% of Hispanic women rated the efforts of the university as between poor and moderately good. In terms of faculty retention, 23% of the Black women rated the performance of the university as poor, 43% rated it as moderately good, and only 14% rated it as good or better. Sixty-seven percent of Hispanic women and 62% of the Black men rated the university's performance as between poor and moderately good. Negative views on the role of departments were more widely divergent, but none of those surveyed ranked their departments as outstanding.[17]

These results show persisting institutional problems. Women of color were identified as facing particular barriers as they struggled in the face of both gender and racial prejudice. Although the Michigan Mandate made some progress in increasing their representation, only 3.1% of tenured or tenure-track faculty were women of color. The proportion who achieved promotion was lower than that of either men of color or White women.

We also heard stories of women being discouraged from using the modified-duties policy by male colleagues and chairs, with the suggestion that they would be seen as taking undue advantage of the system. And some White men continued to believe that Michigan had come to a point where faculty were not thought of "in terms of racial or ethnic background … but in terms of the people themselves and their expertise," an assumption based not only on the university's rigorous selection policies but also, perhaps, on their continued innocence about the significance of their own and others' racial, gender, and ethnic positionings.[18]

Rutgers University–Newark: Racial Diversity as a New Institutional Mission

As we saw in Chapter 3, Rutgers University–Newark (RU–N) hired some African American faculty in the 1970s and 1980s, but the shift in emphasis toward research as a result of membership in the American Association of Universities later on in that decade meant that affirmative action issues were not at the forefront of the university mission. Some attempts have been made over the years to recruit and retain minority faculty. We heard of a short-lived committee that discussed how "minority faculty could be made to feel comfortable here" and a postdoctoral fellows program designed to attract faculty of color.

The issue of identity politics has complicated faculty diversity efforts. An African American member of this short-lived committee reportedly said that he would welcome Whites into African American Studies as a way of countering its ghettoization, unconsciously echoing Arthur Powell's concerns about the Academic Foundations Department. But both a Hispanic faculty member and an Asian American faculty member told us that the student members of their ethnic group needed more faculty to represent and mentor that group. (It is interesting that these proposed hires were not described as benefiting the student body as a whole.)

However, since his arrival first as dean of Faculty of Arts and Sciences Newark (FASN) in 1999, Provost Steven (Steve) Diner has charted a new direction for RU–N. As the Michigan Mandate had linked excellence and diversity as part of an institutional mission, Diner made an institutional commitment to diversify the faculty in his statement of goals for 2004:

> We are justly proud of our status as the most diverse national university in the U.S., but our record in faculty and senior staff diversity is not nearly as good. We must build a faculty with the background and experience to serve our student body effectively. In particular, we must substantially increase the number of Hispanic, African American, and other underrepresented minority faculty at Rutgers–Newark, and increase the diversity in the ranks of upper campus administrators.[19]

Diner has tied diversifying the faculty to the university's mission as an urban university. As the dean of FASN, he keyed hiring to three initiatives to recruit people in clusters as scholars of urbanism, ethnicity, and globalization and to connect them to three campus centers—the Cornwall Center for Metropolitan Studies, the Institute on Ethnicity, Culture and the Modern Experience, and the Center for Global Change and Governance. Since becoming provost, he has expanded that vision to support centers in the School of Criminal Justice, the Law School, and the Business School. "We don't have the critical mass in any one discipline, so one way to attract people is to build thematic emphases across disciplines." Diner's 2004 call for more minority faculty is consistent with a new university-wide initiative, the Faculty Diversity Initiative, which President Richard McCormick launched late in 2004 to increase the number of minorities at all Rutgers campuses. The program funds 50% of a line for 3 years.[20] The appointments would not be made otherwise and thus contribute to the diversity of a department or school. RU–N received support for three such hires in the 2004–2005 academic year and for five such appointments in 2005–2006.

This vision of an urban university with ethnic diversity is tied to making the city an explicit center of scholarship. As Gray Roth put it:

> Steve was very smart in defining "urban" in a scholarly fashion, rather than a service fashion, and that made it acceptable, then, to start talking about urban focus, and urban commitment, and roots in the community. It was embraced, really as the campus's mission, as opposed to individuals, or individual offices. ... And Steve was cutting-edge,

because urban was about to kind of reemerge, nationally, as a renewed scholarly focus.

This urban focus includes not only faculty of color but also White faculty with the same research agenda. However, the junior faculty on whom this vision rests are subject to multiple pressures—teaching seriously under-prepared students, engaging with the Newark community, and realizing a research agenda with minimal support and no graduate students. As assistant professors listen to the provost talk about the importance of working in the community, they wonder to what extent that statement will hold true when they come up for tenure. Although the dean talks about the importance of ser-vice, the department chair tells them, "Be careful, ultimately it's going to come down to publications." The chair's caution speaks to not only the quantity of publications required but suggests that research based in the community may still be suspect, revealing the persistence of traditional scholarly norms even as Diner is challenging them.

These problems are exacerbated for faculty members of color. Belinda Edmondson explained, "If you are seen as essentially representing the com-munity then you are not seen as scholarly. ... Also, we have huge student com-mitments as mentors because there are so few Black faculty." As one recent article on the position of women of color in the academy pointed out, this is further complicated by service demands on them:

> On the one hand, there is too little support for the work that is valued (research); on the other hand, there is too much demand for work that is not rewarded (committee work, student club advisor, etc.). ... Institu-tional reward systems can deny tenure and security of employment to those who spend more time on service than on research, even when the service is designed to meet institutional needs.[21]

It is not surprising that junior faculty at RU–N described these pressures more often than our respondents at the other two institutions. And in spite of Diner's experience that RU–N faculty hold up as well throughout the tenure process as colleagues from the other two campuses, many respondents tell stories of negative tenure decisions and faculty of color leaving who were not replaced. One issue may be that Diner has not been around long enough—he has been provost only since 2002 and was dean for only four years before that. But there are also intractable stresses on building and retaining diverse faculty cohorts. Research pressures and varied teaching responsibilities, which are heavy in some departments, are a stark reminder of the lack of privilege for faculty at RU–N, on top of which the scarcity of resources means, for exam-ple, that there is no such thing as a "nurturing leave." McCormick's Target of Opportunity program is for junior faculty only. If the examples of Michigan and Stanford are relevant, they will have far less impact on transforming the institution than will senior faculty—or their influence will take a long time to be realized.

There is also little talk of recruitment and retention of female faculty—the focus is on minorities. Support programs are informal, as are many efforts at RU–N. For example, we heard of efforts in the dean's office to mentor junior female faculty by helping them prioritize their time commitments and "juggle all this work and life together." There is no child care center on campus (RU–New Brunswick has three). The associate dean's position seems reserved for a woman, if past practice is an indicator. But we heard from several women that they had been told that the institution was not "ready" for a female dean. There were few female chairs in FASN in Norman Samuels's administration; today, under Diner, there are eight. Samuels's administration has been characterized as male-dominated, although some feel the culture is just beginning to change.

In terms of heterosexual privilege, things are also beginning to change. Maggie Shiffrar told us that this year Diner, for the first time, had a reception for gay and lesbian faculty and staff: "Diner has made this a good place for gay and lesbian faculty, staff, and students."

Stanford: New Institutional Discourses on Diversity and Gender

If Phase Four is about the need to link excellence and diversity on the institutional level, then what we find at Stanford is not so much a series of major public institutional policy shifts, such as we have seen at Michigan and RU–N, but rather an intense discussion in many sectors of the university about what transforming Stanford's vaunted standards of excellence might mean for the institution. Nearly 20 years after the Michigan Mandate, thoughtful faculty and administrators are beginning to discuss the need to link their standards of the "best possible faculty" with diversity goals. Provost Etchemendy's remarks quoted at the beginning of this chapter exemplify that thrust. In a discussion at a community forum in March 2001, at the beginning of John Hennessy's presidency, Al Camarillo of the History Department noted, "The biggest disappointment, the most persistent problem, the most aggravating issue in my entire career at Stanford has been recruitment and retention of minority faculty. ... I submit to you today it is a crisis."[22]

One explanation for this crisis is the conservative turn of Gerhard Casper and Condoleezza Rice's administration, which Renato Rosaldo characterized as "making it clear that diversity issues didn't matter. They were off the table." Ramon Saldivar, another Chicano faculty leader, told us Provost Rice was concerned with diversity but was convinced that success in the university was a matter mainly of each individual's talent and effort. "Her position was that the presence of minority scholars in the university indicated that although institutional barriers might exist, really talented and capable people could achieve success. She would cite her own case, or Al Camarillo's, or Renato Rosaldo's as evidence for the primacy of individual talent. I certainly agree with this position for the most part. I depart from it to the extent that it forgets how extraordinarily fortunate some of us have been in achieving success in the university, how circumscribed our chances were, how historical factors worked in our favor, and, more important, how crucial it was that there were others like us in the academy to mentor, guide, and advise us in our success."

Paula Moya, who recently gained tenure at Stanford and is known for her work on the epistemology of identity, told us what it was like to be a woman of color at Stanford living with this ideology. She pointed out that the discourse of individual achievement relies on a hidden support structure that women and minorities often cannot access:

> It is very difficult to be a person of color in an institution like Stanford for the same reasons that it is difficult to be a woman here. Sometimes the difficulty comes in the form of a subtle dismissal in which we might not be granted the same kind of credibility that White people are. Sometimes it comes in the form of lack of mentorship, in which an untenured faculty member is not really told what she needs to do and then she finds out too late that she missed something important, or made a crucial error. Another serious problem is becoming isolated. Or they face a kind of patronizing by their senior White colleagues. A consequence of this is that because they don't have the same kind of expectations as White junior faculty, they may not deliver as much. It is very complicated.[23]

Claudine Gay's experience is a concrete example of these dynamics. An African American political scientist who studies the role of race in politics, Gay came to Stanford in 2000 and received tenure early, in 2005, because of competing outside offers. Despite her success, she has found few if any colleagues who share her intellectual interests; they are focused on the institutional side of politics, and she does quantitative studies of mass political behavior. Because she received tenure as her fourth-year review was beginning, there were no formal or informal reviews of her work, and tenure was a surprise to her. When the chair asked why she was so surprised, she thought:

> I've never gotten any indication that I'm doing fine and that people have read my work and find it interesting. I had no way of knowing. All the positive feedback was coming from outside Stanford and definitely not from my colleagues at Stanford. It was a true surprise to me. Obviously they think positively enough to promote me but I had no idea what the discussion was about. There was nothing in writing.[24]

Although Gay finds her chair and colleagues friendly and respectful, she believes they have yet to understand the issues for someone who is the only woman of color in the department. To her mind, the issue is being framed as satisfying the individual rather than changing the department: "What do we need to do to keep Claudine here as opposed to making this a place where someone like Claudine would want to stay?"

In response to realities such as these, Etchemendy appointed the Diversity Action Council in 2002, chaired by the anthropologist Renato Rosaldo. Fifty faculty members joined subcommittees focused on undergraduates, graduates, faculty, and staff. When the council presented its report to the Faculty Senate in May 2003, Provost Etchemendy took the lead in asserting that becoming world class is tied to becoming more diverse, reflecting Rosaldo's insistence that the public support of senior administrators was key. In the diversity effort, Rosaldo said, faculty transformation is central. "Our committee concluded that the most important challenge is to recruit faculty in the areas that really respect and want to work on issues of diversity, and who welcome diverse perspectives and the opportunities that they bring into the classroom."[25]

The psychologist Claude Steele, who was elected to the National Academy of Sciences in 2003, chaired the faculty committee. In his report to the Faculty Senate, he said, "We believe that, other than Asians in natural sciences, engineering, and medicine, there are only about 15 or so minorities in the country who would be viable candidates for tenure at Stanford. ... These 15 would be those accomplished few who could be recruited from other universities at a senior level ... true stars."[26]

We asked Steele why he said this. He responded:

> I really wanted to provoke people, so that they would not be complacent and think that you could pass over a minority candidate so easily. ... And to be prepared for competition; this is a very small and distinguished pool of people ... and that they would cost money. People were surprised and some concluded that in that case they shouldn't go after tenured people. Which is not something that people would say if we were talking about engineers or psychologists ... we have to play as aggressive a game here as you would at building any other dimension of the university.

Why not just hire junior people? "We have done that and have made good progress here. But it is a very laborious effort at a place like this." Steele is asking for the norms that drive Stanford—hiring "stars" as a way to add to the stature of a department and its rankings—to be applied to faculty of color as well as engineers and psychologists. Like Michigan leaders, he also knows that institutional change requires supportive senior faculty in positions of authority.

Ramon Saldivar, however, wondered about the standards being applied. To look at only a "small and distinguished group of people," he said, replicates Stanford's problem:

> Excellence is defined in terms of achieved publications, prizes received, grants awarded, quality of undergraduate and graduate degrees. And

what do you find in our hiring? Huge surprise! Guess who has the most publications, the most prizes, the largest grants, the Cambridge, Oxford, and Ivy League degrees? Is it surprising that White male candidates usually get the nod ahead of African American, Latino, Native American, Asian American, or women scholars? Those very few minority or women candidates who do have the numbers of publications, the prizes, the grants, and the degrees are like the rarest of diamonds. Which university in the world would not want to hire any one of them?[27]

Saldivar takes a different tack, even though he buys into the consensus at Stanford that university hiring should take place with excellence as the chief criterion. He asked, "What of the next tier of still highly qualified candidates, who may have only slightly fewer publications, prizes, grants, or less prestigious degrees? ... It requires more of a gamble on the future development of scholars in this tier. This is what needs to occur if diversity in faculty hiring is to be achieved. To be truly effective the system of university faculty hiring requires fundamental structural change." He went on to ask:

> What would happen if instead of searching for the unique individual with unique qualities, we searched for candidates whose "excellence" was not a result simply of their own personal successes but also emerged from their ability to play a larger collegial role in furthering the research and teaching goals of the institution? ... By thinking of the roles an individual might play in the context of a university's mission to create new knowledge, disseminate it to new generations of future scholars and researchers, and contribute in practical terms to the creation of a good society, we might be able to get a very different profile of excellence in the hiring process than is presently the case.

Attention to female faculty members' status has also changed with the current administration of President Hennessy and Provost Etchemendy, described by Patricia Jones, vice president for faculty development, as "two wonderful guys who are very supportive of women." As provost, Hennessy had hosted women faculty to small group lunches to discuss their experiences as women at Stanford. The Provost Advisory Committee on the Status of Women Faculty (PACSWF) was announced in the spring of 2001 as a follow-up to the MIT conference on women and science. The committee was charged with considering "how Stanford University can enhance its ongoing efforts to increase the representation of women in the professoriate and address the professional well-being and success of women faculty."

Their final report, issued in May 2004, found no significant gender differences for the university as a whole in measures of overall satisfaction or in non-salary compensation—such as initial salary offers, start-up funds, laboratory space, and moving allowances.[28] The "Faculty Quality of Life Survey" accompanying the report noted that in terms of general satisfaction and workplace experiences, factors important to all faculty included "work climate, a sense of inclusion in the school, department and university, and financial stress." But the survey also revealed some gender and racial differences. Female faculty had more concern about quality of life than did their male colleagues. Women rated their work climate less favorably than men did, were less likely to feel included, and were more likely to report gender discrimination. (Thirty-seven percent of female faculty members felt they had received differential treatment based on gender during the past three years, with descriptions ranging from insensitive behavior to perceived discrimination.)[29] Female faculty members were more likely than their male colleagues to report work and family stress, and they particularly sought quality affordable child care. Women also experienced greater workload pressure, especially relative to advising and mentoring, and this experience was particularly pronounced among women of color.

In terms of general satisfaction, White and Asian male faculty provided the most positive ratings, whereas female, non-Asian minority faculty provided the least. Male full professors expressed the most positive general satisfaction; female associate professors expressed the least. Echoing the findings of the national research on these issues, both male and female faculty of color across all ranks and departments mentioned the following issues that separated them from their White colleagues:

- additional service demands, in terms of both committees and mentoring, compounded by a perceived need to participate in activities that might benefit their racial or ethnic communities;
- a sense that their scholarship is undervalued, particularly if it deals with race;
- tokenism reflected in committee appointments, related administrative activities, and high-visibility events; and
- perceptions of subtle forms of differential treatment based on race, for example, not receiving the active mentoring provided to nonminority peers.[30]

Minority female faculty pointed to systemic issues affecting women of color most severely—especially the significant needs of minority undergraduate and graduate students for mentoring and advising. Women of color found life at Stanford the least satisfying of any group. Milbrey McLaughlin, who headed up the survey, remarked:

I was surprised by the responses from the women of color. Where there was an identifiable group that was unhappy, not about discrimination necessarily, but just unhappy, or had some concerns, [it was women of color]. It kind of made me wonder if there were things that I had not seen, were not sensitive to. I have a number of students, who are of color, and [they say] that it's [very] difficult to talk about race. [31]

Other variations showed up by school and discipline. Although female faculty in law, natural sciences, and engineering were as satisfied as their male colleagues, female faculty in the social sciences, clinical sciences, and education expressed a lower level of general satisfaction and inclusion than the men. Some said that "ingrained attitudes" about women were why they did not feel valued. Provost Etchemendy told us what he learned about this issue from discussions in the PACSWF. It might be that some disciplines are more "aggressive":

> In some disciplines the dominant culture tends to be unfriendly toward what many women feel is their more natural way of behaving. For whatever reason, sociological or otherwise, many women find it harder to interact in a very aggressive way. ... There are disciplines where that sort of interaction is a crucial part of the disciplinary interchange; it has become part of the culture. I think economics is an obvious example. [32]

Several other issues emerged from the report. In a small number of schools or divisions, it noted that men on average receive higher initial salaries than women and larger start-up funds, which may reflect the fact that more men than women are hired at the senior level. [33] The report noted a theme of male "high flyers" or "stars," men "recruited or retained through exceptionally high compensation and other forms of recognition." The authors were concerned that

> [when] the most highly compensated faculty are male, that pattern may perpetuate gender stereotypes. Men [may seem to be] the most celebrated or deserving academics and the most likely to attract outside funding and high reputational rankings for their departments. A link between gender and "star power" may itself contribute to the fact or appearance of bias that the University seeks to alter.

The report suggested that women were less inclined to engage in strategic use of outside offers, due to socialization patterns, or were less able to do so, due to family constraints. But the problem was seen to lie with the women, not the men. In her response to the 2003 preliminary report, Phyllis Gardner, a professor in the Medical School, remarked that the findings of "overall satisfaction" might mask the significance of this "star" issue:

> As I listened to [the discussion of] the high outlier, [I thought] someone is selected as the golden boy; it's always the golden boy. [He] is not a minority [or] a woman, and that person is regarded as the great star of the future, and he is given just a little bit more or even a lot more. He is the head of the parade. The distance between him and the rest widens with time. He gets promoted more quickly, and the salary disparity

grows. Sometimes those "golden boys," in my mind, are not necessarily better than anyone else, but it becomes a self-fulfilling prophecy.[34]

In the October 12, 2004, Faculty Senate meeting, which discussed the PACSWF report, Provost Etchemendy announced that he had decided to fast-track the plans for a child care center and accepted the recommendation for a faculty panel, the Panel on Gender Equity and Quality of Life, to look at these discrepancies in the compensation data.[35] The panel has since gone on to address the issue of these outlier "golden boys" and concluded that their higher salaries and other forms of compensation can usually be attributed to senior lateral hires—either buying faculty away from another institution or retaining one through a salary increase. This causes women's salaries to be lower because, as Jones said, "How many senior women stars are there?" Acknowledging that women don't play the "offer" game for a variety of reasons, the Faculty Women's Forum, an organization of female faculty recommended by PACSWF and founded in 2004, is offering a series of programs, including a six-session workshop, Faculty Women Forum on Leadership, Negotiation, and Influence, led by Business School faculty.

The PACSWF report concluded with a set of recommendations regarding recruitment practices, retention strategies, compensation and support, and academic climate and work–family policies. Although we applaud its thoroughness, we wonder why it did not evoke the same call for institutional change as the report of the Diversity Action Council. Asserting that President Hennessy and he are absolutely committed to needed changes for female faculty, Etchemendy described the goal here as simply, "a community in which equity, fairness and mutual respect are a matter of course in every regard."[36] But the construct of female faculty in the report is heavily invested in female gender schemas. There is much discussion of "family obligations," "geographical constraints," and the "inability or disinclination to drive hard bargains," with no indication of the kind of diversity that women might contribute to institutional discourses. The call for a fair and equitable community implies that women should be "just like them" and thus be treated as individual professionals, with workshops to help them become more aggressive in the compensation game—and to function similarly in so-called aggressive departments. The acknowledgment of the need to establish "a profession and institutions in which individuals with family responsibilities are not disadvantaged" is the closest the report comes to appreciating gender differences at an institutional level.[37]

Renato Rosaldo said that he regretted that there were two separate committees on race and gender. The PACSWF reported that "many women's issues are crucial not only for women (but) ... also of particular concern for groups that may experience disadvantages related to race, ethnicity, sexual orientation, family status, and related factors." Tying these issues together is likely to move Stanford toward a better understanding of privilege in that both persistent and varying patterns of advantage will become clearer.

Pat Jones believes Stanford has already gone through its institutional transformation with regard to diversifying the faculty, citing the commitment of the administration, the statement on faculty diversity, and other major efforts to increase the representation and success of both female and minority faculty.[38] There is an emerging sense of university-wide responsibility for this initiative. Sally Dickson, an African American appointed as associate vice provost for faculty development in 2003, told us they are "trying to change the culture of recruitment. This is a different way of doing business which recognizes, to paraphrase Professor Hazel Markus, that it takes a village to recruit. It cannot be done by one person; it takes the dean, the provost, this office, faculty, students, and the community."[39] Jones said that although there has been no dramatic jump in the numbers, they continue to go up steadily. There are very few departments that have no women among the faculty. Stanford has recently established a Diversity Cabinet, chaired by the provost, that is composed of senior administrators with line responsibility for faculty diversity, undergraduate and graduate education, admissions, student affairs, Faculty Senate representation, and human resources. The director of the Center for Comparative Studies in Race and Ethnicity (CCSRE) is also a member. The provost described the function of the Diversity Cabinet as keeping the issue of diversity at the forefront of the university's agenda. The cabinet is expected to provide strategic advice on how to continue to improve campus diversity.

Not only are concerns about diversifying the faculty being raised at the highest level of the administration, but the administration of the university has also changed: four of the seven deans were women in 2003–2004, and, further, responsibility for many sciences resides with Sharon Long, Humanities and Sciences dean, and Pamela Matson, dean of the School of Earth Sciences. When we asked President Hennessy if this was an institutional strategy on his and Etchemendy's part, he demurred, saying "I think it is a coming of age of women in senior roles in the disciplines at sufficient numbers that there are now highly qualified individuals who are candidates for dean. It is something whose time has come. … Certainly women bring different perspectives to things."

Two of the female deans confirmed Hennessy's "coming of age" theory. Pamela Matson was surprised when she was appointed dean of the School of Earth Sciences in 2003–2004 because "I am not in a discipline that is central to the school." Previously very visible as director of the interdisciplinary Undergraduate Earth Systems Program, she explained that appointing female deans made sense because "university leaders discovered that among the people who were really active and care about the university and can juggle multiple jobs are some good women." Sharon Long said that female deans were hired because

Stanford has "a culture, while not universal, but impressively, that values teams, is very democratic, has a can-do attitude, and asks, Who's going to help?"[40]

Yet the idea that diversity undermines true excellence keeps tripping up members of the faculty and administration at Stanford. Michele Elam, an associate professor in the Department of English and the Research Institute of Comparative Studies in Race and Ethnicity (RICSRE), who is of mixed race—African American and European American—said that Stanford has a commitment to diversity. Yet, like many others we talked to, she said some of her colleagues still unnecessarily set diversity at odds with the idea of "only hiring the very best. That ideal isn't up for inquiry or what we define by the very best. These assumptions particularly run up against one another in search committees."[41]

Although people like Ramon Saldivar call for a redefinition of excellence, even he keeps getting pulled back to the abstract idea of the "best possible faculty." The practice of making appointments only in departments (even though a handful of people have joint appointments in programs such as the Institute for International Studies) also makes for structural rigidity, an issue we explore further in Chapter 5. Pat Jones told us that there had been a discussion of other ways to make appointments but that a decision was made not to establish a formal committee. Interdisciplinary areas may be transitory, and faculty members are expected to first be outstanding in their disciplines.

As we can see by looking at the stories of the Michigan Mandate, RU–N's urban hiring initiatives, and the work of the Diversity Action Council and PACSWF at Stanford, Phase Four marks the beginning of explicit institutional discourses of diversity, constructed not only in terms of individual faculty but as aspirations for institution-wide excellence. Powerful White men have begun to advocate for institutional change. There is an increasing belief that pre-eminent institutions must have both women and people of color in senior positions and among the faculty, because their presence both alters faculty recruitment policies and changes institutional discourses. Some begin to question the construction of the professoriat on a one-career model of the life course, noting that many junior professors today are part of a two-career family structure. Maternity policies and nurturing leaves address the issue of women's life course. There begin to be critiques of a highly individualistic model of success, divorced from any social context, and a recognition that women and people of color need a cohort to support them.

Differences among women in terms of their ethnicity and their academic disciplines, as well as differences between women of color and men of color, begin to receive institutional attention. Domestic partner benefits are won, and gay and lesbian studies begins to grow out of the efforts of faculty already there. Yet the unquestioned identification of "excellence" with Whiteness, maleness, and heterosexual and social class privilege persists, as does myopia to the group advantages of White men. For the beginnings of those understandings, we turn to Phase Five.

Phase Five: Shifting the Focus From Excellence and Diversity to Privilege and Diversity

In Phase Five the persistent dichotomy between diversity and excellence comes to be understood as the unconscious association of excellence with Whiteness, maleness, and cultural and social class privilege. The discussion of privilege becomes an overt part of institutional discourse. The identification with individual achievement, and its blindness about group advantages, give way to awareness of the silent and unseen laws that work for and against specific groups of people. As Elizabeth Cole suggested in the quote that opened this chapter, "bringing in people who are different [doesn't] fix everything"; instead, the difficulties of making the patterns of privilege more visible, so that they can be challenged, begins.

The Faculty Women Forum on Leadership, Negotiation, and Influence at Stanford may reveal some structural aspects of privilege at Stanford in its investigation of male outliers. The focus on the urban mission has started to integrate the discourses of scholarship and ties to the community at RU–N. However, it is only at Michigan that university policies and practices have begun to explicitly alter long-standing and traditional arrangements. Women and minority administrators have used their positions of power to build cohorts of faculty through practices of cluster hiring, leading to the formation of a critical mass of minority faculty members. Policies have been put in place to encourage and reward interdisciplinary scholarship. Tenure policies are being reconsidered. The campus culture is shifting from one in which junior faculty members must prove themselves against all odds to one of greater support, suggesting an institution capable of nurturing its members. Women of color have begun to assert their own place for the first time, and within these new critical spaces overt discussions of privilege have begun to take place, in terms not only of gender and race but also of class. In each of these areas there are struggles and uncertainties over the directions to be taken, but these very struggles show an institution in transition.

What are the explicit practices and structures supporting these changes? Dean Terrence McDonald explained to us the LSA policies on hiring in general, within which diversity hires can be made:

> Each department has done a five-year plan, which an elected college executive committee reviews. At the end of that process, after taking a lot of things into consideration, each department is assigned a guaranteed number of positions for five years. They can apply to go above it. But when they are below it, they just go ahead and hire. We require faculty searches to develop diverse hiring pools and each year train search

committee members in ways to do that. Both my office and the Provost's Office have funds to permit additional hiring for opportunities that might be discovered in regular searches and one of those categories is the opportunity to add diversity to the faculty.

The use of such funds to do cluster hiring in CAAS and American Culture over the past decade has built both programs. Nancy Cantor said cluster hiring was important: "Often what happens to faculty of color in particular is that they get isolated. What you want to do is build a critical mass. The cluster hiring wasn't only faculty of color. It was around particular fields so that you build a sense of intellectual camaraderie and purpose that become very supportive for individuals."

In the case of CAAS, in 1998 the administration appointed James Jackson as its director, building on the earlier accomplishments of Earl Lewis, who had been director from 1991 to 1993.[42] Both had been the dean of the Rackham Graduate School, and they used their university-wide reputations and strong support from the LSA dean and the provost to strengthen CAAS. Kevin Gaines, currently the director, told us, "James felt that CAAS was in an ideal position to fulfill the mandate for diversifying the faculty, and that we were able to do that as well as, if not better, than any other unit in the college. I think he single-handedly took it upon himself to expand CAAS. We partnered with History, with American Culture, Anthropology, and English."[43]

Jackson said, "The only reason I took on this task was to demonstrate that it could be done. When I went over to CAAS, there were about six faculty. I think there are closer to 50 now, who are affiliated with the center." He accomplished this goal by working with other departments on joint hires, "trying to convince people about their collective interests with regard to having people with these particular qualities. … You had to know how to go out and find them. You had to know how to attract them. You had to know how to convince them to come to Michigan." Jackson is very proud that all the people he helped hire have gotten tenure and in turn influence the institution. Gaines, who was brought in by Earl Lewis, told us that CAAS and American Culture sought both senior and junior people. "They were going to find the leading scholars in these areas who will very shortly be in positions of leadership. At present, we have this pyramid that is extremely wide at the bottom."

Michigan's policy of cluster hires is one strand of the university's commitment to institutionalizing diversity; the transformation of the tenure system is another. Growing out of a report by the ADVANCE program, discussed later, and an ACE project, the Committee to Consider a More Flexible Tenure Probationary Period issued its report in June 2005.[44] Why is flexibility needed? Differences among individuals lead to different rates of productivity, such as career paths where some faculty begin as postdoctoral fellows and others do not, and to variations in the quality and quantity of mentoring they receive and in the personal and family demands they experience. Joint appointments and interdisciplinary research put multiple demands on assistant professors. Outlets for scholarly publication have diminished. Funding is increasingly directed to larger, multi-investigator projects, requiring time for junior faculty to establish those collaborations. It is more challenging now to amass a record of accomplishment that will earn tenure in a fixed period of time.

Because of these individual differences, and the changing demands of scholarship and publication, the existing tenure process, dating from the 1940s, is much too rigid and should vary as well. Differential treatment is more equitable than uniform treatment. "With customized policies that accommodate to different circumstances, the University can respond in a more tailored and nuanced way to individual faculty issues. Treating people differently in ways that correspond to their circumstances is, in that sense, fairer." The Committee sees these changes as supporting ambition and risk taking for those who seek to work at the frontiers of their disciplines and encouraging more ambitious lines of scholarship and creative work, rather than requiring people to play it safe to get tenure in a restricted time period.

The report recommends that each school and college identify a presumptive time to tenure and then create consistent policies that may accelerate or postpone the tenure review for faculty members depending on their situations. This would require an extension of the maximum probationary period from the current 8 years to 10 years, although 6 years would remain the norm, so that units would have the freedom to provide longer probationary periods. The provost or the chancellor would ensure that unit policies define fair and clear criteria for decisions about accelerating or postponing the tenure review. The authors believe that the cumulative effect of these changes in the timing of tenure will make Michigan a national leader in recognizing and responding to changes in faculty work. After broad consultation, they hope to have recommendations by summer 2006 so that schools and colleges may begin consideration of their policies in the 2006–2007 academic year.

The impact of a critical mass of faculty of color as a result of years of cluster hiring has shown how complex it is to construct a truly diverse campus culture, an environmental shift not possible in a setting where there is only "one of" any group. We heard often that the University of Michigan is the best place in the country to be working on these issues. But the critical mass does not solve the problems—it simply creates the conditions to work on them. Elizabeth Cole, paraphrasing C. Wright Mills, said, "Having enough people together means it doesn't feel like your private trouble anymore, but a public issue. I feel like that is a luxury. ... There are enough women of color here that I can even afford to not like some of them. It is not like every single one has to be my ally, no matter what. That is stupendous."

On the other hand, one untenured faculty member was also worried about the university's commitments to supporting and sustaining this new critical mass of scholars:

> I honestly think that we are going to face barriers from very ingrained notions about how many people of color should be the critical mass in a given program. The idea is that we all come up in these different categories, Asian Pacific Islander, Native American, Latino, in one year and the Executive Committee will understand that we are all necessary; we produced our books and everybody is happy. It may be irrational of me, but I really fear that this sort of "one of" rule might rear its head again: do we really need this many people of color in one program? I am sure that once my book comes out, those biologists and sociologists on the Executive Committee will, even if it comes out with ... some important press, will look at it and say, "What is this?"

The stresses of this phase include the complexities surrounding the institutional commitment to interdisciplinary work and shifting ideas of what counts as scholarship and faculty achievement. Maria Cotera characterized Michigan as "the best of all possible worlds for doing this work. It doesn't make it a perfect world and there are serious problems, but nevertheless, given what the world is ..." She cited the power to hire people in joint positions on campus and the unusual commitment to comparative studies in race and ethnicity. But she also noted anomalies in her role at the intersection of American Culture and Women's Studies. "We are jointly appointed precisely because our work sits at the intersections of these two discourses. ... It is hard to find a place that feels entirely like home, because whereas in one place you feel like issues of gender and sexuality are not being discussed in any real way, in another place you feel like race is really marginal to the discussion of gender."

Women faculty of color point to other ways that race is gendered. Some minority men are part of the star system at Michigan, the image of the "big men of color on campus," according to one. Said another, "They are macho numbers crunchers, who reproduce the White old boys club." Most tenured women of color are associate professors, and for that reason alone they are not a part of the star system. Aside from such stresses, male faculty of color also benefit from gender privilege. Alford (Al) Young is a tenured African American sociologist. He said:

> Things happen to my wife because she is a woman. It is almost like two separate universities. I do think there is a strong gender component to how people view diversity at Michigan. For me this ties to Michigan's period of activism, which was very male-centric in the '60s. There is still a culture of accepting men's voices on issues. It is always safer for me to raise a concern about diversity, even if it is ignored. For a woman to do it

would be more of a challenge, and possibly have some repercussions. ...
I think it is less safe for any women to be progressive here.[45]

Young's partner, Carla O'Connor, agreed. She said that although she was part
of informal support networks for women of color, they needed to be quiet
about their child care responsibilities, and that there is also the challenge of
creating a public persona. "I am bubbly—that is just who I am. I wonder if
as an African American woman, that makes me more approachable. If I had
a more reserved orientation, there would be a sort of double jeopardy. More
reserved African American women—I think it is definitely working against
them. It is a gender, race kind of thing."[46]

In a 2001 study, "Assessing the Academic Work Environment for Faculty of
Color in Science and Engineering," a quarter of faculty of color reported expe-
riencing racial or ethnic discrimination at Michigan within the past five years.
And, as at Stanford, the most unhappy group at Michigan was also women of
color:

> Women scientists and engineers of color felt they had less influence
> over educational decisions than their colleagues, received less attractive
> offers and counteroffers, and received less mentoring. Moreover, they
> rated their departmental climate as significantly less positive in terms
> of scholarly isolation, gender egalitarianism, and the rating of their
> department chairs as fair and committed to racial–ethnic diversity.[47]

Another discourse that has emerged at Michigan in the current period is
about social class. It is in the discourses around class that people officially
seen as "diverse" in other ways begin to reveal some of the deepest cultural
barriers that maintain their marginalities. Some people have indicated that
their class backgrounds have complicated their racial and gender positions.
O'Connor said:

> I come from a low-income background, and sometimes I feel like I am in
> a different world from many colleagues. I feel they have frames of refer-
> ence I can't even begin to imagine. I can't think of any specific examples,
> but just references they make to culture or art. I have no idea what they
> are talking about or whom they are talking about. It is in those moments
> I realize how big the class divide is and how privileged academics are in
> terms of their social origins. For me, between the class divides and the
> race divides, I really try to avoid informal faculty gatherings.

Class consciousness is important because the academy expects professors
to have, as Terrence McDonald explained, "the same ease of presence as someone who was born in faculty housing." Such assumptions mean that many
aspects of the academy are seen as not needing to be explained or named—
people will already know what they are. As McDonald noted in his quote that

opened Chapter 1, although his class background helped him understand race and gender issues, issues of "belonging" and understanding difference based on a variety of factors remain for many people. bell hooks wrote about the pressures to assimilate in class terms that she faced as an undergraduate at Stanford, reflecting the pressures to "cover," in Kenji Yoshino's formulation. "Demands that individuals from class backgrounds deemed undesirable surrender all vestiges of their past create psychic turmoil. We were encouraged … to betray our class origins. Rewarded if we chose to assimilate, estranged if we chose to maintain those aspects of who we were, some were all too often seen as outsiders."[48]

To sum up the institutional accomplishments and challenges in Phase Five, we think that the arrival of a cohort, or critical mass, of White women and faculty of color ushers in a recognition of heretofore unnoticed structural privilege; this recognition in turn permits and necessitates institutional changes in policies and practices. A cohort of diverse senior faculty, along with committed White administrators, takes the lead—in the case of Michigan beginning with Duderstadt and continuing with Lee Bollinger and Mary Sue Coleman. Joint appointments and cluster hiring recruit new faculty members. Although expectations for excellence in scholarship increase, institutions become explicitly focused on the range and complexity of faculty needs. Tenure and promotion policies are examined, and changes are proposed. The most marginally positioned group—women of color—are at the intersection of new discussions about integrating race and gender in relation to privilege. New theories of intersectionality inform previously unmarked categories of race, gender, sexuality, and class. And, as we will see in Chapters 5 and 6, shifts begin to occur in university structures and the new forms of scholarship that these structures enable and support.

A Scientist and a Woman?

There is another important aspect to the narratives at all three institutions, and nationally, about diversifying the faculty by race and gender. A major set of issues, consistent with but also different from the general narratives around female faculty, has arisen in the specific case of women in the sciences and engineering. These differences are tied to disciplinary hierarchies. The sciences and engineering are often seen to be the most powerful and richest departments in the university, both nationally and particularly at Stanford and RU–N, because of their records of external support and business and government's reliance on them to keep the country competitive economically and militarily. These status hierarchies in the disciplines have correlated negatively with receptivity to including women.

Respect for the "scientific method" as the least interpretive, least culturally inflected, and therefore most "free" of bias of all the academic disciplines has functioned as a gatekeeper in all the academic disciplines and insulated them from gender critiques.[49] This epistemology, which Sandra Harding characterizes as an internalist scientific epistemology, "has assumed that the representations of nature's order that the sciences produce can be mirror-like reflections of a reality that is already out there and available for the reflecting."[50] Advocates of this perspective have argued that gendered perspectives have little or no bearing as scientists work to achieve this "mirror-like" perfection. This ideal helps to explain why feminist gender critiques of science and engineering have lagged behind those in the humanities and social sciences and why women scientists and engineers have been such a small proportion of scientists. As a way to illustrate how discourses about women in science have changed over time and the specific story in each of these institutions, we present an abbreviated description of phases in the entry of women (particularly White women) into these fields.[51]

Phases One and Two

The Cold War expansion in the sciences of the 1940s and 1950s left little room for women in universities' celebration of the male scientist as cultural hero. The positionalities of male scientists were officially considered irrelevant, at the same time that women's gender positions and their gender scripts were seen to make their lives incompatible with those of a university scientist. The slow growth in the numbers of female scientists during Phase Two, during which those who made it were constrained to "become just like them," may be best illustrated by the remark made to us by Catharine Stimpson, dean of research in humanities and social sciences at New York University. She said that for some women, "being a scientist is more important than being a woman."

RU–N was ahead of the other two universities. Judith Weis, who has been in Biological Sciences since 1967, "pre–women's movement," as she said, attributes her comfort there to a department with a tradition of hiring female scientists. There were three tenured women when Weis arrived, including Helen Strausser, who took her under her wing. (Strausser, along with Dorothy Dinnerstein, was one of the scientists who filed Newark's sex discrimination complaint, along with a zoologist and a physicist, all full professors.)[52] This tradition of receptivity to female scientists continues today. Female scientists in particular told us that they thought that it was easier for them at a less competitive place like RU–N than elsewhere and that being a productive researcher in the sciences trumped gender distinctions. Maggie Shiffrar in psychology, who came to RU–N from the National Aeronautics and Space Administration, said, "This campus is a whole lot easier to be a woman at than a whole lot of other places I have been!"

Phases Three and Four: Challenging the Norms and
Combining Diversity With Excellence

The successes of women during Phase Three, particularly in biology, may be partially attributed to the sizable number of women attracted to the field. That women as women were beginning to be accepted can be seen in the career of Pat Jones, the first woman hired in Biological Sciences at Stanford in 1978. The current chair, Robert Simoni, said that Jones's gender had little to do with her appointment, because beginning in the mid-1970s, at first half of their undergraduate majors, then more than half of their PhD candidates, and eventually half the job applicant pool were women. "So we've had the good fortune and sense to hire the best candidate available by our judgment, irrespective of any other issue. And I say this for a reason. We've been really quite successful at hiring women." It was not an issue of affirmative action but rather, with such talented applicant pools, an issue of "nondiscrimination"—they would have had to go out of their way *not* to hire a woman. He was on sabbatical at the time Jones was hired but said, "My guess is that there was little or no discussion that she was a woman. She was a top-notch scientist and she would be an extraordinary teacher. Both were true."[53]

Unlike Estelle Freedman, Pat Jones perhaps personifies a *kind* of excellence that her male colleagues believed could be maintained as they added women to their ranks. President John Hennessy, former dean of engineering, recalled that after they hired the first woman, the Engineering School also changed: "All of a sudden the culture opened up the number of female applicants." Jones, who has been department chair, confirms Hennessy's belief that departmental change begins with the success of the first woman. Biological Sciences is an exemplar of enabling junior faculty to succeed, according to Jones: "Since I came 40% of the hires were women and all of them got tenure. ... All assistant professors have been tenured so it's the men too. We usually have an assigned mentor to make sure the junior faculty members are doing OK."[54]

The experience of Jones and earlier generations of women scientists in these three universities suggests that the accomplishments of women scientists in Phases Two and Three are less contentious in the sciences than in the humanities and social sciences. We believe that precisely because the standards for success in the sciences are easier to quantify, the women who met them by being "scientists" seem to have escaped certain kinds of gender discrimination.

The complexities around these issues are suggested by the reported experiences of Stanford engineering faculty today. The happiness of the 20 or so women there was an unexpected finding of the "Faculty Quality of Life Survey." McLaughlin had this hypothesis: "By the time you get to the School of Engineering at Stanford, you've already climbed some fairly steep hills and are getting lots of support and there's not the sort of internecine battles about research paradigms that there are in other areas." Women may face less discrimination in disciplines whose focus is the "real" world, over more historicized, socially connected approaches where their gender position is more suspect. Could it be that male engineers who work on "real problems" are less invested, or seen to be less invested, in gender differences than are men in the humanities and social sciences? If you can solve the problems and be a member of the team, does your gender (or perhaps your race) matter that much? Some doubt all of this and attribute female engineers' contentment simply to their lower expectations for job satisfaction than women in the humanities or social sciences.

When and how have the standards of scientific excellence become explicitly linked to the practice of a diverse group of researchers? For the female scientists and others we spoke to, new subject matters challenging frameworks in other academic disciplines, such as those involved in Estelle Freedman's tenure case or the Stanford core debates, were not so much at issue in the sciences. Rather, there is the realization, or suggestion, that women are particularly talented at certain aspects of science that are becoming central to the whole field, particularly the life sciences and interdisciplinary approaches to scientific problem solving. These realizations, particularly at Stanford, have led to conversations at all levels about how to understand and judge the role of the women in this work. Although all emphasize the scientific and scholarly credentials of these women, they wonder if the unitary model of the male scientist might also be changing.[55]

Both Pamela Matson and Sharon Long are members of the National Academy. According to the former, "the recognition that comes with that helps." But Matson also told us about the acceptance she felt for meeting her home responsibilities, in sharp contrast to the experience of Carolyn Lougee three decades ago. Matson believes women's progress is tied to efforts of earlier generations and wants to support the younger women (and men) in her school:

> One of the things I've always loved about my job is that I can be many things; I can be both a scientist and a woman. I love the fact that I go out in the field and do muddy fieldwork and come back and put heels on; that I can be a researcher and mentor to my students, and be a loving and warm parent and don't have to hide any of it. I don't want to trivialize what it means to be a woman by using those terms, but I've never had to choose to be one or the other. The people who've been my mentors and my bosses never drew that line.

We will see more of the role of women in the sciences at Stanford in the discussions of interdisciplinary research approaches in the next two chapters.

Another place to note the effects of being a female scientist, rather than simply a woman who became a scientist, is in the story and research focus of Paula Tallal at RU–N. Few faculty members, men or women, are more privileged and respected than she; indeed, when Norman Samuels brought her and her husband to RU–N, he recognized, he told us, "that she would be the star." Tallal's story combines scientific privilege and gender discrimination. She and Ian Creese ran separate labs at the University of San Diego for many years, and yet Tallal, who consistently received the largest grants in her department, was not initially on the tenure track and thus not promoted to associate professor for 10 years. Her work, as she described it, is not only multidisciplinary but considered "soft" because she is concerned primarily with children's language and learning problems:

> In the field of neuroscience, anything to do with cognitive performance has always been considered softer than the cellular, molecular—what is real or hard science versus softer science. Anything to do with children would have been considered even more so. And if you move toward anything educational, it's even considered less scientific at some level.[56]

Her status at RU–N is ensured, and like Matson she says she wants to use it to promote women and minorities at the Center for Molecular and Behavioral Neuroscience. They have minority graduate students and a gender-balanced faculty whose specialties run contrary to stereotypes. "We had three molecular faculty members, hard molecular, and all three were women. And the behavioral cognitive numbers have been two women, the rest men. So it hasn't divided up the way that most traditional programs might have thought it would."

MIT's study on the status of female faculty in science, now nearly a decade old, set off a national debate about the place of women in science-related disciplines, particularly regarding unexamined gender bias in the sciences—what it is and how it operates in the culture of departments and laboratories. Representatives from both Michigan and Stanford attended the 2001 MIT conference on women in the sciences and engineering.[57]

Efforts to increase the number of faculty women in the sciences and engineering at Michigan had been painfully slow: there were a total of 2% for female scientists in both LSA and engineering in 1980, 5.5% in 1990, and 10% in 2000. Comparable figures for the same dates overall in LSA were 14% in 1980, 21% in 1990, and 35% in 2000. Currently Michigan is tackling the full inclusion of women in the sciences on an institutional level and the transformations that full inclusion might entail through the ADVANCE program, funded by the National Science Foundation (NSF), and its partner, STRIDE (Science and Technology Recruiting to Increase Diversity and Excellence). Begun as a way of increasing the number of women in science and engineering, the University of Michigan applied and received an NSF–ADVANCE grant in 2001 to improve the campus environment for female faculty in basic sciences and engineering, looking particularly at the question of unexamined gender bias. The goal was to shift "from a painfully incremental process of change … to a more dramatic process of transformation" by increasing the successful recruitment, retention, and promotion of tenure-track women in those disciplines.[58] Their approach, said Stewart, was to buy into the NSF's logic that "we need a powerful group of women faculty, especially as something that trickles down to graduate students and post-docs."

The project's interventions included efforts to make women more competitive through a gender equity resource fund for personal work-related expenses, a departmental transformation initiative to support changes in departmental environments, and perhaps most effective, a campus climate initiative focusing on activities (workshops, focus groups, climate surveys, consultations on increasing pools of female applicants) designed to improve the campus climate for female scientists. For example, a drama group called the Center for Research on Learning and Teaching Players presents ADVANCE-sponsored sketches such as "The Faculty Meeting" and "Mentoring Junior Faculty" that graphically portray gender and racial issues at play in specific situations. Faculty advisory teams are available for recruitment, hiring, and targeted consultation with department chairs. As a way to address their "extreme isolation from one another," the grant funds a university network of female scientists for sponsoring speakers, retreats with junior women, and social events.

A unique aspect of the Michigan proposal was the use of social science research to think about science. This comes in part from the strength of the social sciences at Michigan and in part because Abigail Stewart, President Lee Bollinger, and Provost Nancy Cantor were all social scientists. Stewart told us:

> We at IRWG have lots of social science resources. We saw that social science has lots of knowledge that would be useful in figuring out how to do this transformation—organizational behavior knowledge, institutional change knowledge, knowledge about how bias works, how people think psychologically, and also ideas about collective identity. We have theory about the social construction of knowledge and the construction of identity. And the sciences don't have the kinds of theoretical tools for thinking about social phenomena. That is really a useful insight. [So] we keep putting the tools out there. We keep trying to say there is a way to understand this and, honestly, they are sponges. They love learning about the research.

ADVANCE has created a network of female scientists and engineers that has exposed and addressed their isolation from one another, as well as influencing how other female faculty view scientists and vice versa. Stewart said, "I think many social science and humanist faculty thought of scientists in general as benighted, in some way lesser because of their lack of understanding of things we did know something about. I am very happy to have moved on that. I know a huge number of female science faculty now and have enormous respect for them but also a lot of fun with them."

At least partially as a result of ADVANCE, 39% of tenure-track hires were women in 2004, up from 15% in 2001. When the grant was funded, of the 55 departments in sciences and engineering, only one was headed by a woman; today there are eight.[59] Departments are also attracting better scientists. According to Stewart:

> An LSA department hired two women last year who were highly sought after. They were definitely able to get better women scientists than men. So they totally get it now. One said she didn't go to the better ranked institution because they talked about how excited they would be to have her as a woman. Michigan, because of our training, knew better. We recruited her for her science and nobody said we want you because you are a woman. The women scientists have explained that we know that you want us because we are women. You don't have to rub our noses in it. Just talk to me about how my science fits into your department.

When a team from the NSF did a site visit in September 2004, it saw an institution making progress, concluding, "Michigan is ahead of other universities in the pool in taking courageous stands and investing resources on behalf of excellence through inclusion." The team noted that there was an increase in the number of departments that had moved from "token" representation of women (less than 18% of tenure-track faculty) to "minority" representation (18% to 36%) but that retention was still a major issue.[60]

Phase Five: Dismantling Privilege

While the ADVANCE program at Michigan has directly addressed reforms in institutional structures and practices to benefit women in the sciences, new research at Stanford is also beginning to explore institutional barriers to women's success. There are promising new initiatives at IRWG at Stanford to examine women's different life experiences, particularly in relation to female mathematicians, scientists, and engineers. Londa Schiebinger, a leading scholar in the history of science, has been director of the Institute since 2004. Her work has shown that the structure of universities, not women, are the problem; her goal at IRWG is to move the debate away from questioning whether women are good at math and science toward transforming institutions and removing barriers to women's success. Noting that "our culture is quick to jump to biological explanations for social inequalities," Schiebinger critiqued the "assimilationist model" of the academy that requires "women to think, act, and perform like men in order to find a place for themselves in professional life. So as not to disrupt their professional lives and appear weak, some women schedule births on weekends or over summer breaks in order to make reproduction invisible to professional colleagues and avoid being stigmatized for it."[61]

IRWG has decided to launch a multiyear study of Dual Career Partners in Academia, under the hypothesis that dual-career models adversely affect academic women more than men. Among heterosexual couples, women tend to marry men of higher status than their own, and consequently professional women are more often than men in couples with other professionals. Second, many women practice disciplinary endogamy—marrying within their particular discipline:

> While only 7 percent of the members of the American Physical Society are women, for example, an astonishing 44 percent of them are married to other physicists. An additional 25 percent are married to some other type of scientist. A remarkable 80 percent of women mathematicians and 33 percent of women chemists are married to men in their own fields. Married and domestic partners in dual-career relationships suffer decreased job mobility and the benefits in terms of opportunities, experience, salary, and working conditions that mobility can bring.[62]

This kind of attention to dual-career couples in the sciences and engineering stands to expose the structural aspects of universities that hold women back and may lead to the kinds of fuller exploration of the dynamics of male privilege, particularly in the sciences, that would characterize the beginnings of Phase Five. These new perspectives are important because they push institutional efforts in the sciences toward the kinds of "cluster hiring" approaches that lead to the critical numbers needed for real change. For example, in the School of Engineering, Dean James Plummer told us that broad-based faculty searches, "area searches," are a matter of course now because such searches are more likely to turn up women and people of color.[63] The dual-career study should shed light on such complexities, including generational changes as more women and people of color enter science and engineering fields.

Schiebinger asserts that the challenge is "to shape educational institutions like Stanford to be places where all people—women and men—can flourish and produce the very best knowledge that human beings can produce." Her point that the "very best science" needs to be produced by a variety of researchers reflects Phase Four thinking, namely that excellence must be diverse. The approaches of women and members of minority groups may offer fresher and fuller perspectives on scientific problems, whether it be Paula Tallal's combining "soft" issues or cognitive performance with "hard" molecular science, or Jim Plummer's new focus on area searches to turn up a range of candidates.

However, Schiebinger has other things on her agenda that suggest Phase Five. She wants to look at how gender molds knowledge and the implications not only for the disciplines but the university and even the workings of science labs. She believes that the humanities and the social sciences understand the value of new ideas and perspectives, but not the sciences.[64] New standpoints have the potential to offer new and important kinds of knowledge more available to those on "the borderlands," as philosopher of science Sandra Harding puts it:

> The needs and desires [of women and racial/ethnic minorities] are not the ones that have found expression in the design and functioning of the dominant institutions. ... The experiences and lives of marginalized peoples, as they understand them, provide distinctive problems to be explained or research agendas that are not visible or not compelling to the dominant groups.[65]

Conclusions

The changes over the past two decades were unimagined when the academy first grudgingly cracked open its doors to women and people of color. The University of Michigan has appointed its first female president, Mary Sue Coleman, and she, in turn, has appointed a woman, Teresa Sullivan, as provost. Three of the seven deans at Stanford are now women. James Jackson heads the prestigious Institute for Social Research at Michigan and Claude Steele heads the Social Science Institute at Stanford. Only RU–N has yet to move beyond staffing all powerful positions with White men. Yet given all the laudatory efforts to diversify the faculty in these three universities, why does the number of women and minority faculty remain so low? Faculty of color number about 21% at Michigan, 18% at Stanford (of whom 12% are Asian), and 23.5% at RU–N (14.5% of whom are Asian). The numbers of women faculty are, respectively, 28%, 24%, and 34.2%.[66] At RU–N the percentage of women on the faculty reached 30% in 1983 and is slightly improved 20 years later.

James Jackson believes the answer lies in the persistence of White (and male and class) privilege through practices of denial. He said it is much easier in the military and in business, where there is less chance of obfuscation of the issues and the bottom lines are obvious. White faculty members think they have done well because they work harder:

> Nobody wants to hear about how what happens to a person in the third grade plays out with regard to when they get ready to enter college. It is all too complicated. We have a simple explanation—I worked like a dog to get where I got. That person didn't. It is no accident that Whites do not want to discuss the issue of White privilege. They get very uncomfortable when you start talking about that. Why is that? Whenever you bring up privilege, then the explanation with regard to my success has to become much more nuanced. Well, maybe it did have something to do with the fact that I grew up in Grosse Pointe. How could that be? I would have been successful whether I grew up in Grosse Pointe or in some rural part of Mississippi. Of course, that is not true.

Dean McDonald agrees that privilege still operates: "Well, of course there is White skin privilege. I think male privilege. I don't think there is any way we are cut off from the rest of the country in that respect. I worry about the way female faculty and faculty of color get evaluated in their teaching."

Although we have seen numerous efforts at Stanford and Michigan to deal with women's gender roles, Virginia Valian's thesis that the gender schemas assigned to women do not fit the qualities valued in professional roles in large part still holds sway.

Mark Chesler, who has long studied faculty responses to diversity issues, recently wrote a paper that explored the difficulties for faculty sympathetic to diversity. Echoing Jackson and McDonald, he believes that Michigan is representative of a culture of academic privilege: "There is something about the precious and protected nature of academic culture that reflects entitlement." He said that although many faculty support diversity-related changes, some are opposed, and many are in the middle. As for women and faculty of color, there have been many efforts to support their entry and advancement and to alter the surrounding climate. Especially noteworthy have been targeted hiring and change programs and projects like ADVANCE:

> At the same time, significant problems remain. I think a lot of female faculty and faculty of color are angry at the pace of progress. They often have to deal with student disrespect in the classroom, are taxed by the demand to mentor and advise large numbers of women students and students of color, serve on multiple committees as token representatives, and meet a variety of other service responsibilities. Many also have courageously led the way to challenge campus patterns of discrimination and exclusion. Indeed, we are losing some women and women of color because of this overload and because they don't feel supported by colleagues. Many of the cadre coming up experience considerable pain, before and after tenure.

He wrote about a whole culture that needs to be remade, because most colleges and universities have at least a passively racist and sexist organizational posture. Race and ethnicity, gender, and class "separately and together, affect faculty members' " lives inside and outside the classroom. "The intersection of these identities has powerful effects on the quality of personal and institutional life." He called for change in the monocultural nature of universities:

> We need to challenge the microaggressions experienced by female faculty and faculty of color, the fears and ignorance expressed by some White and male faculty, and the norms and reward structure that so often relegates teaching and overt action to reduce discrimination to second-class activities. They need to respond to the pain and struggle reported by many faculty members and the ways in which collegiate

life is different for many White women and people of color than it is for most White men.[67]

If these new discourses by and about women and faculty of color show anything, it is that entrance into the academy, even as institutions change policies and practices, is not the same as being fully at home there. Patterns of expectations for behaviors and scholarship still associated with the dominant group seem to require compliance, assimilation, and "covering," even as their students and colleagues continue to make specific demands on them that are not made on White men.

To pursue some wider institutional effects of their presence in the academy, we now turn to an examination of some of the departmental, disciplinary, and interdisciplinary structures that have both fostered and impeded the progress of female faculty and faculty of color within each of these institutions. Finally, we discuss the new scholarship of these newcomers and how their institutional contexts have both helped determine and been affected by the advances in their research.

5

Structural Privilege, Interdisciplinarity, and Calls for Change

Because of their extraordinary ability to organize in one single structure research fields, individual careers, faculty hiring, and undergraduate education, disciplinary departments are the essential and irreplaceable building blocks of American universities. ... Disciplines as social structures are extremely solid because they are based on an organizational form—the department—that is as essential to the university as it is to the discipline it embodies. ... Disciplines provide crucial supports for and definition of academic and intellectual identity.[1]

Andrew Abbot—"The Disciplines and the Future"

I think one of the major issues is a structural one. Stanford has departments and it has programs. Programs crosscut departments and sometimes crosscut schools. Stanford has been rigid about not making faculty appointments in programs; tenure-line appointments have to be in a department.

James Gibbs—Professor Emeritus, Stanford University

The University of Michigan has been very good at allowing people to move a quarter or half of their line to another unit. That mobility is very unusual. UM made a commitment in the early '90s that the next configuration of a great university was going to be one in which people were going to find their intellectual interests converging with those of people in other units and in which the structures would provide for that fluidity of intellectual interests.

Sidonie Smith—Chair, English Language and Literature, University of Michigan[2]

We turn in this chapter to an examination of the question of what makes specific academic departments and interdisciplinary programs powerful within their institutions. The stories of faculty hiring and institutional adjustment surrounding Phase Four and Phase Five hint at institutional transformations because of efforts of the newcomers and their allies. Whereas underrepresented faculty had to adjust in earlier phases, in later ones they have challenged institutional structures, policies and reward systems.

At first glance, the clout of both departments and interdisciplinary programs in all three institutions seems related more to their influence in the outside society than to their specific contributions or roles inside the institution. When we asked informants to tell us which were the powerful campus departments, they made lists consistently based on the same criteria: national rankings, the presence of PhD programs, the amount of external funding, the number of majors, and their contribution to the overall reputation of the university, whether in science and technology or in the social sciences. This was brought home to us when Stanford president Hennessy humorously said, "Electrical engineering and computer science are the departments that we would die to keep number one. Yes, we care about all the rest of the departments, but if we lose those two, we are in big trouble."

At the core of these institutional structures, as Andrew Abbott observed, are departments, primarily organized by academic fields, that have long been among the most important sites for the distribution and legitimation of power in the university. It is there that faculty members work out the legitimacy not only of their scholarly and teaching agendas but also of their own place in a small community—a community that has particular relationships to the wider communities of the university and the discourses of the national disciplines. They also work out how to exercise individual judgments about the general and official expectations of their university, goals worth setting and ideals worth pursuing, and standards of behavior defined as acceptable through informal social networks in departments and committees.[3] It is in these contexts where many of the microaggressions experienced by faculty newcomers referred to by Mark Chesler occur.

We also examine the relationships of departments with interdisciplinary programs and the ongoing patterns of privilege that those relationships reveal. We look particularly at the growth of women's studies, African American studies, and ethnic studies as prime examples of interdisciplinary programs that have challenged departmental and research status quos. Why is it that programs that incorporate diversity, unlike other interdisciplinary efforts, seem marginalized? As their faculties set out to change the way knowledge is constructed and transmitted, they bumped up against the power/prestige hierarchies of the scholarly disciplines and structural arrangements that constrained them. In contrast to Stanford's practices in particular, Michigan's ability, as described here by Sidonie Smith, to tenure people in interdisciplinary programs rather than only in departments makes for a greater stability and success for these programs at Michigan than elsewhere. This success, in turn, supports a culture of fluid boundaries in which people's intellectual interests determine the configuration of their line rather than their original disciplinary affiliation. At Rutgers University–Newark (RU–N), interdisciplinary work is supported through three centers, whose effects on academic departments and on the institution as a whole have been very different.

The stories at these universities also illustrate the status differentials among them. Faculty at top institutions such as Michigan and Stanford, although meeting more rigorous standards for tenure, enjoy lower teaching loads and more support for their research. The research elites set terms for scholarly success that can lead to pressure and alienation at institutions in the middle such as RU–N. Extending the lament of faculty members stated in Chapter 2, Randall Collins lays the problem on the doorstep of the disciplines: "Professors still define themselves primarily in terms of the intellectual content of their disciplines, and this gives enormous ... power to the research elite. The strains ... for many scholars lower in the hierarchy seem likely to remain merely localized, personal troubles. It seems likely that there will be little overt resistance as the disciplines become much more severely stratified."[4]

Rutgers University–Newark

Powerful Departments and Programs: The American Association of Universities and the Call of Science

The most powerful departments at RU–N are those meeting the criteria listed earlier, including their contributions to the campus's reach for research university status and increasing parity with the flagship, Rutgers University–New Brunswick.[5] With only $22.6 million in research expenditures annually, they aspire to improve their national rankings through beefing up departments, founding centers, or developing collaborative programs with nearby universities that attract external grants, chiefly in the sciences.[6] The history and workings of the Center for Molecular and Behavioral Neuroscience (CMBN), which many say is the most powerful entity on campus, provide a classic story of the costs and benefits of pursuing preeminence in one area, in a university with limited resources and a culture formerly focused on teaching and service.

The Center for Molecular and Behavioral Neuroscience

CMBN has fulfilled Provost Norman Samuels's vision of the campus "gem," a place representing "pure research, pure academic accomplishments, and winning acclaim in the professions." A decade after its founding, *Rutgers Magazine* reported, "CMBN has been the model for numerous neuroscience centers that have since come into existence. ...The Center ... has been recognized as one of the premier facilities of its kind."[7] Its power is attested to by many RU–N spokespeople. CMBN is responsible for a large proportion of research grants obtained by the university, accounting for 22% of total external awards in 2004.

Paula Tallal, the codirector, told us how Samuels wooed them. Her narrative shows from the inside what others less well placed see from the outside:

They gave us the opportunity to build a research institute according to our own vision of where neuroscience was going, which would be much more interesting across these multiple domains. It's fair to say that we were about 15 years ahead of our time in doing cognitive neuroscience, one of the fastest growing areas of neuroscience. We were basically focusing early on this whole idea of integration. And the opportunity to build that was really quite exciting.

We had a very forward-looking provost and faculty who saw that this could be something that the university could have as a center of excellence. New Brunswick had several centers of excellence, but Newark didn't have any at the time.[8] So, we became the flagship here. ... But we also had to have a marvelous partnership with the administration, which we had right from the beginning. We required the appropriate resources to be able to build a beautiful building,[9] and say what it needed inside in order to recruit faculty ... to come into Newark. It wasn't such a high-level name university. But the resources that we were able to garner are spectacular and difficult to replicate.

Samuels grew the original $2,000,000 in initial funding for the Center, as one of Rutgers University's six Centers of Excellence, to $25,000,000, primarily with internal resources. The Center began with 14 faculty lines, a postdoctoral program, an agreement to keep their indirect cost recovery, and their own computer center and business office. This level of support was contentious on campus and had far-reaching effects on the departments of Psychology and Biological Sciences. Not only did Samuels prevent the departments from hiring—by taking open lines and reassigning them to the CMBN—but only Joan Morrell of the Institute of Animal Behavior (IAB) was invited to join the Center. Reporting directly to the provost, Creese and Tallal were given full authority to hire "those who could sign on to the vision of the Center, with no obligations to the RU–N faculty," according to Samuels.

Barry Komisaruk of the IAB was passed over, even though he had an active and continuously federally funded research program in behavioral neuroscience and had been instrumental in obtaining support for the Center. He had also fought mightily with the scientists to have behavioral and molecular neuroscience included in the Center's name and activities. Komisaruk told us that when Samuels restricted all neuroscience research to the Center, *he* was pressured by the administration to forego neuroscience research because it would overlap with that being done in CMBN. (Komisaruk said Samuels admitted to him later that the prohibition against others performing neuroscience research had been a mistake.) Maggie Shiffrar concurred, "We couldn't hire anybody in psychology who might overlap with the kind of research that was being done in the Center. That is problematic because ... the areas in psychology where you can get grants are areas that overlap with them."

The effects of all this on the Psychology Department were profound. In the 1970s, the department had been divided into the IAB, the Institute for Cognitive Study, and the Development and Life Span program, where, according to Lillian Robbins, "most of the women were." Those less able to get outside grants, mainly the female developmentalists, managed the heavy undergraduate teaching load. The power struggles with CMBN added to tensions already there. Because of the chaos and demoralization caused by these conflicts and because he was tired of resolving fights in the department, in 1994 Provost Samuels stepped in and, over the objections of a majority of department members, brought in an outside chair. Steve Hanson was hired from industry, and by all accounts he decisively turned the department around. Seeking to beat CMBN at its own game, he emphasized a new specialty, Functional Magnetic Resonance Imaging (FMRI), which brought in needed external resources. He focused on building the research- and grant-based aspects of the department at the severe expense of the undergraduate program. He was asked to step down as chair in 2004 and was replaced by Maggie Shiffrar, who intends to rebuild the department and improve their graduate program: "I'd like to make Psychology a bigger presence on campus and get more faculty involved."

Biological Sciences, the other department that the Center should have strengthened, was also severely weakened, according to some. Edward Bonder, the chair, recalled that when he came in 1987, RU–N was trying to retain the "mission of being an undergraduate institution that values teaching excellence and likewise has a commitment to research." To overcome inadequate resources and staffing and to increase external funding, the department decided to concentrate on hiring in several specific areas, namely, ecology and evolution, and cell molecular biology.[10]

But Bonder added that the department has had to wait for new staff, affecting its ability to gain outside funding:

> We have maybe $2 million in external funding, and that will vary, but we are down. ... We have 3 new faculty out of 18, and then we have a number, as all institutions do, who are not researchers. They bear the brunt of the teaching. So, you are looking at a huge loss of our potential grant funding. ... One way is to put more burdens on resident faculty, or just hire adjuncts. It is the same problem all research universities are faced with: How do you balance that?

However, our interview with Dean Edward Kirby suggests progress. Bonder mentioned a hitherto unfunded 1995 proposal for a PhD program in cellular and molecular biodynamics, but Kirby said that they were recruiting in that program. "We're hoping once we get senior leadership here, that we will get a Howard Hughes Medical Institute Grant that brings together areas in the biological sciences, biophysics, structural biology, and biochemistry—a real multidisciplinary approach to science."[11]

Kirby told us about another interdisciplinary effort, the Meadowlands Environmental Research Institute, that involves geophysics, toxicology, and community ecology. He was enthusiastic about the ways RU–N is putting faculty together around institutes or centers or big ideas, which he sees as a benefit to departments. However, perhaps reflecting his understanding of the effects of CMBN, he added, "But not at the expense of solid academic departments. That's absolutely critical."

The story of the CMBN and the Biological Sciences and Psychology departments is a stunning example of how the operations of privilege interact with internal and external forces. Samuels's desire to create something "big and new" as a way to signal that Newark was a research university coincided with the national trend of funding for molecular biosciences over research in the life and environmental sciences. And although CMBN stood to become a model of interdisciplinary work in its fields, bringing together aspects of biology and psychology under one roof, its effects on the both the Psychology and Biological Sciences departments have been severe and demoralizing. Edward Bonder, among many others, sees contradictions between the urban mission of the university and the power of CMBN: "Our diversity is the undergraduate population." Biological Sciences, with the same number of faculty as CMBN, engages with these undergraduates, and CMBN does not, because there is no undergraduate major in neuroscience. Bonder concluded, "I guess money talks in that case."

The Cornwall Center and the Institute for the Study of Race, Ethnicity, and the Modern Experience

Two other interdisciplinary centers, the Cornwall Center and the Institute for the Study of Race, Ethnicity, and the Modern Experience, are tied to the city of Newark and deal with education, economic and community development, race relations, and health care. They are both structured to promote interdisciplinarity in the service of scholarship, community engagement in Newark, and synergy among faculty members across departments. Diner characterized them as "the heart and soul of what we try to do, and the way we try to gain distinction."[12] However, neither of these have anything like the resources of CMBN, and there is some disagreement about how much they engage with academic departments on campus. Their relative lack of power, compared with that of CMBN, means that they have had little effect on departmental policies and structures. Rather their power lies in their ability to bring individual faculty members together around the strongly articulated agendas of urban scholarship and outreach. As Diner said, "I think there is no question that they engage extensively with faculty who have interests in ethnicity, public history, and urban affairs. Students in a variety of programs undertake internships or engage in research at these centers, particularly the Cornwall Center."

The Cornwall Center, which occupies an attractive, sparkling, newly renovated five-story brownstone at the edge of campus, opened its new headquarters in May 2003, thanks to a $2.4 million gift from the Fund for New Jersey. Provost Diner described it as "one of my creations when I came, and that's the focal point for faculty interested in urban issues." Its two-pronged goal, according to the campus newsletter *Rutgers–Newark Connections,* is "to advance research on cities and metropolitan areas, and to apply that research to urban public-policy issues and neighborhood revitalization."[13] Its new director, Stephanie Bush-Baskette, is an African American whose academic work has been in crime and delinquency and who was also a New Jersey state assemblywoman and a commissioner in the administration of Governor James Florio. In a recent interview Bush-Baskette elaborated on her goals:

> I want the Center to be viewed as a dynamic place … to work on issues that have an impact on the quality of life—housing, social justice, education, health, community and economic development. This could include faculty who want to work with us on projects, people from other campuses at Rutgers as well as other institutions [and graduate students]. I also want the community to see us as being a natural link to the university and to research-based information. That's already happening, and it's happening very quickly.[14]

The Center pulls in faculty members through small grant programs in the range of $10,000 to fund research in Newark and other cities. It holds faculty research forums, sponsors other speakers, funds graduate assistants, and provides resources to help faculty design undergraduate courses using the city as part of the curriculum. For example, a political scientist is designing a course on campaigns and elections in which the students will learn how to poll Newark voters. There is no release time provided for such efforts, however.

An examination of the Center's *Urban Research Inventory 2000–2002* reveals a plethora of grants made to faculty members in the Law, Nursing, and Business schools and the liberal arts for research, outreach, and community development in a variety of fields. Most of the grants are for social science projects, but there are science and humanities projects as well, and some are funded by outside foundations and state or federal agencies. Almost all entail investigations and interventions into various aspects of the life of Newark and its surrounding areas.[15]

The Center also sponsors and serves as an umbrella for a vast array of RU–N outreach and service projects, ranging from school interventions to several law clinics, health clinics such as one for women with AIDS, neighborhood improvement programs, minority business initiatives, and the Greater Newark

Safe Cities Initiative, funded by the state of New Jersey and run by the School of Criminal Justice.[16] However, the Center is widely perceived as being primarily concerned with outreach programs to the community. One faculty member said, "The Cornwall Center makes little effort at outreach within the faculty or the curriculum. It seems essentially an 'in-group,' shutting out many who might contribute."

The Institute for the Study of Race, Ethnicity, and the Modern Experience, founded in 1996, is a much smaller operation. Its headquarters is the office of its founder, Clement Price of the History Department. With a meager budget and little space, its programs minimally fund research and outreach programs, with little or no impact on the RU–N curriculum. Instead it sponsors various conferences, fellowships, and lectures, such as the Heningburg Civic Fellows Program, which pulls in "four community leaders and activists" a year for "intensive discussions" with scholars around urban issues. The Marion Thompson Wright Lecture Series is an annual one-day conference to bring together community members and faculty around a specific theme—W.E.B. Du Bois in Africa or the 50th anniversary of Brown.[17] The Geraldine Dodge Fellows, junior faculty funded to conduct research, meet together to share their ideas. Each of these initiatives has different funding, which makes running and growing the Institute very difficult.

In an interview, Price described the Institute's founding and history as a place where faculty and members of the community can come together. Their forums around issues of race and ethnicity help make the campus home to a "free exchange of ideas about race." The city has learned to take advantage of what scholars know:

> The name was inspired by the new scholarship on the social construction of culture, the perceptions of culture. I was a one-man institute, some people still call it Clem's institute, which I don't like because now it's much heftier than it was in 1996 and '97. ... I think the Institute has made ... Newark, despite its reputation, a city at peace with itself in terms of discussions about race and racism, and Whiteness and Blackness. You can't do it in Brooklyn or Washington, DC.
>
> We were thinking out of the box on how we could serve this community. The group that most benefits from the Institute are these recently hired assistant professors who are two or three years away from tenure. ... They are all participants in the Institute's work and beneficiaries of the Institute's synergy that is partly social, partly academic. Their work has a potential public resonance.

Charles Russell, the codirector of the Institute with Price, described their program of outreach to new faculty members. He and Price raised money to support colloquia and to provide release time for faculty to pursue their scholarship and develop courses. He added, "part of our role, which has been the most delightful, is very consciously nurturing the younger ones."

Sherri-Ann Butterfield, one of these younger faculty members, credits the Institute for her involvement with Newark, which she prizes, and with promoting interdisciplinary connections:

> The Institute is how I have made all these connections with faculty members and other departments. It brings scholars together in a way that allows us to be actively involved with civic issues and relate it back to our research. In a metropolitan area like Newark, they strive to improve the education and health of their children, housing, and the economic stability of residents; all this is directly related to our research.

What is the impact of their work on the campus? Fran Bartkowski, the former director of Women's Studies, regretted that the Center and the Institute did not have more to do with gender issues. The African-American and African Studies Department (commonly referred to as African American Studies) is more connected to the Institute. Belinda Edmondson, the outgoing chair, welcomes the connection, although emphasizing that the Institute is committed to all ethnicities:

> The Institute has been a real boon to us. I wish we had more connection to them, but it would also be problematic because it is not necessarily about African Diaspora people. They have a strong emphasis on ethnicity, but ethnicity is ethnicity. They've done terrific research on Jews in Newark, on Asian populations, all of which is important. ... But the Institute cannot be a substitute for building our department, which concentrates on African-descended peoples and has a commitment to undergraduate education.

Edmondson supports Evelyn Hu-DeHart's observation, summarized in Chapter 1, that because race and ethnicity are divergent experiences, the structures of African American studies departments and programs cannot be synonymous with or contained within programs or institutes with a broader ethnic studies focus.

African-American and African Studies, Women's Studies, and the Future American Studies PhD

Unlike Women's Studies, African American Studies has its own faculty lines and is a department and not a program. Yet Edmondson thinks they are marginalized as a result of their history. We wonder what kinds of microaggressions she might be remembering as she thinks about the treatment of African American studies faculty on campus. She told us:

These departments were conceived, essentially, in the same way that women's studies was, as political entities—and they have been perceived that way by the administration for a long time. They're not necessarily seen as scholarly. ... We're not treated as part of the academic community, and so the faculty starts to isolate themselves, a problem from both sides. So we become very marginalized from much of the intellectual life of the rest of the academic community.

Much of the literature in African American studies also emphasizes these non-scholarly origins as contributing to the marginality that Edmondson and Arthur Powell of the Academic Foundations Department expressed. It denies these programs' value as producing legitimate scholarship and their part in a "multiracial movement for social justice that forced colleges to begin the long, hard process of real and substantial change—both intellectually and institutionally."[18]

Because of this sense of the isolation of the department, Edmondson voiced numerous fears about the impact of cross-listed courses on departmental autonomy. Even though she thinks the administration realizes the centrality of the department in a university with an urban mission, she worries about two faculty lines that have gone unfilled. (There is currently a search for someone who will be affiliated with both African American Studies and the joint PhD in American Studies.)

They want African American historians, they want people who work on the Caribbean and Africa, but they're not necessarily going to see them housed here. ... One of our specialties is to be interdisciplinary, and I have advocated this cross-listing of courses with other departments; however, it is dangerous if you cross-list all your core courses out of existence ... then there's no raison d'être for existing.

Uncertainty about faculty positions available for program course offerings among competing units is a common narrative at RU–N. (By contrast, as we see below, Michigan has guarantees related to faculty lines.) As for Women's Studies, Fran Bartkowski described its history over the years, noting with pride that this program was the first established on the three Rutgers campuses (in 1970). The major dates from 1989. The program recently added a graduate concentration connected to six different MA programs on campus. Bartkowski doesn't think that departmental status or a freestanding MA would work well at RU–N. This approach reflects their history; in the early 1980s Women's Studies received a $75,000 grant from the Department of Higher Education for "curriculum transformation" across disciplines:[19]

Across campus courses were being rethought. People could redo their syllabi and think about what they were teaching in light of new scholarship on race, class, and gender. ... So I didn't feel that a struggle worth taking on was to insist on becoming a department as opposed to a program. A women's studies department made huge sense at RU–New Brunswick. But here, it seemed to me much more crucial to have gender, race, and class discussions going on across the campus in different departments.

However, her rationale ignores the power differentials embedded in being a program and not a department. Jyl Josephson, Bartkowski's replacement, divides her teaching between Women's Studies and Political Science, where she was hired with tenure in January 2004. Wanting Women's Studies to have both a scholarly and an activist emphasis, Josephson connects the program explicitly to Diner's urban vision. She imagines women's studies courses being offered in the community and is planning internships in the city for her students.[20] We wonder if Josephson, whose goals for Women's Studies seem tied to the curriculum rather than to scholarship, will in time have regrets similar to Bartkowski's that the Center and the Institute do not have more to do with gender issues.

Finally, many told us about the proposed PhD in American Studies, which is designed to build on RU–N's strengths in the areas of race, ethnicity, and urban studies and establish RU–N's first humanities PhD program. As the brochure describes it, the proposed program will emphasize both public scholarship and community outreach. Charles Russell described why he thinks RU–N is a perfect place for such a PhD and his frustration over the program's long failure to come together:

> With the Cornwall Center, with the Institute, we had centers of inter-disciplinarity ... and applied research; ... so we designed a program to emphasize public scholarship. Through it we would try to move to some of the most interesting issues in American studies, the relationship of the academy to the public sector. So we designed a program that would have half our students be trained to be academics, and the others to be in the public sector, but all students would get training in public scholarship. ... There are a lot of needs in the humanities and social sciences but it's piecemeal, and collectively there's no vision of what to do.

Searches for a director failed twice. Russell was recently appointed acting director for three years to get the program up and running and to prepare the ground for a future search for a director. Russell's appointment and the current search in African-American and African Studies are steps in a positive direction. Meanwhile, under the leadership of Alan Sadovnik in Urban Education and others, a joint PhD program in Urban Systems is planned for the fall of 2006. It combines emphases in urban health, urban environment, and urban educational policy and is cosponsored with the New Jersey Institute of Technology (NJIT) and University of Medicine and Dentistry of New Jersey (UMDNJ).[21]

This look at selected departments and centers at RU–N reveals that "catch-up" institutions are heavily influenced by the need to respond to external forces, particularly in pursuit of state and federal funding. The state of New Jersey has a history of funding campus initiatives—not only CMBN but also the Cornwall Center and curriculum integration in women's studies. Indeed New Jersey stands out in its recognition of the societal benefits of intellectual work. But we learned of no major federal funding in the humanities and social sciences. The campus is also subject to agencies' recent emphasis on collaboration across institutions. According to Diner:

> The new University Heights Science Park was established by the four public higher education institutions of Newark (known as CHEN, Council for Higher Education in Newark) to promote economic development and neighborhood development in an area that sits between the campuses of NJIT and UMDNJ in the area we call University Heights. It uses the presence of research science, technology, and medicine at the universities to attract related businesses to this area of Newark. It is also responsible for the development of a new magnet school, Science Park High School, which will be closely aligned with the universities.

RU–N's focus has been to build strong centers with connections to the outside, particularly with CMBN but also with the Cornwall Center, as a way to build its reputation as a research university. But the differences between CMBN, the Cornwall Center, and the Institute are striking examples of the privileges awarded to and enacted by the sciences through the world of external funding. CMBN has had powerful effects on the institution, both building its reputation nationally and weakening several other departments in the process. By contrast the Center and the Institute, operating respectively with few or no real resources, have had little overt impact on departmental decisions and on the curriculum. Nevertheless, they have been able to foster a new culture for interdisciplinary thinking and relationships for individual faculty members—newcomers and others.

Stanford

The Sciences, Engineering, and Humanities at Stanford Today

In our interview with Stanford President Hennessy, he succinctly laid out the role of the "external environment" and the ways in which the institution matches the externally funded predominance of the sciences and engineering with internal support for the social sciences and the humanities:

> The real question is, what does the external environment impose on the institution? And how do we internally respond to try to balance those forces? From the central university resources, we disproportionably support the humanities and the social sciences. We support fellowships in humanities and social sciences. We don't support them in engineering. They are tubs on their own bottom.

Now, there is no doubt that society has or our government has decided that the sciences and engineering are critical to various other issues, such as economic growth, national security, and health care. That does allow growth there. Look at the Medical School, which has grown incredibly under the influence of the NIH budget. Then you ask, how do we bring some counterbalance to that? We do, and the humanities have actually grown faster over the past decade, in terms of faculty, than engineering has.

Because of its wealth and national standing, Stanford seems less influenced by pressure from corporations to pursue applied research that fuels the economy than are catch-up institutions such as RU–N. Hennessy, the first engineer to serve as president, has been described by Provost John Etchemendy as "the embodiment of everything that has made Stanford one of the world's great universities."[22] No stranger to the corporate world, Hennessy has a strong position on the university's involvement with the federal government and corporations. In spite of their powerful roles in funding and shaping university research programs, the university should ultimately remain independent of both. Harkening back to David Starr Jordan, the first president of Stanford, who said that "the life of the university is original research," Hennessy stressed the primacy of universities setting their own research agendas and cautioned against the idea of universities as generators of economic growth:

> Instantaneous, real-life applications of discoveries are not what make research universities important. Rather their fundamental contributions are the "great leaps forward"—the discoveries that, in many cases, are only understood to be remarkable in retrospect. Unlike corporations, universities can set distant research horizons, and they should avoid becoming engines for small incremental changes to existing technologies.[23]

James Plummer also emphasized the long-term and broad-based nature of the research agendas of the engineering school: "We tend to work on long-range, really hard problems. We have a major new program in energy technology, the Global Climate and Energy project, and it's taking a broad-brush look. ... So I think the goals need to be long range. The mission needs to be long range. But that's not inconsistent with results that have a short-term impact."

What have been the effects of the power of engineering and the sciences on Stanford as a whole? On one hand, there is a common complaint among humanists and social scientists that the sciences and technology areas, particularly engineering, are increasingly dominating the university. This perception overlooks the fact that building world-class programs in key disciplines of particular relevance to the Silicon Valley has been going on for half a century, since Terman's era. In the past 50 years, university faculty, staff, and graduates have launched some 1,200 companies. This domination is also strongly linked to external funding. For example, Timothy Lenior, until recently a historian of science at Stanford who specializes in the history of the Silicon Valley, noted that the percentage of the total operating budget of Biochemistry that comes from external grants ranges from 70% to 98%. Electrical Engineering is often in the high 90th percentile, as is Genetics. These are "indeed steeples of excellence," he said, concluding with the observation that engineering and biomedicine actually fund the humanities.[24] Echoing this point, Plummer said engineering's preeminence comes not from university support but from its "entrepreneurial faculty":

> With only 13% of the faculty we have 25% of the students in the engineering school. ... Yes they have an advantage, because we're here in the Valley, and they can establish connections with corporations and get research money that way. But most of the research money here comes from the federal government, not from companies. This happens only because engineering faculty are out there in an entrepreneurial way, trying to get funding. ... Faculty look at the engineering school and see apparent wealth ... and they say, how can you build that? It's not done by the university. It's done by entrepreneurial faculty.

Etchemendy, a philosopher, told us that because of the competition for top-flight humanists, humanities faculty are actually paid better than engineers, because they match outside offers in the humanities to keep the best faculty. They do not need to do that in engineering. Recalling his time as associate dean for the humanities, Etchemendy said:

> Many, many deans have recognized that if we could just bring our humanities departments up to the level of our science or social science departments or engineering departments, then we would without question be the strongest university in the world. Anyway, I don't think that engineers are really privileged in the way that the humanists think they are. Engineers feel that they ought to be more privileged than they are.

Dean Sharon Long, whose responsibilities include the sciences, social sciences, and humanities, although admitting some disparities, emphasized the complexities:

> Stanford is a complex enough place with distributed enough talent and deep enough values that it's not driven by the Valley or driven by engineering. Nor are the humanities or the social sciences marginalized. They might find it convenient to feel that way, but I don't think so, they're just different.

Indeed, further investigation of the history of the place of the humanities at Stanford indicates that every president since Richard Lyman has worked to correct these disparities of emphasis. Donald Kennedy founded the Stanford

Humanities Center and Gerhard Casper sponsored symposia and humanities fellowships.[25] This support for the humanities continues in the administration of John Hennessy. In his inauguration speech in 2000, he noted that although Stanford had fostered the humanities since its origins, differences between the sciences and the humanities remained. "[Outside funding] has no doubt been the dominant source of that disparity and has led to an inequality in total resources, if not in institutional emphasis, and a consequent concern that we are not doing enough for the arts and humanities at Stanford."[26]

Stanford now has a humanities lab, which enables humanities scholars to undertake the mid- to large-scale team-based research projects that have traditionally been the domain of the natural and social sciences. It has an epistemological twist as well: to supplement traditional humanities training with hands-on experiences in a true laboratory setting. The Stanford Humanities Lab promotes a model of the humanities that is flexible and cross-disciplinary at its core—Big Humanities, along the lines of Big Science, which has a primary goal of changing the funding imbalance between external funding for the humanities and the sciences.[27]

Yet at Stanford we were told that the status hierarchies among departments and disciplines are reflected in a pecking order around scholarly research methodologies. According to Cecilia Ridgeway:

> Sure there is a pecking order. ... Not officially published of course, but there is an implicit one among the sciences, social sciences, and humanities essentially. It exists amongst the students as well as the faculty. Science and engineering probably have a hierarchy amongst themselves, but I can't say I know all the details. Amongst the social sciences it's basically economics, then psychology, which is a top-ranked department in its discipline, basically the two individual sciences. ... There are people by the way in psychology that are quite critical of that too, as there are in economics. These are just dominant perspectives. ... And then I would say political science. Sociology and anthropology are there toward the bottom. Feminist studies by the way is below all of them.[28]

This pecking order ties departmental status to primarily "value-neutral" research methods and epistemologies and favors the study of the individual and the individual unit over the group. For example, economics, often associated with positivist research epistemologies, has a reputation of being exceptionally rigorous; it also has a very low tenure rate. By contrast fields associated with social constructivism and qualitative approaches to knowledge are seen as having a lower status. Like the lineaments of the Stanford style, these ideas are conveyed both formally and informally, by means of the social relationships by which people are inducted into departmental and institutional norms.[29]

Multidisciplinary Programs: The New Mark of Stanford

In interviews and in the *Stanford Report,* we were told that one of the marks of Stanford is its multidisciplinary approach to solving problems and constructing knowledge. Hennessy sees research today as inherently more multidisciplinary because it is driven by the large-scale problems we face:

> We are certainly going there because the problems we want to work on are problems that demand that sort of organization. They will not be amenable to the single faculty member working alone or working with a small team of graduate students solo. ... They are much more cross-disciplinary in the nature of the problem. ... It can be a new drug or medical device that changes the world.

Stanford has chosen to use university resources to address global challenges that are likely to be around for the next 50 years. Their topics are governance and political institutions, human health and well-being, the environment, and the general biosciences, or Bio-X, Biology for the Twenty-First Century, which brings physics, engineering, biology, and chemistry together. With regard to health and well-being, Provost Etchemendy explained, "If you are dealing with AIDS in Africa, you have got to bring in the resources and insights of a wide variety of disciplines, from sociology, political science, obviously medicine and all of the subdisciplines. ... That forces you to adopt interdisciplinary perspectives."

However, this new focus on interdisciplinarity is in tension at Stanford with the claims of traditional disciplines and departments to retain their autonomy. Dean Long insisted that however important interdisciplinary initiatives are, expertise must be measured primarily through a discipline. True stars were both leaders in their own disciplines and influential beyond them:

> I feel that the way to have great interdisciplinary work is not to find people who are average in a bunch of things. The best way is to find people who are superstars in a discipline, but who have the creativity and interest and drive to work across. So a discipline is still the entry. But being graded in a discipline and having the drive and creativity to reach across isn't enough. You do have to be able to learn the vocabulary of the other field, which might be mathematics, for example. ... We think that this is the way to be an excellent institution, and we also think that Stanford can do it better.

Long said that one of the big challenges she has as dean is dealing with the tensions between disciplinary and interdisciplinary work. These tensions also revolve around how departments are positioned in the university. The two largest undergraduate majors at Stanford are economics and biological sciences. Both departments are often ranked as number one in the country, and their size and power matter. Both chairs are suspicious of interdisciplinary approaches.

John Pencavel, chair of Economics, told us that the "general posture" in economics is that "if the university has this pot of money, that they're going to spend, and they say to you, you're going to benefit, this is for interdisciplinary research, we say, we'd rather have our fraction of the money direct."[30]

Referring to institution-wide initiatives such as Bio-X, Robert Simoni, chair of Biological Sciences, said, "The whole notion to set up these kinds of institutes is largely a directive from the top that the university invests in the future in that way, rather than within existing departments and programs. A profoundly important decision." He is worried that abandonment of disciplinary and departmental programs may damage the biological sciences department. Referring to three faculty members who reside in the Clark building with Bio-X, he said:

> If this trend continues, departments would be nothing more than budgetary, and appointment and promotion units. There'd be no intellectual coherence. … To have people picked out here and there for other people's visions defeats our planning. It may turn out that to the institution, it is a great advantage. That is not yet proven, and the risks are great.

One of the strongest proponents of interdisciplinarity at Stanford is Pamela Matson, who described herself as a "biogeochemist, really an interdisciplinary field." In the sciences, particularly at Stanford, women are seen as especially interested in, and able to, work at the intersections of traditional disciplines. Matson said, "If the university can support people who want to do interdisciplinary work they will be helping women and vice versa." James Plummer mentioned, "The intersection of engineering and life sciences seems to be an area that women are attracted to. So we just started hiring there, but two of the four first hires were women."

Another advocate for interdisciplinarity is the sociologist Karen Cook, who upon assuming responsibility as the dean for the social sciences at Stanford in 2001 convened a group of faculty advisors to explore the challenges faced by social science researchers. The result was the Institute for Research in the Social Sciences, launched to produce cutting-edge multidisciplinary research in the social sciences. Its Faculty Steering Committee represents a widely diverse group of faculty. Current initiatives include the American National Election Studies (funded by a grant from the National Science Foundation [NSF] of $7.6 million), designed to untangle the causes of voter participation and candidate choices in the 2008 U.S. presidential election. Another, in collaboration with the Center for Comparative Studies in Race and Ethnicity (CCSRE), is a lecture series, "Confronting Katrina: Race and Class and Disaster in American Society."[31] Collaborations such as these draw on the expertise of many faculty, including women faculty and faculty of color, and may loosen up departmental structures.

The CCSRE, Feminist Studies, and the Institute for Research on Women and Gender

The establishment of the African and African American Studies Program in 1969 awakened the need for ethnic studies among other student groups—the first courses in Asian American studies were taught in 1970–1971. There was an attempt in 1972 to establish a program in Asian American studies, but it was not implemented. More than 20 years later, on the morning of May 4, 1994, Chicano and Chicana students began a hunger strike with four demands, one of which was a Chicano and Chicana studies program. Within a week, Concerned Students for Asian American Studies surreptitiously entered the Faculty Senate chamber through a locked door and chanted, "Asian American studies now—not another 20 years." Although President Casper, in his State of the University Address on May 12, spoke out against "the politics of ultimatum," he supported Dean John Shoven's proposal to set up working committees to study each group's demands. Shoven asked the two committees to work in parallel, considering whether "ethnic studies should be placed, for instance, within American Studies or whether the School of Arts and Sciences should establish comparative ethnic studies."[32]

The result was CCSRE and its associated research program, the Research Institute of Comparative Studies in Race and Ethnicity (RICSRE). Developed by Al Camarillo, Claude Steele, and others in 1996, the curricular program offers about 130 courses per year in interdisciplinary majors in Asian American, Mexican American, and African American studies and comparative studies in ethnicity, which has the largest number of majors. According to its mission, the Research Institute strives to "create an integrated community of scholars with a diversity of perspectives addressing the problems of how to foster a stable, inclusive, democratic society that successfully incorporates diverse people, institutions, cultures, and practices."[33]

With the perspective of a decade, the administrative dean for CCSRE, Sharon Long, extolled its benefits to faculty and students, saying that it draws people from all over the university. "The Center for Comparative Studies in Race and Ethnicity has been one of the biggest successes for undergraduate education and for faculty. ... A lot of research projects have come out of this. It is sort of grass roots. A structure supports it, but it has to be faculty who come together in order to move forward."

Claude Steele, who was the director of CCSRE at the time we interviewed him, was more measured about the position of CCSRE in Stanford's hierarchy, noting that, as at RU–N, programs such as this tend to be marginalized in part because they are not departments but also because of the challenge they present to power and rewards in the academy. Until very recently, when the new director, Lawrence Bobo, was hired to be half-time in the CCRSE and half-time in sociology, there were no faculty lines in CCRSE—all faculty were hired and tenured in academic departments. However, Steele imagines a time when being knowledgeable about the comparative studies of race and ethnicity is the mark of an educated person:

> I believe that the scholarship [of RICSRE] should be central to the institution. It tends to be marginalized. And so the next big frontier, I think, is going to be getting institutions to the point where you can't consider yourself an educated person without really having had some serious involvement with that kind of material, with that aspect of being an American. … Just being a Europhile is not sufficient. … You really need both.

In the spring of 1974, the Center for Research on Women (CROW), now the Institute for Research on Women and Gender (IRWG), was formed "to create and advance cutting-edge research on topical issues relating to gender by harnessing the intellectual power of Stanford faculty and visiting scholars from around the world."[34] In 1979 the director of CROW formed a task force to determine whether Stanford needed a women's studies program and, if so, what form it should take. The program grew out of the scholarly interests of faculty rather than of student advocacy and thus was grounded in a research model from the beginning. [35]

The decision to name the program "Feminist Studies," rather than the more widely used term "Women's Studies," was grounded primarily in feminist scholarship as well. Although opponents saw the name and the program as too political, the founders saw feminism as "an analytic approach to a particular subject matter. This approach assumes that gender inequality is 'problematic.' It is a social fact that is intellectually interesting and worthy of scholarly analysis."[36] Nan Keohane, who was a faculty member in political science at the time, reportedly argued for Feminist Studies, holding that it is better to be feared than pitied.[37] Because of political resistance, Feminist Studies was first offered through the Individually Designed Majors program. Although the Feminist Studies Program Committee could coordinate courses and advise students, students had to present proposals to the Individually Designed Majors program committee, and some of the members routinely discouraged them.[38]

The first five-year review in the spring of 1986 was so positive that the committee recommended degree-granting status. Nevertheless, in a formal memo in 1987, Dean told the director of the IRWG that it was "inconceivable to him that Stanford would grant a degree called Feminist Studies."[39] However, the next 5-year review, in 1990, was so strong that the program was finally awarded degree-granting status as an undergraduate major. Feminist Studies continues to receive strong reviews. Penny Eckert, the current director, made the following distinction about Stanford students: "My Feminist Studies students hate the party culture and love the term *feminist*. The larger undergraduate student body doesn't like or understand the term but generally holds basic feminist values. For them being a feminist is a little like wearing a bike helmet. It's considered not cool."[40]

In an effort to bring Feminist Studies and IRWG in closer alignment with one another and with the humanities and sciences, IRWG moved in September 2001 from the Office of Research and Graduate Policy to the School of Humanities and Sciences. According to Barbara Gelpi, professor emerita of English and former acting director, this happened under the aegis of Dean Sharon Long, "someone who has power and who will listen to what is happening to women." Now, half a century after the new "male scientist heroes" of Terman's era, IRWG is creating a critical mass of thinkers who study gender influences on the theory and practice of the sciences and engineering. Later, IRWG plans to devote similar energy to research on gender in the arts and humanities, business, law, and medicine.[41]

What does this look at Stanford tell us about what makes specific academic departments and interdisciplinary programs powerful? National rankings certainly matter. In the School of Humanities and Sciences, eight departments across all disciplinary categories are ranked in the top five by the National Research Council. In the School of Engineering, there are five departments ranked in the top five.[42] Without PhD programs, neither CCSRE nor Feminist Studies are ranked, contributing to their being at the bottom of the pecking order in the university.

However, this pecking order at Stanford is also tied to the structural relationship between programs and departments. As Simoni and James Gibbs have indicated, Stanford rarely allows joint appointments. But as Bobo's appointment may indicate, this rigidity may be changing. Even though a recent decision was made not to set up a formal committee to investigate other ways of making faculty appointments, the topic is now a part of the institutional discourse. Will Stanford's new emphasis on interdisciplinary programs loosen up this rigidity? Departments seem intent on maintaining the power to recruit and tenure their own members according to their own criteria. People like Simoni are unlikely to give up this central piece of their identity and power without a fight. Yet in his reflections on his five years as president, John Hennessy twice mentioned the need to do something about the fact that departments still primarily carry the decision-making appointment authority. He asked, "How do we make the whole greater than the sum of its parts?"[43]

The relationship between departments and interdepartmental centers and institutes also raises questions about the "Stanford style." Stanford's expectation that everyone be a star in her or his discipline works against structural change. One informant told us, "This is a very centrist place, which effects implementation of the new." However, as we will see in the next chapter, changing ideas about the relationship between the best scholarship and diversity may be the crack in the wall that changes the power relations between departments and interdisciplinary programs.

Michigan

Departments and Disciplines at Michigan: The Social Sciences and the Role of the Institute for Social Research

Michigan's story diverges from those at RU–N and Stanford for two reasons. The sciences take somewhat of a back seat, and structures of interdisciplinarity have a long institutional history. At Michigan, because institutional preeminence belongs to the social sciences, the most powerful departments and the most powerful disciplines are those concerned with the social world and its challenges. Moreover, the social sciences have always been interdisciplinary at Michigan. In many departments, the boundaries within fields in terms of subfields, and the boundaries between fields, have generally been porous and negotiable. Thus the power of the social sciences has produced and in turn benefited from an institution-wide acceptance of new ways of configuring power, structures, and knowledge. It is arguable that the social science mission of the university has also led to definitions of its public mission in terms more of social rather than of scientific problems.

Michigan's social science preeminence is mainly identified with the Institute for Social Research (ISR), a major interdisciplinary unit of the university, which combines the Survey Research Center (SRC), about 75% of ISR, and other centers, including the Research Center for Group Dynamics. "ISR has contributed powerfully to the body of knowledge about human behavior and social interaction, collecting data of interest to the general public, to decision makers in government and the private sector, and to scholars everywhere."[44]

Today ISR occupies a unique position at the university. It has its own faculty and financial independence, factors crucial to its growth over the years. ISR raises all of its funding but retains indirect costs from grants and contracts. In sharp contrast to the policies of CMBN at RU–N and in keeping with the interdisciplinary approach with which it was founded, an extraordinary number of faculty in academic departments have joint appointments with ISR, such as anthropology, history, psychology, and sociology. According to Steve Raudenbush, formerly a senior scholar at ISR, place also matters: "In terms of interdisciplinary social science, it's happening essentially within the confines of one building. People have offices in the same place and have seminars so that they can then collaborate on projects."[45]

Raudenbush told us that SRC faculty are predominantly older, male, and White, "because there's tremendous continuity in the Survey Research Center. So, over many, many years there are people there who are associated with very well-known national studies." Their commitment to increasing diversity is shown by the recent elevation of James Jackson, a longtime associate and former associate director, to the directorship of ISR.

The connections of the social sciences to ISR helped ensure departments' high place in the national rankings. The College of Literature, Science, and the Arts (LSA), whose reports combine rankings from the National Research Council and *U.S. News and World Report,* noted that 24 of their programs in the social sciences and sciences are ranked in the top five. In the engineering school, which relied only on *U.S. News,* the number is four.[46] However there is another, more subtle story of ongoing gender privilege within these departments, a story that surfaces in some accounts and not others. Jacque Eccles of the Psychology Department, Women's Studies, and education, drew for us a picture of the gender dynamics within psychology. Some subfields traditionally had more women, and other fields were thereby let off the hook:

> There has always been a very, very strong interest in women and diversity in social psychology and in personality. The department was probably one of the first that had a reasonable representation of women. In part that was being carried by particular areas. The increase in the proportions of women in clinical, cognition and perception, and biopsychology has been more recent. The fact that it was high in some areas left other areas off the hook to even have to think about it.[47]

Eccles also told us that men in developmental psychology were much more likely than women to have an affiliation with the Center for Human Growth and Development—an interdisciplinary research institute at Michigan—which gave them more research space and time. Yet all faculty members were evaluated by the same yardstick:

> On the evaluation committee there is no discounting for the people who buy themselves off on grants or have these privileged research positions. They are quite likely to get very high ratings because of the amount of research they do, and the fact that they are required to do less teaching is not really taken into account. So you look at them and say, oh, he has done more research. I say, well, he has a half-time research position. He should have to do twice as much to get the same rating as the full-time faculty precisely because the full-time faculty members (more likely to be female) are teaching more. No, no, no. In addition, men, on average, guard their research time very closely. Many of the men do not do their fair share of teaching or service. They get the big raises, because they spend their time on the thing that the university is best at understanding, going out and getting offers.

Similar complaints were echoed by Howard Kimeldorf, the chair of Sociology. He said that ISR creates enormous opportunities for some faculty—a source of inequities in the department because ISR sociology faculty do less teaching and more research, leading to higher salary rates for their proportion of time in ISR.[48]

The Sciences and the Humanities at Michigan

The preeminence of the social sciences has meant that the sciences and the humanities, in their different ways, have struggled more at Michigan than at Stanford. The sciences in LSA and the departments in the College of Engineering at Michigan do not suffer from a lack of funding. However, one point at issue is the relative power of different subfields, such as the two separate departments in biology. Deborah Goldberg is chair of the Department of Ecology and Evolutionary Biology (EEB); in 2001 it split from the Department of Molecular, Cellular, and Developmental Biology (MCDB), largely because EEB's focus on field biology and biodiversity was seen to be at odds with MCDB's lab-based emphasis on model organisms.

Not being at the top of the rankings is a complex issue for Goldberg. She said the low ranking of MCDB ("about 30-something") comes from its competition with the comparable department in the Medical School, competition that EEB, located only in LSA, need not meet. "We like to say we are in the top 10. ... We think we certainly belong in the top 10, and I think most people would probably agree. We, of course, want to be moving into the top 5, and I think we have every possibility of doing that."[49]

Martha Pollack, associate chair of Electrical Engineering and Computer Science, told us that her department is in the "top 12": "In my field there are sort of a top three or four universities, and they are absolutely, absolutely, absolutely first rate. ... Then I think there is sort of the next 8 to 10. We are in that group. Some of us will be a little better in one area and a little better in another area." She was ambivalent about the ranking system:

I think in terms of getting a sense of who is moving up in the world, what new hot areas are being valued, how you are viewed externally—I think the rankings are important for that. But I think they are taken much too seriously. ... I have been telling both graduate students and faculty candidates that if you pick a university on the basis of it being 6 instead of 9, you are fooling yourself. That is not a reason to make a distinction.[50]

The question of the status of the humanities also seemed no problem for most people we talked to. Julie Ellison, of English and American Culture, painted a picture of strength and confidence in humanities departments. Unlike Cecilia Ridgeway at Stanford, she thinks women's studies at Michigan is solidly grounded: "Once we had both women's studies and the Institute for Research on Women and Gender, under Abby [Stewart]'s leadership—that was a very strong moment."

Ellison, who served as associate vice president for research, learned how difficult it is for humanities colleagues to obtain external funding, particularly for multiyear, multipartner projects. It is not part of their culture to frame scholarly projects in ways that make for good matches with foundation or agency support. A former graduate dean told her that when he met with division chairs to ask what infrastructure they needed, "the scientists and social scientists all got together and came up with coordinated answers to that question, and the humanists didn't know what the question was. They did not operate strategically as a bloc." Ellison believes this sense of marginalization has to do partly with the fact that they haven't historically navigated the institution in the same way and don't think opportunistically about institutions in general. "That's a completely solvable problem. Indeed as humanists develop collaborations with performing artists, work on digital projects, interact with fields such as museum studies, and pursue community-based teaching, their valuing of infrastructural support changes."

Like Stanford, Michigan supports programs in the humanities where external funding is severely limited. Marvin Parnes, vice president for research, said funding maintains vitality in the faculty members' intellectual life:

> We have a program conjointly with LSA, where we give term awards. What many of our humanities faculty want is time off. We do competitive term awards for people. We also top off salaries for people who get prestigious fellowships, where it really doesn't cover their costs, their writing, so for the humanities we try to protect some of their funding.[51]

Interdisciplinarity at Michigan

A major narrative at Michigan concerns the appreciation of interdisciplinarity, the easy acceptance of multiple subfields inside each department and discipline and the low boundaries between the disciplines. According to President Coleman, "Interdisciplinarity is the key watchword. It is what made Michigan great. I think it is going to be key in the future. I think those universities that can really continue that trend, can get people to work across disciplines will be ahead. That is going to make for the great university of this century."

Jacque Eccles said of Psychology, one of the largest departments in the university, "Everyone used to kid, and the deans got worried about it, that the modal appointment in the department is zero time. There are 150 people who fill 70 slots, because the majority of faculty have joint appointments with research and others programs on campus that are as different from each other as they are from other fields. You often have better allies in some of the other departments than you have in your own department. ... New programs emerge all the time. ... You create new programs and these boundaries change."

Richard Gonzalez, chair of Psychology since 2002, described some of Michigan's interdisciplinary innovations:

> We created the Culture and Cognition program as a subarea in psychology. ... We started the Developmental Psychopathology and Mental Health program, which is a merger of clinical and developmental, bringing the two disciplines together to study the development of disorders

in children. ... Then we started the Cognitive/Cognitive Neuroscience program. It was the first program here that merged the two disciplines. Faculty sort of developed their interests. All of our success stories came from the bottom up, with administrative support.[52]

We were told that Sociology, Political Science, and Economics were more protective of their boundaries, both topically and methodologically, although sociology began to move toward broader epistemologies in the 1990s. The historians we spoke to echo this theme of border crossing. Sonya Rose, chair of History, emphasized that history became more interdisciplinary as cultural history influenced the discipline.[53] There are numerous joint appointments with American Culture, the Center for African American and African Studies (CAAS), and Women's Studies, and History spans the humanities and social sciences divide. Candidates for tenure can be considered by either the social sciences division or the humanities division, depending on the faculty member's research.

Humanists also spoke about their low boundaries and the permeability both among themselves and with other units. English chair Sidonie Smith used the example of her discipline to describe the complex issues of mapping specific research topics onto disciplines and academic units. Noting that English is particularly strong in gender and sexuality studies, with about 25 or 30 women and men exploring such issues, including race, in literary and cultural texts, she said that "many with appointments only in the English Department would position ourselves as doing interdisciplinary work." Because there are "degrees of interdisciplinarity within literary studies and across the disciplines of the humanities and the social sciences ... there is not one mapping of your appointment status to your interdisciplinary reach." Disciplinary affiliations and identity matter, however. "Historians do different things with texts than literary scholars." Furthermore, "disciplinary attachment is different than the attachments made possible by the artifactual history of a particular department, college, and university, and by the history of the emergence, identities, and institutional structures of interdisciplinary units."

In terms of the sciences, Deborah Goldberg echoed Smith's point that interdisciplinarity is about crossing somewhat arbitrary, historically constructed lines. She also remarked on the extent to which major funding agencies often require interdisciplinary research. This emphasis is reinforced in LSA by tying seed money to research collaborations with faculty outside each college. Unlike universities that "talk the talk" about interdisciplinary research, Martha Pollack thinks Michigan really does walk the walk. Even more important, "there are mechanisms in place to get the money divided up and to get the credit divided up. The administrators know how to deal with that, and the faculty does, and that is not true at all universities."

Marvin Parnes summed up the Michigan style when he said, "There has always been an effort to promote innovation, novel research, interdisciplinary research." It is this openness that helps Michigan to take advantage of the "big growth in the availability of external resources." Internal funding for interdisciplinary projects is also strong. A flyer for a summer 2005 interdisciplinary humanities project announced that funding up to $15,000 would be awarded to three to five interdisciplinary groups. "All participants may work within the humanities or the group may include humanists and scholars from other fields (such as the social sciences, arts, sciences, or professional schools)."

These stories show Michigan's imagination in creating ways to hire and support new people for new interdisciplinary fields and new kinds of scholarship. Administrative support fosters intellectual affiliations across traditional lines. At Michigan, departments do not hold sway in the same way that they still do at Stanford and elsewhere, although the traditional disciplines, as Abbot observed, still provide crucial academic and intellectual identity.

CAAS, American Culture, Women's Studies, and IRWG

At Michigan, CAAS, American Culture, and Women's Studies are well-supported units. In contrast to programs at Stanford and RU–N, in these programs the majority of their faculty lines are shared by joint appointments with other units and departments. Lines are shared across American Culture and English, for example, or Women's Studies and Music.

CAAS did not begin with these flexible structures. According to Kevin Gaines, the present chair, CAAS began in 1970 as a result of the Black Action Movement I and was marginalized at the beginning. Declining the chance to recruit a nationally prominent scholar (such as St. Clair Drake at Stanford), Michigan hired Harold Cruz, "a prominent African American cultural critic, who was a true public intellectual," to lead the program. But the administration was uncertain of its long-term commitment to the program—Cruz was not an academic. As a result of the student unrest on campus in the mid-1980s, the fortunes of CAAS began to change, in large part because there was a continuous line of administrators who, according to Philip Deloria, were "very, very committed to building a diverse faculty, who supported programs like CAAS and Ethnic Studies within American Culture."

Elizabeth Cole, an African American psychologist, with joint appointments in CAAS and Women's Studies, emphasized James Jackson's effect on the program when he became director, as well as its challenges for the future now that CAAS had grown so much:

> CAAS got a lot of institutional capital when they hired James. Putting James into this position and giving him the resources to hire people make me think that the administration wanted to change its status. ...
> He had a real vision of a Diaspora focus, that it was important to keep

African, African American, and Caribbean studies all together, that ... intellectually something was going to happen that wasn't happening anywhere else.

Junior faculty members have been getting tenure, and the Center received an award for curriculum restructuring. Despite these markers of success, Cole believes that on some level CAAS has got to be on probation. She said that the administration will ask, "Now that we have given you all these resources, what do you have to show for it?"

Kevin Gaines, whom Cole described as "highly respected," emphasized how joint appointments made under James Jackson worked to prevent marginalization in CAAS. "James felt strongly that CAAS would grow and stabilize itself in partnership with other units. CAAS is able to hire its own faculty 100%. ... But it is really a last resort. Our growth has been maintained by these kinds of partnerships. Also it prevents us from being marginalized."[54] He summed up the benefits of this structural approach and pointed out that it was only possible because of CAAS's "parity" with academic departments, a sharp contrast to Belinda Edmondson's fear, at RU–N, that joint appointments would swallow up the much weaker African American Studies:

> What is unique about CAAS is that other prominent African American studies programs hired all these stars. But at Michigan we have achieved this success with the multigenerational model, where we have hired both at the senior level and really top junior people. We have promoted them in ways that probably wouldn't have been possible at some Ivy League institutions where the relationship between the African American studies program and the departments does not have the parity and the shared mission that we have had. Our model is founded on a shared commitment among the departments that we have worked closely with.

Another interdisciplinary program that has benefited from Michigan's structures and commitments is American Culture. American Culture was created in 1952 by students and faculty in the English Department, who wanted "a grasp of American experience broader than could be provided in the study of any one discipline." In the early 1970s, influenced by the 1960s social movements, the program expanded as it responded "to the growing awareness in our society of the diversity and complexity of cultural experience in America."[55] By the early 1990s the program encompassed Latina/ Latino Studies, Asian American Studies, and Native American Studies. At the end of the decade, 12 positions were allocated to enhance the ethnic studies programs under its umbrella.

Sidonie Smith told us that this major infusion of resources was in part a strategy related to institutional concerns about the possible outcomes and effects of the Supreme Court cases: "The university put significant resources into attracting and retaining faculty of color and faculty whose scholarship contributed to the study of communities of color in the U.S. It did so in order to secure the university's ongoing attention to scholarship in these areas and to provide support for young scholars and role models for graduate students." In his interview Philip Deloria, the present chair of American Culture, expanded on these institutional benefits:

> Now we end up having one of the strongest Pacific Islander faculty in the country here in Michigan. And it is an amazing group of people, and … I believe the program turns in interesting ways on the Pacific Island faculty, who engage other ethnic studies faculty, each around distinct issues that are usefully compared with the Pacific. Since I came, in 2001, Native American studies had a similar kind of explosion of faculty. It went from one faculty member to nine. Some of them are not in the program in American Culture but are faculty associates of Native American studies, for example, in anthropology and information systems and law.

Decisions about joint faculty members' duties raise interesting issues around the "relationships of power" between American Culture on the one hand and English and History, for example, on the other. With most faculty having 50–50 split appointments, it is difficult to determine which is the home department. However, as Deloria observed, "Michigan does a very good job of sitting down with faculty and administrators to try to figure out what is best for the faculty member, but also meets the needs of the unit."

Women's Studies began in a marginal position similar to that of CAAS. The Women's Studies Program was founded in 1973 by a grassroots group composed of students, faculty, staff, and community women. They developed the first introductory course in 1972 and wrote a proposal to create a women's studies program in LSA, asserting "that feminist questions could inform scholarly work to produce new theory and knowledge."[56] Kathryn Kish Sklar, a 1970 PhD graduate in history, recalled that feminism began to emerge as a force on campus within the context of the Black Action Movement, antiwar activity, and the sex discrimination complaint. Although the latter "posed serious financial challenges to the university," the emergence of feminism created a constituency that made "it possible to think of women as serious subjects of academic study."[57] Like resistant faculty at Stanford, however, some questioned the academic respectability of women's studies and saw the proposal as another "wacky '60s student idea" brought forward by those at the margin of the university.

The founding mothers were realistic about the workings of privilege in the university and made highly respected senior scholars the leaders of institutional transformation, a strategy used decades later during the Michigan Mandate and the Michigan Agenda for Women. But gender politics was less subtle in the 1970s. The senior women, particularly Elizabeth Douvan, were characterized as wise protectors, holding "back the onslaught of the outside world." But Douvan was also described as the wily female: charming, witty, calming, optimistic, and politically savvy. In an environment and an era of White male control and distrust of women, this was a portrait of a person with little real institutional power.

Like CAAS, the Women's Studies Program at Michigan initially chose joint appointments. The current director, Valerie Traub, told us that Women's Studies was one of the units to pioneer this approach:

> In Women's Studies a decision was made early on that it wanted joint connections more than it wanted to have its own 100% lines. ... Women's Studies was really on the forefront of being the guinea pigs for this—both at the untenured and tenured level. ... We began with one FTE [full-time equivalent of a faculty position], Barbara Reskin, and later [Abigail] Stewart, a social scientist, and Domna Stanton, a humanist. They both had 50% appointments and made up one position.[58]

While eventually Women's Studies gained a few of their own lines, from the beginning the emphasis on joint appointments meant they were able to ally themselves with both "insider" departments and "outsider" departments such as CAAS. With them they were able to not only make joint hires but to explicitly challenge departmental and disciplinary boundaries. Since that time, interdisciplinary projects have become the primary mark of their work.

Stewart, who directed Women's Studies from 1989 to 1995, described the important challenges of the 1990s. They had to overcome the program's initial failure to gain external funding, a prime mark of scholarly productivity, and therefore academic reputation, at Michigan:

> The founders wanted Women's Studies to be a place where research was funded and supported. And they got some pittance of funding and were told they should go out and get external funding. The first proposal they wrote wasn't funded, and it became an embarrassment and a shame. And so they stopped talking about it. It became a thing that was unimaginable. We were a teaching unit.

Women's Studies also had a collective governance structure, selected by many such units as an alternative to the hierarchies of patriarchy. When Stewart arrived in the late 1980s, she observed that it was "clear the program was burning itself out with its collective structure." More important, deep racial issues surfaced. As the numbers of graduate students and undergraduate students of color increased, there were no such gains in the numbers of faculty of color. "The White faculty had no tools for dealing with this, no conceptual tools, no personal tools, nothing. No self-awareness. Pat Gurin, who chaired the internal review, played a huge role in working through the issues around race."

To address these problems, review committees in the late 1980s evaluated all aspects of the Women's Studies Program. Their work bore fruit; in 1990 the program was reorganized and given additional resources and support.[59] Their 2003–2004 long-range plan recognized the importance of the institutional context in shaping their scholarship. "We aspire to create and improve institutional structures for the production of new knowledge and the support of faculty and students dedicated to feminist scholarship."

The institutional context contributed to the program's success. President Duderstadt's leadership and support mattered—the Michigan Agenda for Women created a climate that fostered success for women.

Duderstadt also helped with the founding of IRWG in 1996. Stewart, the founding director, remembers how a group of feminists went to meet with him to propose it, with the encouragement of Edie Goldenberg, then dean of the LSA:

> I remember he had basically two questions. How many institutes like this are there nationally? And I said 60. And his jaw dropped. He had no idea. He thought it was going to be none or one. So he asked, Why don't we have one? I mean, of course, this is the Michigan attitude. If there are 60, how did we miss the boat? ... We didn't have one because there had never been support for a program with a research mission that engaged the faculty. ... The second question was, Is anybody willing to lead this thing if I agree to it? And so, Edie said, Abby will. She knew the answer had to be yes and there had to be a name. So he literally said okay, let's do it and walked out.

Beginning with substantial funding from Duderstadt, the institute's current budget includes substantial internal support and external funding. Stewart told us that a key issue has always been the "intersectionality of identities." She said, "Many programs in IRWG have focused as much on race as they do on gender or focus on them together. The theoretical advance of intersectionality has helped everybody deal with it. So it is just not possible to be thinking about gender and not thinking about other identities."

IRWG seeks to be an umbrella organization, not only for bringing together interdisciplinary research but also for public dialogue on social issues.[60] An example of that is IRWG's stance as the Supreme Court cases progressed. In a strategy to divide women and people of color, anti-affirmative action arguments often obscured the ways such legislation would also harm women. Stewart recalled, "One of the things that we did was to repeatedly articulate the question, Why is this issue being framed around race and not gender?"

Why are women's studies and IRWG at Michigan so well equipped to explore so many of these issues? Part of the answer lies in the Women's Studies

Program's commitment to create and improve not only institutional structures but a campus culture that does the same. The structural changes the university community set in motion when diversity programs were granted the authority and the power to hire and tenure their own faculty began a significant institutional shift. The major factor in a faculty member's departmental or program alignment is one's scholarly affiliation rather than departmental designation. This may be the main structural difference between Michigan, and Stanford and RU–N.

Conclusions

How do the phases of diversifying the faculty relate to the institutional changes we have documented here? In Phase Two and Phase Three, faculty newcomers advocate for changes in the curriculum, object to unfair tenure decisions, and begin to point out some institutional practices and policies that are not working for women and people of color. However, they do not call for structural change.

As we have seen from examples in these three places, it is only in Phase Four that campus leaders and their allies first link excellence and diversity and begin to examine the institutional structures, policies, and practices that hold change at bay. Ramon Saldivar's notion of "institutional collectivism" signals a shift from the individualistic idea of the "one best faculty member" whose worth is measured simply by her or his personal successes to an ability to play a larger collegial role in furthering the goals of departments, schools, and the wider institution. Faculty members and administrators recognize, in Saldivar's words, new roles for the individual "in the context of a university's mission to create new knowledge, disseminate it to new generations of future scholars and researchers, and contribute in practical terms to the creations of a good society."

As the pressures of the significant cohorts of new faculty characteristic of Phase Four challenge the limitations of traditional departmental structures, people begin to understand that these structures themselves carry privilege in the form of advantaging and reward only certain kinds of knowledge and experience. Phase Five inaugurates the process of countering departmental autonomy with more interdisciplinarity, allowing intellectual interests to trump the allocation of departmental lines and designing institutional structures that are in the service of new kinds of scholarship and faculty rather than departmental power.

We saw this shift in various instances at Michigan where, according to Nancy Cantor, a critical mass of faculty was built—both of color and White—in which there is a "sense of intellectual camaraderie and purpose that becomes very supportive for individuals." Faculty members were able to follow their intellectual interests across departmental boundaries and thus create new knowledge, particularly benefiting the younger generation of scholars and their research as well as their departments and the whole university culture. Leaders in the ADVANCE program saw early on that the social sciences could provide scientists with theoretical tools for thinking about relevant social phenomena such as the social construction of identity, the workings of bias, organizational behavior, and institutional change as they worked to diversify the faculty.

The example of CAAS at Michigan illustrates that a high-quality diverse faculty can be found, that this faculty can be composed of not only the "15 most prominent faculty of color" but also promising junior faculty members constituting a strong pyramidal base. As a different set of people, often in interdisciplinary programs, performs key institutional functions—hiring and evaluating colleagues and recommending tenure—this critical mass mounts a fundamental challenge to the perceived wisdom of leaders in the disciplines, thus opening a new window on the workings of disciplinary and departmental privilege.

What of the other two institutions? The RU–N administrators have the glimmerings of the need to support people's changing intellectual interests as converging with colleagues in other units as they recruit people in clusters to be scholars of urbanism, ethnicity, and globalization. However, it remains to be seen if those initiatives will change departmental patterns of organization or bring the centers more closely in line with academic departments on campus. For the most part, those at Stanford locate their intellectual interests within their disciplines and their departments. Stanford's recent decision not to study the pluses and minuses of faculty appointments outside departments suggests that structures are unlikely to change in the near future. And yet two of the most powerful clusters of departments at Stanford—sciences and engineering—are heavily involved in interdisciplinary work. The CCSRE is a vital intellectual center, if primarily for faculty of color, and its new director has a joint appointment. It remains to be seen if the primacy of departments can hold in this evolving context.

As to the question of marginalizing programs that carry diversity, unlike other interdisciplinary efforts, we propose these explanations. In addition to and compounding the pecking order of disciplinary hierarchies, African American and ethnic studies programs have had a difficult time outliving widely held notions that their origins lay in political turmoil rather than in legitimate scholarship. This disparagement contributes to the "downward construction" of faculty of color that parallels that of people of color in general and is a factor in the microaggressions faced by many of them. In terms of women's studies, many scholars have written about the failure on the part of the academy to take women's studies seriously as a discipline. Marilyn Boxer expressed the conclusions and frustrations of many when she wrote:

The stems of feminism are now deeply planted throughout the terrain of higher education. … [Yet] controversy over women's studies was inevitable. Women's studies entered the academy at a time of significant change in the church, the family, and the world economy. It gained a foothold only when fractures had already appeared in preciously solid walls of resistance to women's historical claims. It is understandable, therefore, that women's studies, which introduced feminist issues into higher education, would be perceived by opponents of change in gender relations as one of the causes of those changes and would be accused accordingly.[61]

It will take a long time before women's studies, like African American and ethnic studies, outgrows the stigma of "parochialism" and "other loyalties" levied at Estelle Freedman so many years ago, a stigma perhaps hiding the degree to which men are threatened by women's entrance into the academy. It also may be that women and people of color associated with diversity programs are less willing to "cover" or mute their stigmatized traits to be more socially acceptable.

Yet the Michigan story affirms how alliances between women's studies and ethnic studies may promote structural change. Such alliances are absent at RU–N, and with the possible exception of CCSRE, we learned of no particular alliances between White feminists and people of color at Stanford. Renato Rosaldo's lament that there were two separate faculty committees on race and gender supports our idea that those alliances are yet to be forged in any institutional way.

6
The New Scholarship of Diversity and Its Relation to Institutional Structures

When talking about the creation of knowledge, people often use the metaphor of building an edifice, constructed one building block at a time. While this may be a useful metaphor in the sense that the creation of knowledge is a communal project with many people contributing pieces, I don't think it is quite right. Building blocks have the same shape and dimension. Thus the metaphor implies that all contributions are the same. But new knowledge—new discoveries, new insights—are never homogeneous. By definition, if your discovery is the same as mine, then yours is not a new discovery.

Provost John Etchemendy—Stanford University, 2003[1]

My own view is that we not only have an obligation to the city but that the city has extraordinary resources for teaching and research and that the mission of the university in the community is first and foremost to tap into the resources that the city offers. This means to be doing research, to be teaching, to be learning. Cultural institutions, scientific laboratories, business, the courts, major law firms, they are all here—and my orientation is to take full advantage of that, because that is the competitive advantage of an urban university.

Provost Steven Diner—Rutgers University–Newark, 2004

The whole notion of diversity is that it really is intellectual and social diversity all mixed in, and that is what interdisciplinarity does. You look at a question or an issue from multiple lenses, jargons, disciplines, and it is the same thing that you do when you say that it is a more exciting environment if people from different life experiences come together. … The interdisciplinary conversation we had was in some ways the most fundamental challenge to privilege because privilege is often rendered in these institutions through the perceived wisdom of leaders in the disciplines.

Nancy Cantor—Former Provost at the University of Michigan, 2005

Our purpose in this chapter is to examine how institutional structures have responded to and helped to shape the scholarly work of newcomers. In what ways have their institutions come to support their research and help make their backgrounds an asset rather than a liability? How has the particular mix of intellectual and social diversity in these three universities influenced the kind of scholarship that is most valued and rewarded? Again, beyond being hired on the basis of their scholarly agendas, faculty make decisions about their scholarship that are supported and shaped by informal networks of support and advice. We saw in the previous chapters how external factors of disciplinary frameworks, national rankings, external funding, and the public reputation of the institution help construct the local conditions under which scholarship is created and measured. These factors are often cited, as we have seen, as constituting barriers to the new kinds of work that White women and people of color have brought into the academy.

But these factors by themselves do not determine what decisions are made in each institution about what kind of scholarship is to be sought after, supported, and rewarded. As the opening quotes suggest, leaders at each of these three institutions have articulated the challenges and possibilities of the new scholarship differently, and these differences say much about the role of the institutional context in the scholarship produced there. At Stanford, the emphasis is on "new discoveries," which will "push the forefront of knowledge further, faster," in Etchemendy's words.[2] At Rutgers University–Newark (RU–N), Provost Steven Diner has for the first time articulated a specifically scholarly urban mission, making a significant virtue out of a hitherto maligned social context. Nancy Cantor credits the interdisciplinarity that grew out of the social and intellectual diversity of the faculty for changing structures and ideas about the scholarship most worth having at Michigan. All of this combined to challenge the privilege of departments and disciplinary authorities. She described how she saw it working: "If you give tenure lines to interdisciplinary programs, then all of a sudden you have a different set of people evaluating tenure and rewarding scholarship, supporting junior faculty in different ways, recruiting different kinds of graduate students, and using fellowship moneys in different ways." Thinking also changed about how to structure a career and mentor junior faculty.

Within this discussion of the role of institutional structures in the construction of this new scholarship are four questions. The first is the question of the importance of the scholar's own gender and racial positioning in the production of such scholarship, and how people at each institution have thought about these connections. The second question is about the changing nature of topics and areas of study. The third concerns the shifts in and expansion of research methodologies. The fourth is the larger public purposes of scholarship as seen by people in each institution and the possible links between research and its social effects—whether in terms of scientific breakthroughs or social activism.

First, how are racial, ethnic, and gender identities and backgrounds thought to affect the nature and value of contemporary scholarly initiatives? Although a few scholars attended to race and gender before the 1970s,[3] most disciplines rested on the unstated assumption that the White male experience is universal, constituting a basis for generalizing about all human beings. The advent of newcomers to the academy exploded for many the myth of the objectivity and applicability of the mainstream work conducted for generations by the White male academic elite. Rather than seeing the new ideas of women and people of color as contributing ideas formerly absent, it was often seen as eroding the timeless quality of this work. Cecilia Ridgeway of Stanford observed:

> Many of the players who are not active feminists seriously don't get it. Many of them are committed to equality, but they don't get how the assumptions about what is an important topic, what is a high-quality journal, what is a well-established standard, how rankings are made, all embody assumptions about what is important knowledge. ... And when you raise that question they secretly think that you're justifying mediocrity, that you're trying to make an excuse. Best work does not need to be excused.

Some argue that the newcomers, by their very positions in the society, have hitherto unavailable viewpoints. Newly tenured at Stanford, Paula Moya articulated the idea of "epistemic privilege":

> Epistemic privilege refers to a special advantage with respect to knowledge about how fundamental aspects of our society (such as race, class, gender, and sexuality) operate to sustain matrices of power. People oppressed in a particular way have experiences that people who are not usually lack—that *can* provide them with information we all need to understand [about] how hierarchies of race, class, gender, and sexuality operate to uphold existing regimes of power in our society. [This is] not an a priori link between social location and knowledge but one that is historically variable and mediated through the interpretation of experience.[4]

She told us later in an interview, "For me the idea behind epistemic privilege has been to look to the perspectives of people whose views are not usually given any airtime, as a way of correcting for the dominant view that gets all the airtime. It isn't a matter of saying that the subordinated person always understands more about everything but rather that in order to really understand the whole, we must pay attention to those perspectives that usually get overlooked. Otherwise we can't really see how power is working."

Another critical issue is how White colleagues change through contact with colleagues from diverse backgrounds. Terrence McDonald at Michigan, a White man, spoke of the evolution of his field of history as a result of the advances of the new scholarship:

> I have been fortunate that I had this sympathy with people who feel uncomfortable. I had real training at the hands of my colleagues— women historians, African American historians and others whom I have come to be friends with—about the theory and practice of race and gender. That has had a huge impact on my teaching and my own work. It is at the core of everything now.

McDonald went on to say that he had seen the spread of these ideas across the university, which made them no longer racially specific or gender specific. He provided this example: "So you have male historians writing about the construction of gender. It may be about masculinity, but it is still there. I can see the impact it is having on hiring. There is no longer the sense that this person is not the best, but the best includes diversity."

Two more aspects of the new scholarship have also had important ramifications within each institution. First, as we will see, especially in relation to RU–N, the topics formerly considered appropriate for scholarly work—in the sense of producing the most prestigious and lucrative results in the wider world of publications, grants, and rankings—were often not those associated with the problems or lives of women, people of color, or oppressed groups in general. But at RU–N, as elsewhere, this may be changing.

The new scholarship has also been associated with the expansion of research methodologies, away from and in contrast to the traditional positivistic research models associated with the Cold War. The disciplines that adhered most closely to that method became the most privileged and powerful. Thus the sciences led the social sciences and the humanities, and within the social sciences, where many methodologies are used, quantitative approaches were seen as more prestigious, more mainstream, and more safe than qualitative ones. Many of the newcomers to the academy came first to the more interpretive disciplines, where they faced contentious struggles over epistemology, topics of study, and disciplinary boundaries. It is no coincidence the resistance to their scholarship has been often safely, and euphemistically, couched in critiques of it as lacking objectivity and rigor.

At Stanford, the Department of Cultural and Social Anthropology split over just such issues, as a result of a struggle powerfully illustrating the impact of "epistemically privileged" newcomers and the resulting contentions over the legitimacy of different kinds of knowledge. Although all three institutions have struggled with these issues, the mix of intellectual and demographic diversity at Stanford has been particularly contentious, as shown by Estelle Freedman's tenure case and the core debates in the 1980s.

The New Scholarship at Stanford: A Department Split Apart

The place of faculty diversity in the case of anthropology leaps out in photographs taken in 1998. Pictures of the Department of Cultural and Social Anthropology and the Department of Anthropological Sciences taken after the split would show the former, with one exception, composed of women and people of color and the latter, with one exception, composed of White men. Yet James Gibbs, a retired long-term department member, described the split in anthropology in that year, which produced these two new departments, as a function of the department's "ethos and history," the Stanford administration's visions for the department, and "intellectual grounds," namely, "changing methods and theories in contemporary anthropology."[5]

To us, the split illustrates the complex interplay of all these factors. The racial, ethnic, and gender positions of faculty provided one basis for a struggle about the directions of a rapidly changing field, some of whose new topics and epistemologies grew out of the "search for a better world" in the 1960s. At the same time the links between the Program in Human Biology (Hum Bio), founded in 1976, and the department contained the seeds of the later split because, as we emphasized in Chapter 5, faculty members at Stanford could not have positions or tenure in a program—they must be located in an academic department. Institutional restrictions fed into issues of personal, intellectual, and methodological identifications.

When the department was founded in 1953, it took a cultural and social approach rather than the more common four-field approach.[6] Archaeology had one representative, and 10 years later a linguist was added. According to Gibbs, in the mid-1960s there was a "live and let live" ethos and a broad range of cultural and social fields represented, including medical and educational anthropology and political economy. Then "in the 1970s the department began to develop a reputation for its emphasis on feminist anthropology, initiated by the work of Michelle Rosaldo, complemented early on by the work of Jane Collier and Sylvia Yanagisako. ... Other more recent approaches ... were interpretive (Renato Rosaldo), symbolic (Carol Delaney), poststructuralist, and reflexive." The department also had a reputation for recruiting women faculty and a graduate student body that was diverse in terms of ethnicity, race, gender, and sexual orientation.

In 1976 a new element was injected into this context. At that time the fields of biology and the social sciences were riven by the sociobiology debate, concerning the relations between biology (i.e., genetics) and culture in determining human behavior. The newly founded interdepartmental program, Hum Bio, inaugurated a search for a 50–50 hire in anthropology and human biology. The position would be in anthropology although the teaching would be half-time in each unit. After strong disagreements about what kind of anthropologist should be hired, the faculty finally selected William Durham, whose field is "co-evolution, or the dual inheritance model of biology–culture relations." Durham's appointment was the first step toward more emphasis on biology in the anthropology department and was followed by a long period of growth in Hum Bio. Other anthropologists began to teach in the program as well, many anthropology courses were listed as part of the major, and, says Durham, "this was probably the anthropology department's most visible extradepartmental contribution."[7]

Durham told us how the department expanded by bringing in an additional archaeologist and a second linguist while maintaining its strength in social and cultural anthropology:[8]

> It was clear from the start that we were token additions to do the other subfields of anthropology. I was to do biological and ecological anthropology. John Rick was to do archaeology. Earlier they had hired Jim Fox to do linguistic anthropology. So it was a sociocultural department with the three of us as subfield satellites. We got down to our work and built large undergraduate enrollments. Between John, Jim, and myself, we taught about half the students in the department. The Dean's Office saw this, and as the years went along, said, "Gosh, wouldn't it be great if we could diversify and add strength in these high-enrollment subfields of anthropology. How about giving the department a couple of positions?" That's how a lot of the tension started.

In 1985 Dean Norman Wessells proposed a new Program in Human Origins in the Department of Social and Cultural Anthropology, for which he offered two faculty positions. Wessells, a biologist, had been greatly influenced by Don Johanson, a physical anthropologist at Berkeley, renowned for discovering the fossil Lucy. According to our interview with Gibbs, Wessells wanted the proposed program to be housed in anthropology as a way to link the natural and social sciences. The program also was to have strong curricular links with the Program in Human Biology. "Sylvia Yanagisako … maintained that evolutionary studies contributed nothing to these pursuits. In her view, the proposed program in human origins 'was a clear attempt to change the character of the department and the subdisciplinary balance.' "[9] Even though they were offered two new faculty positions, the cultural anthropologists resisted it because it would take away from their cultural–social mission.

Jim Gibbs, described by some as the one faculty member who could have held the department together, elaborated in an interview on how the department's ethos and history contributed to the resistance to evolutionary studies.[10] He said that one point of resistance was that people such as Renato Rosaldo and Yanagisako, who received their doctoral training in the 1960s, had an image of anthropology as creating a better world. The new scholarship on women, race, and ethnicity as well as Marxist theory provided the intellectual underpinnings for this hope.

Although affirming these points about changing methodologies, Durham saw the issue as about explicit differences between humanistic and interpretive approaches on one hand and scientific models on the other. Would they hire a geneticist who saw the human genome as a source of historical data or one who would critique it as a reductionist, ahistorical way of looking at human evolution?

In effect, there were two distinctive ways of studying culture in the department. One was really grounded in the humanities and interpretative. It was Geertzian in part, but it had a lot of Renato in it. It had a lot of Sylvia and the Colliers [George and Jane]. ... Culture was analyzed as a kind of a text to be read, to be interpreted.

Meanwhile, those of us in the satellites were doing much more of a scientific analysis. Our focus was learning about culture by studying the behavior, the artifacts, and the ideas behind them. We built models and tested hypotheses while they were going about looking for sets of meanings and interpretative frameworks. The tension was at least in part about which methods you use to study culture. The tension came to a head when it came time to appoint new people. Do you appoint more in the "science" vein? Do you appoint more in the "interpretative" vein?

These methodological issues surfaced with the opportunity for a search in anthropological genetics. The scientific anthropologists argued for a person who, according to Durham, "does genetics in order to understand human history. ... Instead of digging down through layers of tuff and ash, you now look inside the cell for clues to history in the gene patterns." His colleagues on the interpretive side objected that such approaches would lead to racist theories and categorizations of humans. Durham sharply disagreed:

There was a strong self-critical force to the postmodern view: Why privilege the Western way of knowing? We need to be critical of who we are and our place in this world, a common postcolonial critique of anthropology. But we said, Look, don't turn your back on the scientific method. Its strength is not a "Western thing"—other peoples have science too. Don't abandon science now, when there is all this new information available from genetics. For the first time we can now look inside human genes for a record of history. Genes can tell us about the history of European peoples, for example. Where did folks come from and when? ... So there you have it: two winds were blowing in anthropology at Stanford. One said those questions are old fashioned and not helpful social science. The other was saying, boy, here is a chance for social science to really reveal things about the past, and we are turning our back on it. It was really tough.

Gibbs attributed the impasse about evolutionary studies not only to episte-mological differences but also to "the old, unstated rule that those faculty closest to the area of a new appointment should have the greatest say in defining a billet and shaping the search." He feels that if the cultural anthropologists had been willing to let their scientific colleagues have the dominant role in doing searches for the Program in Hum Bio, the split could have been avoided. The cultural anthropologists were afraid, he thought, that acquiescing to the scientists' con-trol of the search would have meant "going backward in the department's impor-tant, pace-setting strides toward increased faculty gender diversity and tilting the overall ethos of the department."[11]

In 1993 the department completed one successful search by recruiting Rich-ard Klein, a paleoarchaeologist from Chicago, to spearhead the Program in Human Origins. But they could never agree on a second hire. The dean invited in an external review team, but the compromise proposals for a second hire didn't work. Gibbs concluded, "After years of dissension over the human bio-cultural initiatives, both factions had virtually exhausted any residual feelings of goodwill."[12]

In 1996 Renato Rosaldo, then department chair, suffered a stroke brought on in part by the ongoing tensions in the department and the university. His recol-lections differ markedly from Durham's. Although he agreed that one issue was positivist versus interpretive research paradigms, he also told us, referring to the two departments' photographs, that issues of gender, race, and ethnicity played an important part as well:

> I think that there was an issue that never was allowed to be said out loud in department meetings … that racism and misogyny were very close to the surface. … I think there was an unspoken assumption about the excel-lence and diversity issue: this department's not excellent because it's so diverse. I think the politics of difference played an important role that was never allowed to be acknowledged in public.
>
> The issue about how you do your research, positivism versus more interpretive kinds of paradigms was taken to be the main issue. I'm of two minds. On some days I think the intellectual paradigms were a central issue. I think that they literally didn't know the depth of discussion that is going on in interpretive work. I think they had the idea that it was flying by the seat of your pants rather than a research agenda and methodology. The fields are becoming differentiated enough that nobody can master them both. The people who went to the other department were not attuned in their research to the issues of race and gender. They still are not.

In 1996 Robert Weisberg, a law professor and vice provost for faculty rela-tions, was asked to step in as chair, which was "unheard of at Stanford."[13] Then, in 1997, tenure was denied to Akhil Gupta, described in the *Chronicle of Educa-tion* as a "promising scholar of state-society relations and postcolonialism."[14] The cultural anthropologists felt that the administration was biased against cultural anthropology and a rising star in the field; letters poured in supporting Gupta. "According to Gupta," said the *Stanford Magazine*, "the department's junior faculty, all of whom were on the cultural side, began to feel threatened as the tenure controversy intensified. Some dreaded coming to their offices, fearing hallway confrontations."[15]

President Casper finally awarded tenure to Gupta in 1997, after a second grievance uncovered procedural errors in his case. Meanwhile, however, five disgruntled and fearful junior faculty had written to the dean requesting an investigation into threats made against them; they said they were told that if the department didn't vote a certain way, none of them would get tenure. The dean appointed Iris Litt, from the Medical School, to investigate these charges. She wrote a confidential report to the deans concluding that there was a "hostile environment" in the department.[16]

According to Sylvia Yanagisako, Dean John Shoven told the department about these findings in 1998. In her view, the administration was in an untenable legal situation. On one hand, they could not take action against the senior faculty who had been accused of making threats without risking a lawsuit, because the threatening remarks were a matter of interpretation. On the other hand, they could not allow the situation to continue or they could be accused of perpetuating a hostile work environment that had a detrimental effect on the productivity and well-being of the junior faculty. Department members were told that the department would be split into two departments and that each faculty member could decide which department to join.[17] Most of the cultural anthropologists were enthusiastic about the split. They had proposed it the previous year but were told by Dean Shoven that it was not feasible. Durham disagreed: "I've actually felt that if the administration here had been a little more patient and thoughtful, we might have found other ways forward. I think they saw this situation as quickly headed for trouble, and I think they wanted to put out fires." The split became final in May, 1998.

Each department now has its own faculty, courses, graduate students, and undergraduates; however, students take courses in both departments. The number of faculty members in Anthropological Sciences has gone from 6 to 12, with the 6 new hires being equal between women and men. There are now 14 faculty members in Cultural and Social Anthropology, 9 of whom are women—the photograph would be different today. But there has been a cost to the split. Anthropology was ranked in the top five departments prior to the split; neither is as highly ranked today.

The philosophical differences, the deep divisions in epistemological approaches and topics, and what is counted as valuable knowledge between the two departments are reflected in their different mission statements. The Department of Anthropological Sciences published their statement in the

October 1998 *Anthropology Newsletter:* "[Our] subject matter is the nature and evolution of our species. ... The department is united by a common interest in the interrelations of biology, culture, and environment, and by a commitment to a four-field approach to anthropology."[18] By contrast, the Cultural and Social Anthropology Department's mission focuses on postmodern, reflexive approaches drawn from philosophy and literary criticism. Their big picture concerns the cultural forces that shape contemporary societies and identities. Their work has a political-economy focus, namely, "the ethnographic study of the cultural and social processes shaping our lives and those of other people. ... We will prepare students to anticipate and contribute to debates of global, international, national, and local significance."[19]

The crisis may have been magnified by, in addition to the structural causes, unnecessarily constricting disciplinary boundaries. A major theme in a recent book edited by Yanagisako and Daniel Segal is the importance of what they called "flexible disciplinarity."[20] In the book Ian Hodder, a British archaeologist in the Department of Cultural and Social Anthropology, argued that archaeology could be linked with "classics, history, human biology, cultural-social anthropology, environmental science, and so on." In the United States it is more closely linked to "an overarching model of scientific archaeology, defined in positivistic terms." This particularly American split could have been avoided if faculty members had been willing to form groups around interdisciplinary "themes such as social agency and meaning, materiality, genetics, language, or selectionism. ... In such a context there is no metadiscourse provided by anthropology or any one discipline."[21] The hierarchies at Stanford among the sciences, the social sciences, and the humanities may have played a role as well. Some anthropologists want more connections with the natural sciences. Segal and Yanagisako characterized this as "the fear that too active a dialogue with the humanities will result in the downgrading of anthropology from a social science to a humanities discipline."[22]

Although Renato Rosaldo also saw the politics of difference as playing a role that was never admitted, Durham recalled it differently. He said that the cultural anthropologists asserted, " 'You guys who do the science: you are male. Science is a male thing. We have on our side the entire female faculty. And you are all Anglos. On our side, we are mixed.' I didn't buy it then and I don't buy it now: science is not a male or Anglo thing. The record speaks for itself. We are not racist and we are not sexist." In the middle of the conflict, he said, they hired a female geneticist because "what was important to us was the kind and quality of work that was done, not the gender of the scholar."

Perhaps privileged White men such as Durham could not grasp the urgency that Rosaldo and Yanagisako felt about the racist and misogynistic aspects of sociobiology. Durham, who was an undergraduate at Stanford and recruited to the department while still a graduate student at Michigan, has no sense of himself as a "golden boy." He characterized his department's position as the scientific pursuit of objective truth and sees gender as having little or nothing to do with faculty hiring. The cultural anthropologists' claims to "epistemic privilege," in Paula Moya's formulation, were seen as political special pleading by the scientists, allowing Durham's position to remain as one without perspective—simply an objective search for truth.[23] Yet Hodder may also be correct in that this was a particularly American struggle, one that could have been avoided if departmental structures had been more flexible and each side had sought out colleagues in a variety of disciplines who accepted multiple approaches.

This story shows how complex any rendering of institutional responses to differences in scholarly approaches may be. Although the anthropology story is about epistemologies, topics of study, university policies, disciplinary hierarchies, administrative actions, and racial and ethnic identities, it is also about departmental structures and intractable disagreements about the significance of privilege, epistemic and otherwise.

Other Issues of Scholarship at Stanford

The complexities revealed in the story of anthropology are at play, if less overtly, in other departments at Stanford. Although the split in anthropology was more about a particular mix of intellectual and social diversity than about being "the absolute best," that norm undergirded those debates as well. According to Al Camarillo, the 1987 University Committee on Minority Issues Report had criticized the "Stanford style" as supporting the kind of research associated with traditional scholarly inquiry: mainstream topics, empiricist research methodologies, and publication in top-tier journals. Fifteen years later, however, the 2002 Diversity Action Council involved 50 or 60 people on the faculty in various subcommittees. Etchemendy's vision of diversity as enabling "new shapes, textures, and imaginings of knowledge" evolved in that context—a widely representative community of scholars asking diverse questions. However, the contentions around ideas of the "best" remain, circulating around questions such as what have the newcomers contributed, how might their work be evaluated, and how far can or should these long-trusted norms be changed?

Stanford has also struggled with the implications of feminist scholarship for these norms of excellence. One of the results of Freedman's tenure case was that the first woman was appointed to the Appointments and Promotions Committee in the College of Humanities and Sciences. When Cecilia Ridgeway served on the committee somewhat later, in the 1990s, she found that faculty members were being judged against standards that tended to discriminate against feminists. Well-intentioned committee members used the legitimating language of prestige, which holds that "regardless of your subject matter, if you had something really good to say about gender, you would not publish it in the gender journals but in the most prestigious disciplinary journals in the field."

Ridgeway often found herself making the case in committees that this is a very valuable work, "on the edge." Others would counter, "Yes, but can we really be certain this person is really good or are you just making excuses?" Ridgeway continued:

> Right there is the problem, because anything that is going to be unusual *does need* to be explained. I certainly try to make this argument to people, and they just look at you. They seriously don't get it. When the political stakes are higher then the game of legitimacy is fought much more severely. I think this definitely happens with regard to race and ethnicity every bit as much as it does to gender and feminism.

Nevertheless, Estelle Freedman told us that the presence of women and people of color on the Tenure and Promotions Committee helped to persuade others to broaden their views. "They ask, did we give the benefit of the doubt to this standard-product person that we're not giving to a person with a very different background or perspective? And if you raise those in a collegial way, people whom you might start out thinking of as 'the enemy' not only can get it but also can internalize it."

One of the remarkable things we observed at Stanford is the extent to which their conversations about interdisciplinarity are frequently tripped up by a belief in the primacy of the disciplines. John Pencavel, chair of the Economics Department, articulated this belief most forcefully:

> There's not a topic in human and animal behavior that economists don't work on. We think that our models do pretty well. We think that our methodology is the right one, which is, come up with an idea, and really try to test it. So, we're an arrogant bunch, and we think we know how to do it, and we don't look sympathetically on interdisciplinary research.

In the sciences at Stanford, the question of new topics and new research methodologies, as well as the particular contribution of the possible "epistemic privilege" enjoyed by women and people of color, has been particularly articulated through discourses around interdisciplinarity and the idea of multiple research methodologies being brought to bear on the same questions. In spite of her commitment to "the discipline as the entry," Sharon Long tied her experimentation with new and interdisciplinary approaches in part to her gender. She thinks that "women are much more likely to be original, creative, and flexible":

> I think my own work has been very interdisciplinary. If you were looking at my one lab five years ago, you would have seen more different techniques and approaches and disciplines being used in my one lab than in some entire departments. ... Because my particular approach is

to find the problem, and it's always been the way I approach things. ... I keep shifting strategies and approaches in order to get to a goal.

Dean Pamela Matson also espoused interdisciplinary collaboration as especially suited to women. "When it comes to interdisciplinary collaboration—research, teaching, whatever—women seem to be really good. In preparing for a talk, I more or less accidentally pulled together the literature on women and science and engineering along with the very small amount of literature on interdisciplinary research; the overlap in the needs and approaches of scientists in both groups was amazing."

A lot of women would prefer to be in niches, rather than out there scrambling to be the one famous person in an area. Our deans, our provost and president are truly committed to links across disciplines, the multidisciplinary, interdisciplinary approaches. Maybe the selection of women as deans was in part because they were very committed to that.

President Hennessy gave an example of how ethnic heritage also might make an important difference in creating new frontiers of knowledge. He told us about a researcher named James Leckie, recently elected to the National Academy of Engineering: "He has been working on tracing pesticide residuals in the bloodstream of the children of migrant farmworkers. Environmental contamination of individuals is core environmental research that might not have been done by somebody who didn't have an ethnic affiliation with that group." Interdisciplinary scholarship such as this also promotes social and public agendas in new ways. According to Hennessy, Leckie's research into pesticides raises not only policy questions but also questions about the purposes of the university. "When I look back at our founding grant, it says that the university should try to use its power to serve humanity. Well, the impact of that is an idealistic—but pragmatic at the same time—definition of the role of the university."

Many of Stanford's new interdisciplinary institutional priorities have the public good at their core. This in turn may be redefining the scholarly coin of the realm at Stanford. We asked President Emeritus Kennedy if he saw a new kind of privilege today. He said:

Some of the most privileged of the scientists here, in terms of collegial regard and in terms of public impact, are interdisciplinary scientists who are working on the conjunction between science and public policy. ... There is a nexus of people at the new Institute for the Environment here, in which the privilege is being allocated not to the most highly specialized instrument-intensive kinds of scientists but to the ones whose range is broader and laps over into the policy disciplines.

However, the reflections of progress around interdisciplinary work, including a new openness to different kinds of research in the sciences that serves marginalized populations, must be measured against the persistence of the preeminence of the disciplines and traditional standards. After commenting to us that many of the new problems are "much more cross-disciplinary" in their nature, President Hennessy still is not sure how faculty can be hired and credit assigned:

> If you want to have that impact, you are going to need a wider collection of scholars to think about changes in the way we do things in the world. How do we encourage people to work together, but how do we also look to hire faculty? How do we look to attribute credit? All those things are going to have to be reviewed.

We wonder if interdisciplinary conversations at Stanford will follow the path Cantor observed at Michigan, namely, a fundamental challenge to privilege that resides in departments and the associated perceived wisdom of the "golden boys." Academics still function in a culture of capitalism where the ideal subject is, to paraphrase Moya, "an autonomous individual who has no communal ties apart from those formed through economic exchange and who achieves success through his individual effort."[24] The academic emphasis on trajectories of individual success within a discipline tends to obscure and deny the value of interdisciplinary scholarship, particularly at an entrepreneurial place like Stanford.

The place where we saw the greatest congruence between institutional structures that facilitates faculty's research and the relevance of their positions for scholarly work is the Research Institute of Comparative Studies in Race and Ethnicity (RICSRE). It is likewise the central place at Stanford for examining the links between the new scholarship and institutional change. Hazel Markus, the Institute's codirector, commented on the importance of context—of institutional positionality: "Wherever you are, there are contingencies connected with your identity through gender, race, ethnicity, and these contingencies change as you move from one context to another." She argued that faculty members can change the institution through their research and their teaching.

Markus also told us about the Institute's new attention to racial positions and relations, including ideas about Whiteness—that Whites too "perform" race:

> Race is not just something that Blacks or Latinos or Whites have; rather it is something that they "do." Together people make race and maintain it through their interactions. Race is a system of meanings and practices; it is a device for designating and explaining difference. Race is a social transaction. It comes about between and among people; it requires actors and observers. This is certainly not the way that race has typically been

thought about in the social sciences. But now scholars in the humanities and in the social sciences are really starting to have a shared perspective on how to think about race and ethnicity. A lot of the racism in our society today is less the product of individual prejudicial attitudes or antipathies and more the result of taken-for-granted assumptions, norms, policies, and practices that structure our social lives. That is an important idea because it lets people off the hook and acknowledges their good intentions. So you are not saying that I am a bad or prejudiced White person? No, as an American you are necessarily part of a vast and sprawling set of ideas and practices that has been largely unacknowledged and unchallenged but that has been producing and maintaining inequality in education, employment, housing, justice, and well-being for hundreds of years. Such reframing of the sources of racism can be very powerful in conceptualizing what is necessary for change. In my experience, once given credit for their positive attitudes, many people are willing to think about how to change institutional assumptions and practices.

The context for thinking through these new frameworks is a series of faculty seminars at the Institute, which currently involve 90 affiliated faculty members on campus. They spend two years on topics such as race and genetics, identity, and the meanings and practices of diversity. Paula Moya said her work on epistemic privilege was greatly enhanced by her association with the Institute, which provided for the newcomers to succeed by doing things differently:

I thrived much more as a collective subject than as an individual subject, but all the time understanding that I was going against the grain. My theoretical work is very much engaged with that of Satya Mohanty, who is a man of color—not Foucault, not Derrida, not Bourdieu. He is not White, he is not French. ... I put together an anthology called *Reclaiming Identity*. ... It was a collaborative project in that my coeditor and I worked with the contributors so that the anthology turned out to be a programmatic statement about an alternative way of thinking about identity.

I was told as a junior faculty not to do it. Anthologies don't count. But this anthology wasn't just pulling together essays. It was building my own work as part of a collective project. It helped me clarify my own ideas about my own work. Then when I revised my own book, it was much stronger for having forged through that. Since then, I have gone on to build a national research project, the Future of Minority Studies, that loosely takes up these ideas and is interinstitutional, interdisciplinary, and multigenerational.

I was older when I went to the academy. I had been through a tough marriage and divorce, and I'm not easily pushed around. I knew this was the right thing for me.

Claudine Gay, the African American political scientist whom we introduced in Chapter 4, described the Institute as her intellectual home at Stanford, in contrast to her department, where she has no colleagues with whom to discuss her research. "It's a place where there are always opportunities to talk about your ideas. There are people outside my discipline, whose interests overlap with mine. Because of this, I'm made aware of readings that are really helpful. Because I'm participating in the Institute, my work has gone in a more multidisciplinary direction."

It remains to be seen, of course, how the Institute's work will affect the larger culture at Stanford, where deeply ingrained individualism and the pursuit of disciplinary excellence are still powerful forces and, as Claude Steele said in the previous chapter, where the Institute tends toward being marginalized by others at Stanford.

New Scholarship at RU–N

In addition to the national rankings, external funding, and the intellectual public reputation of Stanford, which influences its capacity to finance institutional structures that support both traditional disciplinary scholarship and interdisciplinarity, there is an endowment of $12.2 billion. Hazel Markus told us that Hennessy and Etchemendy have funded RICSRE and are committed to raising a $5 million endowment helping to identify potential donors.[25] By contrast, as we have seen, RU–N's reach for national research university stature has entailed enormous costs to the institution, financial and otherwise. Besides his commitments as an urban historian, such realities may have helped to prompt Provost Diner to explicitly tie RU–N's scholarly emphasis to its urban mission as a way of distinguishing itself from more traditional universities.

Although RU–N's urban involvements are not new, what is new is an institutional shift toward scholarly engagement with the city. Diner holds that the competitive advantage of an urban university will come from studying "real-world" urban problems using all that the city offers: "cultural institutions, scientific laboratories, business, the courts, major law firms." It also offers collaboration with surrounding institutions of higher education. According to Diner, "Newark is a college town." This research paradigm has the potential to address head-on the economic, social, and educational neglect and racial isolation of Newark and to propose new ways of thinking about its people, its problems, and its prospects. And although Diner means for this approach to attract faculty from all backgrounds—Max Herman, for example, is White—he said, "It does create an attraction for certain minority faculty who are interested in urban issues, issues of race and ethnicity, and/or globalism."

Some faculty members have taken up Diner's vision, and it is clear from interviews with many that they believe that the research they do on ethnicity and urban issues is considered important knowledge. Many of the Cornwall

Center's projects are geared toward the analysis and improvement of urban conditions, in Newark and elsewhere. Max Herman studies the aftermaths of the 1967 riots in Newark and Detroit:

> This project examines the riots of the 1960's and their consequences. ...
> One component ... examines post-riot recovery efforts in Newark and Detroit—assessing the economic and cultural development strategies that both cities have employed in recent years to improve their quality of life and alleviate the stigma associated with past episodes of urban unrest.[26]

Another one, set in Chicago, has investigated real estate speculation as a cause of Black poverty, with obvious implications for Newark and other cities. Conducted by Beryl Satter of the History Department, the title is "The Million-Dollars-a-Day Cost of Being Black: A History of African-American, Catholic, and Jewish Struggles Against Real Estate Speculation in Chicago, 1957–1981." Buildings in deteriorating neighborhoods were sold to Black families at high interest rates. "Black homeowners united in a community organization called the Contract Buyers League engaged in protests and litigated court cases. ... Chicago activists who battled contract sales directly challenged institutional racism. Their struggle complicates efforts to explain the causes of urban decline."[27]

Other examples of research with a public purpose are exemplified by Jamie Lew's and Sherri-Ann Butterfield's work. Both use the shifting terrain of immigrant identity to examine the complexities of present identifications and imagine a more truly multicultural future. Jamie Lew described her work with Korean American teenagers, comparing a group of students at New York's elite high schools with a group of dropouts who have enrolled in a GED program. "I'm examining social class issues and race and ethnic identity and the resources in schools to examine why this gap is happening." She is finding major social class differences wherein the children of entrepreneurs are those in the magnet schools who are doing well and those who drop out are the children of single mothers, who work for the entrepreneurs—in nail salons, on the cash registers—earning a living wage only by working several jobs. Her findings challenge some of the stereotypes of Koreans as the model minority and also reveal how students who fail are ostracized in school and their communities. "If you don't do well in school you're looked down upon as less Korean."

Lew explicitly connects her work to the phenomenon wherein various immigrant groups arrive and succeed but many native-born members of African American and Puerto Rican communities are left behind. She says that if she can show these class divisions in the Korean community, it will help illuminate other complexities of race, ethnicity, and class that are masked by the myth of the "model minority." Some Asian Americans can negotiate the color line, but mobility takes structural supports that many immigrant groups, including many Asians, lack:

> The real reason behind my research is to critically look and say that the model minority discourse for Asians is a fundamental way to perpetuate the cultural poverty argument against other minorities and to perpetuate this American ideal of meritocracy. These are the two fundamental ideologies in our society that we have to debunk and challenge in our education system. And this is the core of why I am doing the research I do and why I'm in this profession.

The descriptions of Sherri-Ann Butterfield's grants from the Cornwall Center have similar themes. In a project titled "Living Between Two Countries and Across Three: Second-Generation West Indians in New York, London, and Toronto," she found that second-generation immigrants change their identity fluidly and constantly, often within the same day. The study also demonstrates the complexity of the social category of "Blackness," in that although concepts of race and ethnicity have become conflated for the African American community in the United States, they have multiple meanings in the contexts of London and Toronto. In a related project, titled "Wear a Slip, but Don't Need a Man: Construction of Womanhood Among Second-Generation West Indian Women in New York City," she pointed out that second-generation West Indian women experience social institutions differently from their male counterparts, because of race–gender interactions that have been largely ignored.[28] In addition to crediting the Institute for her involvement with Newark, Butterfield affirms Diner's idea that such scholarly initiatives build a community of scholars across disciplines.

Work such as this directly addresses RU–N faculty members' concerns that African American students' presence on their campus has been eroding in the face of growing numbers of immigrants from all over the world. It complicates and unseats stereotypes around Asian and Black identities and suggests more complex ways of thinking about the student populations they serve. It would be fitting if faculty research in the nation's most diverse university could lead the way in helping campuses deal with the legacies of slavery, American apartheid, and the causes of African American and Puerto Rican students' continued lack of economic and social progress.

As for the sciences, there persists a residue of resentment regarding the hegemony of certain topics and emphases involving external funding and the power that these have afforded certain faculty. The history of the Psychology Department, which includes both biologically and socially oriented faculty, is a prime example of this trend: scientific faculty, dedicated to external funding for measurable results, teach little and have less involvement with undergraduate programs. Lillian Robbins told us that in the 1970s, "what was most prized was being mathematical and scientific with a capital S." This epistemology, which she characterized as "neuropsychology's values," marginalized the fields of qualitative, child-oriented, social, and developmental psychology. This emphasis had implications for tenure and promotion and "not recognizing the contributions" of some departmental members. Robbins added, "At one time the small graduate programs in animal behavior and cognitive psychology were the big things. The rest of us were the hoi polloi teaching the hundreds of undergraduates."

However, the bifurcation implied here between socially oriented and scientifically oriented research is also being challenged at RU–N, where there are now many scientific research projects that have direct public benefits, such as the environmental work in the nearby New Jersey Meadowlands. And several people told us that research in the sciences was now being carried on "with a human face" and with an eye to practical solutions to real-world problems. Paula Tallal has applied her work on cognitive neuroscience to children's learning disabilities, spending more than 20 years investigating her hypothesis that the cause of language-based learning problems in children is a timing glitch in the brain. A practical therapy was the result.[29] New PhD programs in Urban Systems and American Studies are also focused on topics in public scholarship.

Diner's urban mission doesn't appeal only to newcomers or those with cross-disciplinary interests. Maggie Shiffrar believes the fields of social and community psychology can and should become more emphasized, as they would connect more to the urban mission of the university:

> I think that Diner is right that Newark is an untapped resource, and it has gone especially untapped for the Psychology Department because we are not involved in any outreach sorts of issues, and we should be. There is a core moral issue here. Furthermore, these are very fundable areas. Take, for example, social development. What is it like for children to grow up in settings where they are not getting intellectual or psychological or emotional stimulation? I'm hoping that we can hire some people interested in both applied and basic research that overlap with Diner's vision.

Scholarship at the University of Michigan

As Nancy Cantor observed in the comments that open this chapter, "interdisciplinary conversations" led to the changed institutional structures that support the new scholarship. The clearest exemplar of how the intellectual, the social, and the structural interact at Michigan today is the Women's Studies Program, which has been explicit about the relationship between faculty members' scholarly choices and the institutional settings in which knowledge is produced.[30] For example, in their 2003–2004 long-range plan the faculty wrote:

> Following the lead of feminist theory and epistemology and mindful of a dual commitment to feminist theory and activism, Women's Studies

attends to the relationship between those who produce knowledge and the institutions in which knowledge is created and transmitted. We aspire to create and improve institutional structures for the production of new knowledge and the support of faculty and students dedicated to feminist scholarship.[31]

Interdisciplinary projects are the mark of their work. They characterize the scope of their research under six interdisciplinary themes: gendered lives; gender, culture, and representation; gender and health studies; gender, race, and ethnicity; lesbian, gay, bisexual, and transgender studies; and gender in a global context. They have engaged seriously with the "paradigms of 'intersectionality'—theories and histories of the interlocking and dynamic nature of multiple categories of identity and difference."

[We] also emphasize diversity in [our] methodological approaches. Research areas and methods in which our faculty excel are those that are breaking new ground by generating new forms of connection: the integration of quantitative and qualitative methods; analyses of the intersection of gender, race, and nation; and the genealogical reading of the present through the past.

They define what they do as taking a small step across knowledge enclaves.

They point out that their interdisciplinary collaborations have reshaped the construction of knowledge in both women's studies and many other disciplines, including anthropology, history, literary studies, and psychology. The authors of the plan asserted, "The impact of women's integration into the disciplines, along with the effect of feminist scholarship on the disciplines, has created a network of institutional connections, including intellectual collaborations that enrich our collective life."

Research projects at the Institute for Research on Women and Gender (IRWG) are prime examples of the new frontiers that such interdisciplinary scholarship has been able to cross. The "Global Feminisms Project" is a three-year (2002–2005) collaborative international project that "examines the history of feminist activism, women's movements, and academic women's studies in Poland, China, India, and the United States." Project participants in each country are making videos of women activists whom they choose to represent their country's particular concerns and experiences. Not only is the project interdisciplinary and international in focus, it explicitly challenges Western-centric notions of feminism and the idea that the international women's movement represents a "transfer eastward of Western feminist ideals." This project is a fine example of the ways in which the new scholarship crosses not only disciplinary boundaries but the boundaries between scholarship and activism as well.[32]

But the Women's Studies Program and IRWG are not the only places on campus where improved institutional structures have nourished the production of new knowledge. Faculty members are spearheading shifts in scholarly paradigms at Michigan, inhabiting and benefiting from its culture of interdisciplinarity and the low boundaries between academic departments. Stories of such shifts are laced through many of our informants' accounts, alongside discussions of the importance of faculty gender and racial positions in making change.

Edie Goldenberg described new research in the Institute for Social Research (ISR), in the Law School, and in political science as creating new "pockets of perspective." She noted how understandings changed in a number of disciplines when gender became an important variable for analysis. She mentioned James Jackson's work with the Black Voter Study, which challenged a lot of notions that grew out of the predominantly White sample of the American Election Study. She also mentioned Gavin Clarkson, a Native American whose appointment is primarily in the School of Information, who is expanding research on state and local government to include tribal government by establishing a database on tribal transactions. Goldenberg continued:

> We have a lot of work underway that focuses on the Islamic community, some really exciting projects in ISR and elsewhere, including surveys of immigrants in Arab American communities. We have a number of graduate students who are doing work in the Middle East. There are these "pockets of perspective" that will change the way we understand the world, and the way we go about studying in the future. I don't think such focused work has gone nearly as far as it needs to go.

David Halperin, in English, gave us an extended narrative of the development of gay and lesbian studies over the past several decades, emphasizing the evolution of lesbian, gay, bisexual, and transgender scholarship away from identity politics toward more positional, contextual orientations:

> To the extent that I have any kind of theoretical orientation, it is Foucauldian. Foucault leaves all this stuff open. ... Also I don't have to be afraid of contradiction, because I do want to claim a gay identity for myself and for my field of study, even though I also want to critique it. I think the best way to engage with sexual identities is not to conjure them away through some postmodern sleight of hand but to take them so seriously that they end up falling apart and falling apart, when you find that you can't make them do all the analytical or political work that you need them to do. When you pursue sexual identities back through time and across culture, their eventual breakdown teaches you a lot about historical change and cultural variation. It seems to me to be a much more interesting exercise than deconstruction.

Research methodologies have also changed. Pat Gurin noted that ISR's traditional emphasis on quantitative research has had an overall effect on the social sciences—an effect that changed as more heterogeneity was welcomed.

These shifts have had to do with "hiring a much more varied group of assistant professors." According to Dean McDonald, narrative methodologies are now on the table through the advent of cultural studies. He is pleased that, although there is a fight about its legitimacy, "it is an intellectual fight." People's qualifications are not being questioned:

> Right now, a more contentious issue than diversity is cultural studies. What is cultural studies? Is it rigorous enough? For example, people from the social sciences have issues with people who write books about the scripts of TV shows. What kind of science is this? There is a question about methodology in the humanities which is narrative and built upon examples rather than representation. There is a fight about that. If you are doing a cultural studies approach to race in history, you will be challenged more than if you are doing a more conventional, archivally based historical study of race, for example. There are still intellectual issues, but notice that is an intellectual fight. It is not about the person. I think that is a big and beneficial change.

One of the places where research methodologies are pushing the boundaries most noticeably is American Culture. Philip Deloria said that many of the questions that engage faculty there are about alternative productions of knowledge and alternative epistemologies, ranging from the humanities to qualitative social science. He gave us several examples, the first from Asian/ Pacific Islander American Studies. Vicente Diaz, who originates from Guam, compares native traditions of knowledge and cultural practices as they intersect with Western discourses of colonialism and decolonization. Specifically he studies systems of knowledge from his own culture, navigational techniques originating 8,000 years ago, and how that epistemology informs the theorizing of culture. The following is how Deloria characterized his work:

> If you are coming from Guam, you are from what might be defined as a tiny speck of land in the midst of a vast sea, which can be a way of delegitimizing your position. It's a classically imperial way of seeing. In Guam you don't see it that way at all. In indigenous seafaring, they imagine that the islands of the Pacific are moving, and the canoe is stationary on the ocean. It's a whole different kind of navigational epistemology. You see the oceans as giant superhighways in which you can go in any direction.

Deloria went on to say that this epistemological work is regarded as pathbreaking in American Culture, representing the fusion of indigenous and Western ways of knowing, but that it lies outside the norms of history or other, more disciplinary departments. In another example, Native American Studies wrestles with the scholarly legitimacy of using both oral traditions and colonialism's biased written accounts as sources:

Native studies has a huge debate that has gone on for a long time about what is allowable as a source base. How do we deal with oral history and the oral tradition? Can we take that back four centuries? What do we do with that? How do we respond to historians who would say that such histories are not viable evidence?

Those are big questions in Native studies, as well as the flip side. What do you do with the archives that are produced out of a process of colonization? How do you read that? Can you even use it? Those kinds of questions become really central to that field. And it is one of the places where Native studies finds a lot of interesting overlap with Pacific Island studies, especially with the folks who do Pacific cultural studies. Those questions of epistemology become really important.

At Michigan, as at Stanford and RU–N, much of the new scholarship embraces the connection between research, particularly in the social sciences, and political activism and community change. Many of our informants saw the work on the Supreme Court cases in this light: Nancy Cantor, for example, talked about "scholarly passion, if you will, not just a political or legal passion." Steve Raudenbush, formerly of ISR, defended the use of quantitative methods to address political questions. He argued, "Asking the right questions and having the right kind of data and finding out what kinds of ways you can intervene and what kinds of effects you can have is really the heart of the matter."

Furthermore, he pointed out, "Probably the single most visible question in social science and ISR at Michigan in the past five years has evolved around social and ethnic inequalities and health," a political choice.

In the Sociology Department, long regarded as a bastion of quantitative methodology well into the 1990s, Alford Young told us that he had been recruited because of his interest in qualitative methods and in studying Detroit:

> Michigan was a place I had not thought seriously about. I thought of Michigan sociology and Michigan more generally as a place that quantitative researchers go. But I was told that Michigan was interested in having a greater presence in urban sociology and qualitative methods. I would be close enough to Detroit to do some fieldwork there. There had been a great deal of work on Chicago, L.A., New York. Detroit was perhaps the most problem-ridden city with the least amount of attention on these issues. That is quite directly what brought me here.

There are many other examples of public scholarship at Michigan, including Pat Gurin's explorations into the interface between diversity and democracy and Julie Ellison's initiative "Imagining America." Ellison's national project is designed to strengthen the public role and democratic purposes of the humanities and the arts. Its major task is to constitute public scholarship as an important and legitimate enterprise in ongoing collaborations between academics and partners in public and nonprofit arenas.

Research that crosses the line between scholarship and activism is a particularly salient issue in American Culture. Deloria characterized the challenge this way: "We have been working with the notion that a single act might be defined simultaneously as public scholarship, as service, and as pedagogy. ... In American Culture, those have become really fraught boundaries. Lots and lots of our faculty are really involved in activities that are at once community service, public scholarship, and service learning with students." As Vicente Diaz put it, Michigan held out the promise of "helping to create a place where there is critical thinking about pushing the edges between scholarship and politics. The key phrase for me is always 'in relation.' And so a crucial task is to work through, even fight around, the terms of the relation between scholarship and politics."[33]

However, some faculty members at Michigan have informal networks that provide ambiguous support and advice about connecting their scholarly pursuits to activist agendas in the wider society. Al Young said that he was told that on coming to Michigan, "We are not holding you to research in Detroit—you don't have to do that." Diaz has seen the costs of blurring the distinction between politics and scholarship but holds out for constructing new paradigms:

> It is important to not make activism double for scholarship and still not forget that scholarship is always political. For those of us who refuse to distinguish between the two, our reputations as serious academics are questioned and our survival is at risk. But even if, as is often the case, being reputable scholars puts severe qualifications on our political projects (for native struggles for decolonization, for example), we still need to push the edges of each, to fight for a place where critical thinking in relation to our political struggles can flourish or even develop on its own terms. But because the risks tend to fall on us as individuals, however, I need active support from my colleagues and from the institution, and when this proactive support is absent, and especially when things default to mainstream, institutional practices and customs, the initial excitement goes away and I get real worried.

Former Provost Nancy Cantor, now president of Syracuse University, is co-chairing a panel sponsored by the Imagining America Project to create guidelines for rewarding public scholarship at tenure time. Pointing out in a recent *Chronicle of Higher Education* essay that faculty who engage in community-based projects are often told to postpone such work until after tenure, she argues, "To encourage top-notch scholarship that contributes to public purposes, and to attract and keep a diverse faculty, we should look hard at the culture of the academic workplace and reconsider what constitutes excellence at tenure time. We need to develop flexible but clear deadlines for recognizing and rewarding public scholarship and artistic production."[34]

Some other faculty members also feel vulnerable. An untenured woman of color also sounded a warning about the persistent marginalization of women, people of color, and activist scholarship at Michigan: "We are marginalized not just because of our race and gender but because of the kind of work we're engaged in, the kind of work we produce. The activist work we do doesn't register as scholarly work, even if we write about it. There is a resistance to recognizing activism as a form of scholarship."

Why is Michigan so far ahead in establishing structures that support the scholarship of diversity? We think it reflects the institutional commitment that began with the Michigan Mandate and the Agenda for Women. Nancy Cantor affirmed this when she said that despite those who resisted these initiatives, "different people around specific issues," there was "a huge power base of major leaders in the institution who were not of that persuasion." And she added, "You could always find a lot of women."

Conclusions

Each of these three institutions has displayed a unique response to the new scholarship and its relation to institutional structures. As we compare them, we are particularly aware of the privilege of high endowments. The endowment for the whole campus at RU–N is just more than $45 million.[35] At Michigan the endowment is $4.9 billion, and for the School of Literature, Sciences, and Arts at Michigan, our primary focus, it is more than $421.7 million. As we noted earlier, Stanford too measures its endowment in billions.[36] We are reminded of Jim Duderstadt's point that the tax-exempt status of private gifts and endowment income ends up subsidizing institutions, most often private, and giving them enormous advantages. In *The Future of the Public University in America,* Duderstadt and Womack explained:

> An exceptionally strong economy, coupled with highly beneficial tax policies, has allowed some institutions to accumulate vast wealth through private gifts and endowment income and to focus these resources on selecting and attracting an elite class of students and faculty.[37]

It is within the context of that particular privilege of endowment resources that we make our concluding remarks about the scholarship of diversity and its relation to institutional structures, recognizing that RU–N is significantly disadvantaged here.

At RU–N, Provost Diner has begun to leverage RU–N's progress in the social sciences into a specifically urban scholarly mission, one that so far has shown promise mainly through the efforts of junior faculty members involved with the Cornwall Center and the Institute on Ethnicity, Culture, and the Modern

Experience. We did not find instances where many senior faculty members' scholarly work was facilitated. Although many people speak of these interdisciplinary centers as major forces in representing RU–N's commitments to the larger community, they seem to have had few if any effects on institutional structures, the academic departments, and the curriculum. Furthermore, much of the discourse on the new scholarship was about race and ethnicity rather than about gender. Fran Bartkowski said that there is not a campus culture of talking about gender, even though individual faculty members integrate gender topics into their courses and, most likely, their research as well. However, the efforts to begin an American studies PhD program, one that will explicitly educate its students in various forms of public scholarship, is a hopeful indication for the direction of the institution as a whole.

At Stanford the question of structures that support the scholarship of newcomers has been interpreted in terms of the persistent requirement to be the "absolute best." This aspect of the "Stanford style" circulates throughout departmental discourses and policies. Challenges mounted by the faculty newcomers to the decision of the "best" have included the view that interdisciplinary problem solving is particularly suited both to the interests and talents of faculty newcomers and to complex real-world problem solving. One structural exception to the hegemony of departments is RICSRE, which provides a mix of intellectual and social diversity that is the intellectual home for many involved with diversity issues.

Because of Michigan's 20-year history of diversity work, interdisciplinary pairings, emphasis on the scholarship of practice, and the strength of the social sciences, it is the only one of the three universities that has institutionalized formal structures for the production of interdisciplinary knowledge. These structural arrangements have fostered a vibrant range of new scholarly achievements across all the disciplines, involving White men as well as women and people of color.

Finally, we can see that in each institution, the structures that seem to best support the new scholarship of diversity are those that foster interdisciplinarity in one form or another, whether it be the urban focus at RU–N, the research undertaken in the sciences and by RICRSE and IRWG at Stanford, or the practice of faculty lines following people's intellectual interests at Michigan. Rather than forcing faculty members, whether or not they are newcomers, into the molds of academic disciplines whose boundaries were defined many years ago by male elites, these new niches and bridges create the conditions for new topics of study, seen in new ways. These ideas are examples of various kinds of engagement with the real world, including issues of persistent forms of inequality seen from multiple points of view by scholars previously denied "airtime," in Paula Moya's formulation. Such topics are also studied through a new variety of research methodologies. They create the potential for public scholarship and connections with activist projects outside the campus.

It remains to be seen whether these universities, and higher education in general, will be able to make good on these promises.

7
Privilege and Diversity:
Relating Local and National Discourses

All knowledge systems, including those of modern sciences, are local ones.[1]

Sandra Harding—*Is Science Multicultured? Postcolonialisms,*
Feminisms and Epistemologies

Generalized and generalizing discourses participate in the organization of local sequences of ... action and hence in the ongoing reproducing of the university as a regime coordinating local resources of funding, personnel, teaching responsibilities and so on, with discourses organized extra-locally and hooking up with other universities and other institutions.[2]

Dorothy E. Smith—*Writing the Social*

If you say this about one institution, how does it relate to the next? Are you studying a small corner of institutions and generalizing from this small corner? Could it be more widespread, could this "knowledge" inform transformation in other institutions?

Jill Mattuck Tarule—Associate Provost, University of Vermont,
personal communication, May 2006

These assertions by three feminist scholars push us to ask how what we learned "locally" on these three campuses have connections to and have broader meanings for other institutions. Through campus visits, interviews, and the perusal of institutional documents, we have investigated discourses of institutional change. Because we were interested in privilege as well as diversity, we sought out both campus leaders and those who saw themselves as marginalized, interviewing presidents, provosts and other central administrators, department chairs, and senior and junior faculty members. Most of those we interviewed demonstrated enlightened sensibilities toward gender and race privilege, providing a sharp contrast to those of a generation or two earlier.

While perspectives on these issues are by no means unitary, there are specific "fault lines" that inflect and give institutional form to developments on each campus. Each one offers an institutional model of linking excellence and diversity within its own context. However, if this local knowledge is to be meaningful and useful, it needs to be translated through multiple voices in other settings throughout the American academy. We hope that in the stories of these campus transformations others can see themselves and imagine specific road maps and scenarios for their own institutions.

At Stanford, Michigan and RU—N, as at many other places, female faculty, faculty of color, and their White male allies have diversified their numbers, transformed the curriculum, and become advocates for newly diverse student bodies. In varying degrees they have humanized overly rigid structures and institution-wide polices, changed institutional missions, expanded static visions and boundaries in traditional disciplines, and transformed scholarly research in every field. Their widespread challenges to the cultures of higher education has revealed that racism, sexism, and homophobia are matters not only of individual negative hostile attitudes but also of structures and practices related to both external and internal factors.

They have not acted in isolation, however. Critical factors that positively interact with the phases of faculty diversification include enlightened leadership and hiring at senior ranks; planning that involves administrators and faculty leaders; broad based-discussions about diversity at every level; financial incentives for recruitment; acknowledgments that work and family life intersect; forging alliances between women and people of color; and valuing faculty not only for their individual achievements but for what they can do to further transform the institution.

Indeed we were also struck in our campus analyses by the power of individual leaders in each institution to work within and through their structures and their positions to effect (or resist) change. At the same time that James Duderstadt, building on his predecessor Harold Shapiro's Six-Point Plan, was leading Michigan forward into a new era of institutional diversity, both Gerhard Casper and Norman Samuels, also strongly committed to building their institutions, inaugurated different policies. Harold Samuels's reading of his context led to a decision to build the sciences to strengthen his campus; Gerhard Casper was brought in to restore Stanford's credibility in the 1990s, and he set about re-creating a more traditional undergraduate program. Although all three men were responding to important challenges, the decisions of the latter two tended to undermine diversity commitments. Today, the dreams and accomplishments of Clement Price, Charles Russell, Abigail Stewart, James Jackson, Hazel Markus, and Claude Steele, among many others, are powerful examples of institutional transformation on the ground.

Local Learning for Institutional Transformations

Looking back on the stories of these institutions, what can we conclude about these three decades of "democratizing and unifying" the academy? For many years a common dichotomy in the literature of American higher education has been the opposition between the research and the democratizing functions of the university, a dichotomy vividly illustrated by a 1990s debate involving Paul Lauter, Jeffrey Herf, and others over the future of the university. Lauter argued, "I see what goes on at a university as valuable to the entire community, [and I see] education's potential for democratizing and unifying the sort of very divided community we have now." To Herf, on the other hand, "Universities and colleges are and ought to be elitist institutions. ... The reason we have universities is to pursue the truth about important matters. ... Everything else is secondary."[3]

The most significant paradigmatic shift that we observed was overturning the assumption that these missions are contradictory—that in the current formulation of this elitism versus democratization argument, the goals of achieving excellence and implementing diversity are at odds. As James Duderstadt said at Michigan, diversity and excellence are and must be "tightly linked." And in creating the structures to support these linkages, institutional leadership matters.

At Michigan, for more than twenty years, administrators from presidents to deans to department chairs have increasingly seen the need for departmental and interdisciplinary structures that support the changing intellectual interests of the faculty. Michigan enjoys a campus-wide agreement about the importance of multiple perspectives and multiple research methodologies. These commitments have shaped faculty positions in both departments and interdisciplinary programs. The clear agreements in LSA regarding departmental control over faculty positions, five-year plans, and support for faculty are examples of collaborations between the faculty and the administration that have freed them to loosen up traditional arrangements. The office of Dean Terry McDonald is behind the university's revision and expansion of tenure standards to take account of the different life courses of men and women as well as the changing climate for research funding and scholarly publication. It is only at Michigan that tenured faculty lines follow scholars, according to their interests, into both departments and interdisciplinary programs.

The breakdown of the false excellence–diversity dichotomy in a highly selective institution such as Stanford is best exemplified by the mission statement of RICSRE: "[We seek to] create an integrated community of scholars with a diversity of perspectives addressing the problems of how to foster a stable, inclusive, democratic society that successfully incorporates diverse people, institutions, cultures, and practices."[4] And indeed at Stanford we heard repeatedly that the current administration, including the provost and deans, are committed to both excellence and diversity.

The contentions over Estelle Freedman's tenure case, the core debates, and even the 1998 split in anthropology are difficult to imagine in today's climate. They are in sharp contrast to Provost Etchemendy's assertion that "new knowledge—new discoveries, new insights—are never homogeneous." This reflects a growing, albeit in some departments still reluctant, institutional awareness that the new faculty members have contributed important new kinds of knowledge that has to be taken seriously in an institution devoted to producing only the "best." The missions not only of RICSRE but also of IRWG represent some of the directions that the new scholarship might take, becoming more collaborative and interdisciplinary and less individualized than heretofore. However, we heard no one drawing the conclusion that creating links between diversity and excellence might perhaps entail breaking down departmental and disciplinary barriers. While the power of the central leadership in all three institutions is always mediated by that of faculty and their departments, the power of departments is most intact at Stanford, restricting the thinking about alternative structures that might support innovative faculty work there.

Finally, at RU–N, the challenge has been to determine locally what scholarly excellence means for those in a comprehensive university who are deeply engaged in mass education. Because the university is very differently positioned in the academic hierarchy, the challenges to reconcile excellence with diversity look very different there. An urgent discourse of upward mobility—an effort to give the university higher status—parallels an equally urgent discourse of inclusiveness and commitment to social justice issues. As Norman Samuels said, "To have lost the access and diversity dimensions while achieving success on the academic side would not have been a victory. One without the other would have been less than half. But the two together, that is extraordinary." Yet he reasoned that to put RU–N on the map as an equal partner to RU–New Brunswick necessitated heavy investment in the "potions" and "toys" of science, the coin of the realm in higher education nationally. To him, the diversity of the student body was a given condition of his institution, albeit one that he prized, rather than a goal.

Thus the one structural change towards interdisciplinarity that we saw at RU–N was the absolution of CMBN from most institutional restrictions around reporting lines and use of indirect cost dollars. Neither Women's Studies and African American Studies, nor the Cornwall Center and the Institute, have altered departmental or interdisciplinary alignments. Yet the current provost, Steven Diner, in a different time period, has begun to redefine excellence at RU–N by reassigning to his interdisciplinary urban initiatives the institutional status and social impact heretofore associated primarily with scientific research.

While we have been able to clearly chart the progress of diversity initiatives, we have found the most elusive aspect of this work to be excavating the workings of privilege underneath the discourses of excellence that shore up long-standing practices and policies. Helped by many informants who themselves have been puzzled by the barriers to newcomers, we have learned to look at taken-for-granted assumptions and practices holding change at bay. For example, when people began to interrogate the "Stanford style" or look at the "golden boys," they saw hidden patterns of White, male heterosexual advantage. This form of privilege rests primarily on the belief in an autonomous individual faculty member detached from a group and lacking the markers of gender, race, and sexuality. This focus on the individual obscures the workings of group privilege or oppression that have long advantaged some groups at the expense of others.

Our explorations of the workings of privilege have also been furthered by the ideas of positionality and epistemic privilege. At all three universities, women, people of color, and gay and lesbian faculty members have had knowledge, to paraphrase Moya, about how their and others' positions of race, class, gender, and sexuality operate to sustain matrices of power in universities. In many cases, their reflections on their experiences provided us with information that contributed to our understanding of how hierarchies of race, class, gender, and sexuality operate to uphold existing regimes of power. Sharon Long's and Pamela Matson's discussion of women's penchant for interdisciplinary scholarship show that they, among others, understand Hazel Markus's point that position shapes knowledge production. The research of Jamie Lew and Sherri-Ann Butterfield at RU-N illustrates how their position as women of color shapes their research and may over time give them a particular perspective on their institution.

There is also evidence that the degree of institutional change one perceives depends on where one is positioned. Both at Michigan and Stanford, where there have been studies about the quality of faculty members' lives, women of color see the least change. Faculty of color in all of these institutions say that it isn't as good for them as some administrators and faculty in the dominant culture believe.

It has not been only subordinated persons who have come to understand how ruling regimes work and what that means for institutional change. Following Michigan's Agenda for Women, Duderstadt could admit "that at times my male-biased view of the world was just plain wrong!" Terry McDonald had numerous insights into the workings of White male privilege mediated by social class and their implications for institutional change. According to Abby Stewart, White female faculty in the Women's Studies Program began to discern deep racial issues in the program and their need for tools to deal with the challenges.

When we looked at privilege as a factor of specifically institutional rela-tions, we found other dynamics as well. For example, we saw an inverse rela-tionship between the status of an institution and the sense of belonging felt by female faculty and people of color. "High flyers," primarily White men, in top-tier universities are often highly dominant figures, or to paraphrase Nancy Cantor, embodiments of wisdom in the disciplines. Because White men at institutions such as RU–N are less privileged, their relations with women and men of color may be more equal. On the other hand, it is only at RU–N that no top administrators have ever been women.

Cultures of privilege also have to do with faculty rank and faculty numbers. At Stanford and Michigan, where there are very high standards for tenure, junior faculty members enjoy lighter teaching loads, more financial support for research, and time off from teaching before tenure. A similar cohort at RU–N is not guaranteed such nurturing. Cultures of privilege also change with the numbers. The newcomers, as Steve Raudenbush, formerly of Michi-gan, pointed out, began to change power relations in departments when they were more than "just one." Elizabeth Cole said that there are now enough women of color at Michigan so that "not every single one has to be my ally, no matter what. That is stupendous."

While always specifically local in their origins and effects on people, cul-tures of privilege are also heavily influenced by national norms. For example, looking at the "ruling relations" at each place, we have seen the national power of certain disciplines and fields interacting with local cultures to produce par-ticular centers of privilege and power—such as the sciences and engineering at Stanford, or CMBN at RU–N, or the Institute for Social Research at Mich-igan.[5] The ongoing power of the natural sciences at Stanford and RU–N in particular cast a shadow that has affected the recruitment of diverse faculty, although both institutions—Stanford in its vigorous support for the humani-ties and social sciences and RU–N with its urban initiatives—are seeking more of a balance now. Opening up the sciences to women in particular has been gradual on the three campuses. At Michigan there has been a significant attempt, through ADVANCE, to address these questions, and the new leader-ship at Stanford's IRWG is now also looking at women in the sciences and the ways that Stanford needs to change to support them. Changes at Michigan and Stanford were accelerated by national events such as the 2001 conference at MIT and by supportive internal leadership. Ruling relations are particular and contextual, made and remade in day-to-day interactions, and yet they are always part of a national academic culture.

Today, at each of our institutions, we can see that the equation of excellence with diversity, the achievement of Phase Four, has in all three places, to different degrees and in different settings, led to a public conversation about the opera-tions of privilege and the kinds of efforts needed to overcome them.

The comparable ease with which we found examples of White males and females at Michigan understanding their racial privilege is because the Michigan Mandate linked diversity and excellence more than twenty years ago and because it is only there that there is a campus-wide effort to directly address the structures and practices of institutional privilege. The Women's Studies Program at Michigan has been the clearest about the relationship between "those who produce knowledge and the institutions in which knowledge is created and transmitted." They purposefully "aspire to create and improve institutional structures for the production of new knowledge and the support of faculty and students dedicated to feminist scholarship."[6]

At Stanford, departmental predominance, while challenged by people such as Hazel Markus and units such as RICSRE, may change the most as important scientific "real-world problems" identified by Hennessy, Plummer, Long, Matson, and others become seen as both interdisciplinary and necessarily diverse in their origins and solutions. Three interdisciplinary thrusts are the core of the next major capital campaign. The Bio-X Program in the Clark Center, representing the fusion of biology and medicine, is one. The Stanford Institute for the Environment is the second, and the Stanford Institute for International Studies, which just received a $90,000,000 set of founding gifts, is the third. President Emeritus Kennedy remarked to us that "some of the most privileged are interdisciplinary scientists working on the conjunction of science and public policy." One change that may be afoot is the rethinking of faculty appointments only in departments. In reflecting on his five years as president, John Hennessy asked, "What do you do about the fact that we have departments that still primarily carry the decision-making appointment authority?"[7]

At RU–N, after years of delay, there was inaugurated only recently a university-wide financial incentive to diversify the faculty. The emphasis placed on externally directed centers, whether the CMBN or the Cornwall Center, has seemed to deflect attention from necessary improvements inside the institution and within academic departments. However, Diner's mission has fostered new directions for urban-based scholarship, excellent examples of a social science that critiques and transcends the traditional racial and gender discourses of Black and White.

If we were to sum up the overall effects of faculty diversity on institutions and on the scholarship they support, we would say that another paradigmatic shift accompanying their inclusion is the move towards interdisciplinarity, both in the ways institutional structures have begun to open up and change and in the nature of the new scholarship produced. The work of women and people of color, and increasingly White male scholars as well, complicates and transcends disciplinary borders. This is not surprising, for as Dorothy E. Smith points out, "The experiences, interests, and associations of men of a certain class and race bled into the paradigms of the humanities and social sciences, and even into the natural sciences."[8] Audre Lorde once said, "The master's tools will never dismantle the master's house."[9] If the traditional academic disciplines are powerful examples of the master's tools, then interdisciplinary approaches, "small steps across knowledge enclaves" in the words of women's studies professors at Michigan, may be necessary new tools.[10] Powerful leaders like Stanford's Hennessy agree that following the scientific and social problems of today across disciplinary lines requires the new approaches that faculty newcomers embrace.

National Knowledge: "Why So Slow?"

However, if we step back and look at the progress made in the light of our initial questions, we discern some persistent patterns. If only the percentages of faculty who are White women or minority faculty on these campuses and nationally are taken into account, we have to again ask, "Why so slow?" One answer, at Michigan at any rate, is that although the number of female and minority candidates receiving PhDs has increased, the percentage of tenure-track positions has declined. The increasing number of lecturers not on the tenure track have been mostly women. At Michigan women make up 17% of all full professors, with 2% women of color; 34% of all associate professors, with 7% women of color; and one third of assistant professors (34%), a figure that has been virtually static for more than 20 years.[11] It is hard to avoid the conclusion here that highly ranked universities such as Michigan and Stanford are still male domains, relying on male-based gender scripts for their construction of the ideal faculty member. The numbers at RU–N suggest a similar conclusion.

Widely held beliefs still circulate about the reasons for the small number of faculty of color nationwide—the few people of color seeking academic careers, the stiff competition for people of color with PhDs, and their discomfort in majority White settings. One senior administrator we talked to echoed the views of many when he told us, "Your typical search committee chair here is a White person who probably very much wants to get minority faculty into the pool of candidates but doesn't really know how to do it."

James Jackson attributed these attitudes of helplessness to the persistence of White privilege. The culture of the academy rewards an unthinking association of Whiteness and maleness with being smart enough to be in the academy. "They know that they are here because they are smart. If you are not here, then it is because you are not as smart as I am. ... They say, 'What is a good faculty member? Oh, I'm not sure about that. Good teacher, good researcher, good thinker.'" With these vague standards applied to searches for minority candidates, he said that people throw up their hands, saying such things as "We can't find anybody" or "I just don't know whether they would fit here."

Another persistent and perhaps unconscious dynamic of privilege is that although the new scholarship by women and people of color thrives and is increasingly taken onboard in the academic disciplines, not only do women and people of color lag behind in hiring and retention but women's studies,

African American studies, and ethnic studies programs are persistently in danger of marginalization. At Stanford Claude Steele worries that the Center for the Comparative Study of Race and Ethnicity's courses and programs, although relevant to the whole university community, are experienced by relatively few people. Even though White men like Terry McDonald praise the new scholarship, we have observed that it is more acceptable within a disciplinary context, like history, than in less assimilated interdisciplinary programs.

Cultural patterns of privileging male experiences as the norm continue to mark female faculty and faculty of color as the "other," with uphill battles to make it in the academy. Arguing that the academy takes a passively racist and sexist organizational posture, Mark Chesler wrote, "Race/ethnicity, gender, and class separately and together affect faculty members' lives inside and outside the classroom. We need to challenge both the microaggressions experienced by female faculty and faculty of color and a reward structure that so often relegates teaching and antidiscrimination work to second-class activities. ... We need to respond to the ways in which collegiate life is different for many White women and people of color than it is for most White males."[12]

A final explanation of the question "Why so slow" is the failure of White women and people of color to work together for institutional change, an idea brought home to us by Renato Rosaldo's regret about Stanford's formation of two separate committees on race and gender. The common lament of women of color that they rarely feel entirely at home, because their work sits at the intersections of discourses of gender and race, speaks to the human costs of this separation. The construction of different profiles of faculty excellence is likely to happen sooner with such alliances. The emphasis placed by Dean Matson, among others, on women's preferences for collaborative partnerships echoes Ramon Saldivar's vision of hiring people with an "ability to play a larger collegial role in furthering the research and teaching goals of the institution." Both critique Stanford's model of unique individualistic excellence. By contrast, Michigan's multiple alliances among scholars of race, gender, and sexuality help explain some of their success at institutional change, although some, such as Mark Chesler, argue that much more could be done.

National "Cultural" Knowledge that Informs Institutional Transformation

To further assess the chances for continued progress at Stanford, Michigan, and RU–N, however, we also need to go back to the national picture. In Chapter 1 we argued that intentional postwar governmental policies funded Big Science, institutionalized racial and gender segregation, and democratized higher education, mainly for White men. These developments worked to rigidify the structures, operations, and hierarchies of the academy. We also saw how the equity movements of the 1960s and '70s and the accompanying federal legislation attempted to reverse the 1950s patterns of "intent" and in so doing opened up the academy to White women and people of color. Indeed, several U.S. Senators are currently proposing that Title IX, first passed in 1972, be applied to increasing the number of women in science and engineering as well.[13]

Yet there are forces in American society today seeking to undo the gains that women and people of color have made over the past several decades. At each campus we heard specific narratives of anxiety about an increasingly conservative national picture. This conservatism, first manifest as the "culture wars" of the 1980s, descended on Stanford during the core debates. Current opposition to diversity initiatives and affirmative action has taken several forms. One is the "Academic Bill of Rights" advocated by the conservative activist David Horowitz. The bill calls for political oversight of scholarly and educational work in the name of intellectual diversity. Historian Ellen Schrecker believes that today's assault is more serious than that of the McCarthy era because of its threat to faculty members' autonomy.[14] The aftermath of the Michigan Supreme Court cases also shows some conservatives' determination. Having failed in both the Michigan legislature and the Supreme Court, members of a group called the Civil Rights Initiative have gathered enough signatures for "the Michigan Civil Rights Initiative" for the November 2006 ballot.[15] The initiative would prohibit discrimination or preferential treatment based on race, sex, color, ethnicity, or national origin in public employment, education, or contracting. Programs in higher education would no longer be allowed to consider race and gender—a change that would affect financial aid, particularly diversity scholarships, faculty hiring, and academic services specifically available to women.

Unlike California, where opponents to Proposition 209 allowed the discourse to become racialized and to ignore gender issues, high-profile women such as President Mary Sue Coleman and Michigan Governor Jennifer Granholm asserted that this amendment could affect programs and policies that benefit the lives of women, their families, and their communities.[16] The Michigan Women's Summit 2005: Challenges to Equity, a public education campaign on the benefits of affirmative action and outreach programs for women, produced a study prepared by the university's Center for the Education of Women titled *The Gender Impact of the Proposed Michigan Civil Rights Initiative.*[17]

Jubilation over the Supreme Court victories has also been tempered by persistent racial tensions in the Michigan student body, which is still two-thirds White. One administrator said that because Michigan turns away approximately 14,000 students each year, a White student with friends who were denied admittance might say to a minority student, "If you weren't here, my friend could be." One professor said, "I still see Black students being stigmatized by other students." In fall 2005 there was an incident of racial harassment targeting Asian American students, showing that Blacks are not the only targets. In another case of cultural backlash, the 2005 student commencement speaker at RU–N claimed Jesus as a universal savior—alienating many Muslim, Jewish, and other students and faculty. Several faculty members walked out, and the institution has yet to explore the feelings raised by the incident.

Faculty of color at Michigan see themselves on the front lines of this culture war, characterized by Kevin Gaines as "a product of the rise of the right wing in our national politics, and partly a post-9/11 phenomenon." Gaines described a vocal, sometimes hostile, minority of White students who believe, for example, that American history courses should not discuss race and diversity issues but rather celebrate nationalism. He worries that the race and ethnicity requirement allows students to "delude themselves that this subject matter can be ghettoized in the curriculum and that they are not supposed to encounter it in any of their other courses."

Other pressing national issues include tax policies leading to the greatest income disparities in our history and the decline of state and federal funding for undergraduates. Both are having profound effects on higher education by contributing to the stratification of institutions and their student bodies and making student debt payments increasingly unsupportable. Stanford remains highly selective, and because it has the resources to continue its need-blind admissions policy, it is able to recruit students from all parts of society. But at Michigan, among the younger faculty of color there is a sense that there is little campus discussion of the implications of a wealthier student body. According to Al Young in Sociology:

> We have been talking about the median family income of our students, versus families in Detroit. As at many universities, we are becoming a community of wealthier and wealthier students, from fewer and fewer diverse locations in the state. We register that, but no real discussion there. The university has made some steps, but the people that are on the ground, doing as much as they can, would say they are far away from where the university has been.

At RU–N there is another tricky and challenging discussion about student admissions: Who should benefit from an RU–N education? A committee led by Gary Roth that studied admissions found that recruiting "better prepared" students will not sacrifice the campus's commitment to a diverse student body, because the student body is increasingly made up of upwardly mobile immigrant populations from all over the world. However, this solution skirts the concern of many on campus about the "downward construction" of nonimmigrant minorities, as Hazel Markus put it. Faculty members admit they are much poorer at recruiting and educating native-born African American and Puerto Rican students than immigrants. It will take not only more work to find and support these students but new, perhaps more class-based constructions of their affirmative action mission.

As for the persistent powers of the rankings system, and the pressure of external forces on the university in the form of corporatization and other influences, our informants all emphasized their institutions as active interpreters of outside demands rather than as passive victims. Everyone we spoke to, for example, flatly denied that industry shaped their research agendas, even in the sciences. Stanford may be subject to less external pressure because it is elite and private, and the same may be true for Michigan, because it is elite and nearly private—another mark of privilege. But money matters. Patricia Gumport contends that Stanford is tilted today toward the entrepreneurial model of getting funding because the infrastructure depends on it. "Some of us have this sense of responsibility for the collective, and we try to reconcile those imperatives to keep the infrastructure going with our own intellectual agenda."[18] The elaborate research machine that took off under Terman must constantly be fed.

RU–N is subject to external pressures because it is state supported, and RU–New Brunswick is the flagship campus. Although President McCormick wants to move Rutgers to the top tier of American public research universities, he also understands the importance of applied research and of contributing to the state's economic development in a knowledge-driven economy. The work of the Cornwall Center and other efforts at RU–N are part of this statewide mission.

Looking at the dynamics of privilege and diversity with this national lens as we end this project, we are both puzzled and energized. We are puzzled about how to explain the wide discrepancies between warnings sounded by national publications about the "kept university" or "academic capitalism" versus the sense of autonomy and scholarly integrity described by informants at all three of these institutions. It may be that these commentators are putting their finger on some of the real dangers of the operations of societal "ruling regimes" on the academy—the persistence of business and corporate interests in enlisting universities to feed the engine of profits in a competitive global economy. Whereas people inside American education, feeling successful, satisfied, and focused primarily on matters of importance to the academy, see the role of external funding differently, primarily as feeding an elaborate research machine. Perhaps they are failing to see changes of deep significance to universities. Or perhaps these writers take a longer view than do faculty and administrators enmeshed in their research and their day-to-day lives. Do they see an endangered forest, whereas informants see only their own trees?

As for the progress of diversity initiatives, looking at three institutions in detail also helps to contextualize our answers to the question "Why so slow?" Local knowledge in each institution is being applied to overcome barriers to the progress of women and people of color within them. But another perspective might show us that the 35 years between the sex discrimination suits of the 1970s and today is too short a period of time to overcome the long-entrenched sexism and racism of the academy. Historians of the "L'École des Annales" in France have argued that we measure change in units that are too brief and we need a more complex conceptualization of historical time. They make the distinction between decades, even half centuries, and what they call the *"longue durée,"* by which they mean slow, glacial changes that represent significant shifts in the way people think, changes that require hundreds of years to complete.[19] It may take the innovators of this generation, and the next, of faculty and administrators to fully institutionalize diversity.

Bibliography

Abbot, Andrew. 2002. "The Disciplines and the Future." In *The Future of the City of Intellect,* ed. Steven Brint, 205–230. Stanford, CA: Stanford University Press.

Admissions Office. University of Michigan. http://www.admissions.umich.edu/academics/areasofstudy.html.

Alcoff, Linda. 1988. "Cultural Feminism Versus Post-Structuralism: The Identity Crisis in Feminist Theory." *Signs* 13 (March): 405–436.

Allardyce, Gilbert. 1982. "The Rise and Fall of the Western Civilization Course." *American Historical Review* 87: (3), 695–725.

Alsop, Joseph, and Stewart Alsop. 1954. *We Accuse! The Story of the Miscarriage of American Justice in the Case of J. Robert Oppenheimer.* New York: Simon and Schuster.

Altbach, Philip, et al., eds. 1999. *American Higher Education in the Twenty-First Century: Social, Political and Economic Challenges.* Baltimore: John Hopkins University Press.

Altbach, Philip, et al. 2002. "Race in Higher Education: The Continuing Crisis." In *The Racial Crisis in American Higher Education: Continuing Challenges for the Twenty-First Century,* ed. William Smith, et al., 23–41. Albany: State University of New York Press.

Alvarez, Ashanti. 2004. "Growing the Grass Roots." *Rutgers Focus,* November 15, 3.

American Culture. University of Michigan. http://www.lsa.umich.edu/ac.

Antonio, Anthony Lissing. 2002. "Faculty of Color Reconsidered: Reassessing Contributions to Scholarship." *Journal of Higher Education* 73 (5): 582–602.

Anyon, Jean. 1997. *Ghetto Schooling: A Political Economy of Urban Educational Reform.* New York: Teachers College Press.

Ash, Mary M. 1988. "Do Most Women Believe Changes Are Warranted?" Letter to Editor. *Campus Report.*

Bailyn, Lotte, et al. 2004. *Site Visit Report, U-M NSF ADVANCE Program.* September 19–21.

Baxandall, Rosalyn, and Elizabeth Ewen. 2000. *Picture Windows: How the Suburbs Happened.* New York: Basic Books.

Bechtel, H. Kenneth, 1989. "Introduction." In *Blacks, Science, and American Education*, ed. Willie Pearson Jr., and H. Kenneth Bechtel, 1–20. New Brunswick, NJ: Rutgers University Press, 1989.

Bernstein, Richard. 1988. "In Dispute on Bias, Stanford is Likely to Alter Western Culture Program." *New York Times,* January 19, A12.

Berube, Michael, and Cary Nelson, eds. 1995. *Higher Education Under Fire: Politics, Economics and the Crisis of the Humanities.* New York: Routledge.

Beyers, Bob. 1988. "Faculty Senate Agrees All Freshman Should Study Ancient, Medieval Culture." *Campus Report,* February 24.

Bloom, Allan. 1987. *The Closing of the American Mind.* New York: Simon and Schuster.

Bordin, Ruth. 1999. *Women at Michigan.* Ann Arbor: University of Michigan Press.

Boxer, Marilyn. 1998. *When Women Ask the Questions: Creating Women's Studies in America.* Baltimore: Johns Hopkins University Press.

Brace, Gerald Warner. 1968. *The Department.* New York: W. W. Norton.

Brint, Steven, ed. 2002. *The Future of the City of Intellect: The Changing American University.* Stanford, CA: Stanford University Press.

Brodkin, Karen. 1999. *How Jews Became White Folks and What That Says About Race in America.* New Brunswick, NJ: Rutgers University Press.

Building a Multiracial, Multicultural University Community. 1989. Final report of the University Committee on Minority Issues, Stanford University.

Building on Excellence: Guide to Recruiting and Retaining an Excellent and Diverse Faculty at Stanford University. Executive Summary. 2005. September http://www.stanford.edu/dept/provost/diversity.pdf.

Burghardt, Deborah A., and Carol L. Colbeck. 2005. "Women's Studies Faculty at the Intersection of Institutional Power and Feminist Values." *Journal of Higher Education* 76 (3): 301–330.

Campus Report. 1988. "70 Scholars Endorse Task Force Proposal for Culture Course." February 3.

Campus Report. 1988. "African Study Would Enhance Freshman Course, Profs Say." February 3.

Campus Report. 1988. "Davis: Eurocentrism 'Pernicious' Influence Among Western Academics." February 24.

Campus Report. 1988. "Don't Compromise on CUS Proposal, BSU Spokesman Says." February 10.

Campus Report. 1988. "Historian Degler: No Direct Connection to American Ideas From East Asia, Africa." February 10.

Campus Report. 1988. "Lougee: Core List Impedes Other Lines of Scholarly Inquiry." January 27.

Campus Report. 1988. "Perry Responds to Major Questions About Proposed Change." January 27.

Campus Report. 1988. "Retain Current Western Culture Program With Some Amendments, Professors Urge." January 20.

Campus Report. 1988. "Rosaldo: Stanford Should Develop Models for the 21 Century." February 10.

Campus Report. 1988. "Royden: Review the Core List to Ensure That Unconscious Bias Has Not Crept In." February 24.

Cantor, Nancy. 2003. "A Victory for Justice, and a Vindication." *Chronicle of Higher Education,* July 4, B12.

Cantor, Nancy. 2004. "Introduction." In *Defending Diversity: Affirmative Action at the University of Michigan,* ed. Patricia Gurin, et al., 1–16. Ann Arbor: University of Michigan Press.

Cantor, Nancy and Steven T. Levine. 2006. "Taking Public Scholarship Seriously." *Chronicle of Higher Education,* June 9, B20.

Capizzi, Carla. 2004. "New Era for Rutgers–Newark." *Rutgers Focus,* December 6, 2.

Casper, Gerhard. 1992. "Cares of the University." http://www.stanford.edu/home/stanford/cares/frames/crystal.html.

Casper, Gerhard. 1993. "Concerning Culture and Cultures: Welcome of Freshmen and Their Parents." Stanford University, September 23. http://www.stanford.edu/dept/pres-provost/president/speeches/930923culture.html.

Casper, Gerhard. 1996. "On the Synthesis of Teachers and Students: Remarks to the Meeting of the Senate of the Academic Council." Stanford University, May 9. http://www.stanford.edu/dept/pres-provost/president/speeches/960509synthesis.html.

Casper, Gerhard. 2000. "Transitions and Endurances." Stanford University, March 2. http://news-service.stanford.edu/news/2000/march8/stateutext-38.html.

Castellanos, Jeanette, and Lee Jones, eds. 2003. *The Majority in the Minority: Expanding the Representation of Latina/o Faculty, Administration and Students in Higher Education.* Sterling, VA: Stylus.

Center for African American and African Studies, Michigan. Center Directors. http://www.umich.edu/~iinet/caas/TheCenter/directors.htm.

Chamberlain, Mariam K., ed. 1988. *Women in Academe.* New York: Russell Sage Foundation.

Chang, Mitchell J., and Peter N. Kiang. 2002. "New Challenges of Representing Asian American Students in U.S. Higher Education." In *The Racial Crisis in American Higher Education: Continuing Challenges for the Twenty-first Century,* ed. William Smith, et al., 137–158. Albany: State University of New York Press.

Chesler, Mark. 2006. "Improving the Organizational and Classroom Climate for Multicultural Teaching." In *Excellent Teaching in the Excellent University,* ed. Jerome Rabow, 65–94. New York: Academic Press.

Chesley, Kate. 2004. "Stanford Releases Findings of Three-Year Study on Status of Women Faculty." Stanford News Service, May 27.

Christopher, Susan. 1995. "Required Knowledge: Incorporating Gender Into a Core Curriculum." PhD dissertation, Stanford University.

Clark, Burton, ed. 1987. *The Academic Profession: National, Disciplinary, and Institutional Settings.* Berkeley: University of California Press.

Coleman, Mary Sue. 2003. "Remarks Upon the Release of the 2003 'Women of the University of Michigan' Report." *University Record,* October 21.

Collins, Randall. 2002. "Credential Inflation and the Future of Universities." In *The Future of the City of Intellect: The Changing American University,* ed. Steven Brint, 23–46. Stanford, CA: Stanford University Press.

Cornwall Center Urban Research Inventory. 2000–2002. Cornwall Center for Metropolitan Studies, Rutgers University–Newark.

Cuban, Larry. 1999. *How Scholars Trumped Teachers: Change Without Reform in University Curriculum, Teaching and Research, 1890–1990.* New York: Teachers College Press.

Damrosch, David. 1995. *We Scholars: Changing the Culture of the University.* Cambridge, MA: Harvard University Press.

Das, Veena. 1995. *Critical Events.* Delhi, India: Oxford University Press.

Delgado, Ray. 2004. "Faculty Women's Forum to Be Created, Childcare Center Expedited." *Stanford Report,* October 6.

Delgado, Ray. 2005. "Five Years of the 10th President: Hennessy Reflects on Past, Thinks About Future." *Stanford Report,* December 7. http://news-service.stanford.edu/news/2005/december7/hennessy-120705.html.

Delgado, Ray. 2005. "New Science and Engineering Quad Planned for Campus Core." *Stanford Report,* February 9, 1.

De Vault, Marjorie L. 1999. *Liberating Method: Feminism and Social Research.* Philadelphia: Temple University Press.

De Vault, Marjorie L., and Liza McCoy. 2002. "Institutional Ethnography: Using Interviews to Investigate Ruling Relations." In *Handbook of Interview Research: Context and Method,* ed. J. F. Gubrium and J. A. Holstein, 751–776. Thousand Oaks, CA: Sage.

Dews, C. L. Barney, and Carolyn Leste Law. 1995. *This Fine Place So Far From Home: Voices of Academics From the Working Class.* Philadelphia: Temple University Press.

Diner, Steven. 2004. "Goals for Rutgers–Newark," April, 2. http://www.newark.rutgers.edu/provostoffice/index.php?sId=goals.

Diner, Steven. 2004. "Remarks at the Commemoration of Conklin Hall Takeover," February 24. http://www.newark.rutgers.edu/provostoffice/index.php?sId=022404.

"Diversity Now a Matter of Daily Routine for English Department." 1992. *University Record,* November 23. http://www.umich.edu/urecord/9293/Nov23_92/7.htm.

"Dual-Career Couples in the Academy." 2006. Stanford University. http://www.stanford.edu/group/IRWG/ResearchPrograms/DualCareer/index.html.

Duderstadt, James. 2000. *A University for the 21st Century.* Ann Arbor: University of Michigan Press.

Duderstadt, James, and Farris W. Womack. 2003. *The Future of the Public University in America: Beyond the Crossroads.* Baltimore: Johns Hopkins University Press.

Durham, William. 1998. "Department of Anthropological Sciences—Vision Statement." *Anthropology Newsletter,* (October), 21, 23.

Executive Summary, Evaluation of Developmental Education at Rutgers University–Newark (n.d.), 1–3. Rutgers University—Newark. Academic Foundation Center, unpublished document.

"Faculty Senate Disrupted by Students Seeking Asian American Studies." 1994. Stanford News Service, May 18. http://www.stanford.edu/dept/news/pr94/940518Arc4256.html.

Faculty Senate report, May 1, 2003. *Stanford Report,* May 7, 2003.

Faculty Senate report, May 15, 2003. *Stanford Report,* May 21, 2003.

Faculty Senate report, October 12, 2004. *Stanford Report,* October 20, 2004.

Family Matters @ Stanford for Faculty. 2005. Stanford University. September. http://www.stanford.edu/dept/provost/family.pdf.

Fetter, Jean H. 1995. *Questions and Admission: Reflections on 100,000 Admissions Decisions at Stanford.* Stanford, CA: Stanford University Press.

Flexner, Eleanor. 1959. *A Century of Struggle: The Women's Rights Movement in the United States.* Cambridge, MA: Harvard University Press.

Frankenberg, Ruth. 1993. *White Women, Race Matters: The Social Construction of Whiteness.* Minneapolis: University of Minnesota Press.

Franklin, John Hope. 1947. *From Slavery to Freedom: A History of the American Negro.* New York: Knopf.

Franklin, John Hope. 2005. *Mirror to America.* New York: Farrar, Straus and Giroux.

Frantilla, Anne. 1998. *Social Science in the Public Interest: A Fiftieth-Year History of the Institute for Social Research.* Ann Arbor: Bentley Historical Library of the University of Michigan.

Freedman, Estelle B. 1986. "Women's Networks and Women's Loyalties: Reflections on a Tenure Case." *Frontiers* 8 (3): 50–54.

Furmanski, Philip. 2004. "Memorandum to the Committee on Educational Policy and Planning: Faculty Diversity Initiatives," November 18. Unpublished document.

Geiger, Roger L. 1993. *Research and Relevant Knowledge: American Research Universities Since World War II.* New York: Oxford University Press.

Geiger, Roger L. 2002. "The Competition for High Ability Students: Universities in a Key Marketplace." In *The Future of the City of Intellect: The Changing American University,* ed. Steven Brint, 82–106. Stanford, CA: Stanford University Press.

Gibbons, James F. 2000. "The Role of Stanford University: A Dean's Reflections." In *The Silicon Valley Edge,* ed. Chong Moon Lee, William F. Miller, Marguerite Gong Hancock, and Henry S. Rowen, 200–217. Stanford, CA: Stanford University Press.

Gibbs, James. 1998. "Stanford Anthropology Department Splits." *Anthropology Newsletter* (October), 21.

Glovin, Bill. 1998. "Can You Help My Child?" *Rutgers Magazine,* Winter, 16–23.

Gnagey, Laurel Thomas, and Jared Wadley. 2003. "Cracks in the Glass Ceiling." *University Record,* October 6.

Graham, Patricia Albjerg. 1978. "Expansion and Exclusion: A History of Women in Higher Education." *Signs* (3), 759–773.

Griffiths, S. 1995. "A Class Sister Act." *Times Higher Education Supplement* 1197:20.

Guillory, John. 1993. *Cultural Capital: The Problem of Literary Canon Formation.* Chicago: University of Chicago Press.

Gumport, Patricia. 1999. "Graduate Education and Research: Interdependence and Strain." In *American Higher Education in the Twenty-First Century: Social, Political and Economic Challenges,* ed. Philip Altbach, et al. Baltimore: Johns Hopkins University Press.

Gumport, Patricia. 2000. "Academic Restructuring: Organizational Change and Institutional Imperatives." *Higher Education* 39, 67–91.

Gumport, Patricia. 2000. "Learning Academic Labor." *Comparative Social Research* 19, 1–23.

Gurin, Patricia, et al., ed. 2004. *Defending Diversity: Affirmative Action at the University of Michigan.* Ann Arbor: University of Michigan Press.

Gurin, Patricia. 2004. "The Educational Value of Diversity." In *Defending Diversity: Affirmative Action at the University of Michigan,* ed. Patricia Gurin, et al., 97–188. Ann Arbor: University of Michigan Press.

Hacker, Andrew. 1995. *Two Nations, Black and White, Separate, Hostile, Unequal.* New York: Ballantine Books.

Harding, Sandra. 1998. *Is Science Multicultural? Postcolonialisms, Feminisms & Epistemolgies.* Bloomington: University of Indiana Press.

Hayden, Tom. 1988. *Reunion: A Memoir.* New York: Random House.

Hennessy, John. 2000. "Stanford in the 21st Century." Prepared inauguration text. October 25. http://news-service.stanford.edu/news/2000/october25/inaug_speech-1025.html.

Hennessy, John. 2003. "Stanford and Society: Where Do We Go From Here?" Videotape of *Research Universities 101, Stanford: A Case History.*

"Hennessy, Panelists Outline University's Successes, Future Challenges." 2001. *Stanford Report,* March 14. http://www.stanford.edu/dept/news/report/march14/takingstock314.html.

History of Stanford. http://www.stanford.edu/home/stanford/history/.

Hodder, Ian. 2005. "An Archaeology of the Four-Field Approach in Anthropology in the United States." In *Unwrapping the Sacred Bundle: Reflections on the Disciplining of Anthropology,* ed. Daniel A. Segal and Sylvia J. Yanagisako, 130–142. Durham, NC, and London: Duke University Press.

Hollinger, David A. 1996. *Science, Jews and Secular Culture: Studies in Mid-Twentieth Century American Intellectual History.* Princeton, NJ: Princeton University Press.

Honors College Program Overview, Rutgers University–Newark. 2006. http://honorsnewark.rutgers.edu/ProgramOverview.

hooks, bell. 1994. *Teaching to Transgress: Education as the Practice of Freedom.* New York: Routledge.

Hu-DeHart, Evelyn. 2004. "Ethnic Studies in U.S. Higher Education: History, Development and Goals." In *Handbook of Research on Multicultural Education,* 2nd ed., ed. James A. Banks and Cherry A. McGee Banks, 869–881. Boulder, CO: Jossey-Bass.

Institute for Research in the Social Sciences at Stanford University. http://www.stanford.edu/group/iriss.

Institute for Research on Women and Gender. http://www.stanford.edu/group/IRWG/.

Jackson, Kenneth T. 1985. *Crabgrass Frontier: The Suburbanization of the United States.* New York: Oxford University Press.

Johnston, Theresa. 2005. "No Evidence of Innate Gender Differences in Math and Science, Scholars Assert." *Stanford Report,* February 9.

Joint PhD Program in Urban Systems. http://www.umdns.edu/urbsweb.

Katznelson, Ira. 2005. *When Affirmative Action Was White: An Untold History of Racial Inequality in Twentieth-Century America.* New York: Norton.

Kaufmann, Susan W., and Anne K. Davis. 2005. *The Gender Impact of the Proposed Michigan Civil Rights Initiative.* Ann Arbor, MI: Center for the Education of Women.

Kennedy, Donald. 1997. *Academic Duty.* Cambridge, MA: Harvard University Press.

Kennedy, Donald. 1998. *The Last of Your Springs.* Stanford, CA: Stanford Historical Society.

Kirp, David. 2003. *Shakespeare, Einstein, and the Bottom Line.* Cambridge, MA: Harvard University Press.

Lauter, Paul, and Jeffrey Herf. 1995. "Money, Merit and Democracy: An Exchange." In *Higher Education Under Fire: Politics, Economics, and the Crisis of the Humanities,* ed. Michael Berube and Cary Nelson, 163–198. New York: Routledge.

Lee, Chong Moon, William F. Miller, Marguerite Gong Hancock, and Henry S. Rowen. 2000. *The Silicon Valley Edge.* Stanford, CA: Stanford University Press.

Lemann, Nicholas. 2000. *The Big Test: The Secret History of the American Meritocracy.* New York: Farrar, Straus and Giroux.

Lenoir, Tim. 2003. "A History of Stanford and Silicon Valley." Videotape of *Research Universities 101, Stanford: A Case History.*

Leslie, Mitchell. 2000. "Divided They Stand." *Stanford Magazine.* http://www.stanfordalumni. org/ news/magazine/2000/janfeb/articles/anthro.html.

Letters to the Editor. 1982. *Social Education* 46 (6): 378–380.

Lewis, Earl. 2004. "Why History Remains a Factor in the Search for Racial Equality." In *Defending Diversity: Affirmative Action at the University of Michigan,* ed. Patricia Gurin, et al., 17-59. Ann Arbor: University of Michigan Press.

Lewontin, R. C. 1997. "The Cold War and the Transformation of the Academy." In *The Cold War and the University,* ed. Andre Schiffrin, 1–34. New York: New Press.

Lomax, Ronald J., Thomas E. Moore, and Charles B. Smith. 1995. "The Michigan Mandate: Promise and Progress." *University Record,* April 17.

Lombardi, John V. and Elizabeth D. Capaldi. 2001. *The Top American Research Universities.* Gainesville: The Center at the University of Florida.

Lombardi, John V. and Elizabeth D. Capaldi. 2005. *The Top American Research Universities.* Gainesville: University of Florida, Lombardi Program on Measuring University Performance. http://thecenter.ufl.edu.research2005.pdf.

Long-Range Plan, Program in Women's Studies, 2003–2004. University of Michigan.

Lorde, Audre. 1984. *Sister Outsider: Essays and Speeches.* Freedom, CA: Crossing Press.

Lougee, Carolyn. 1982. "Comments." *AHR Forum: "The Rise and Fall of the Western Civilization Course."* Vol. 87 (3), 726–739.

Lougee, Carolyn. 1996. "Review of *Higher Education Under Fire: Politics, Economics and the Crisis of the Humanities,* edited by Michael Berube and Cary Nelson." *Academe* (July–August), 69–71.

Lovett, Clara. 2005. "The Perils of Pursuing Prestige." *Chronicle of Higher Education,* January 21. http://chronicle.com/weekly/vol51/120/20b02001.htm.

Lowen, Rebecca. 1997. *Creating the Cold War University: The Transformation of Stanford.* Berkeley: University of California Press.

MacDonald, Victoria-Maria, and Teresa Garcia. 2003. "Historical Perspectives on Latino Access to Higher Education 1848–1990." In *The Majority in the Minority: Expanding the Representation of Latina/o Faculty, Administration and Students in Higher Education,* ed. Jeanette Castellanos and Lee Jones, 15–43. Sterling, VA: Stylus.

Maher, Frances, and Mary Kay Tetreault. 1997. "Learning in the Dark: How Assumptions of Whiteness Shape Classroom Knowledge." *Harvard Education Review* 67 (2): 321–349.

Maher, Frances, and Mary Kay Tetreault. 2001. *The Feminist Classroom: Dynamics of Gender, Race and Privilege.* Expanded ed. Lanham, MD: Rowman and Littlefield.

Markus, Hazel Rose, Claude M. Steele, and Dorothy M. Steele. 2002. "Color Blindness as a Barrier to Inclusion: Assimilation and Nonimmigrant Minorities." In *Engaging Cultural Differences,* ed. Richard A. Shweder, Martha Minow, and Hazel Rose Markus, 453–471. New York: Russell Sage Foundation.

Martin, Jane Roland. 2000. *Coming of Age in Academe: Rekindling Women's Hopes and Transforming the Academy.* New York: Routledge.

Massey, Douglas S., and Nancy A. Denton. 1993. *American Apartheid: Segregation and the Making of the Underclass.* Cambridge, MA: Harvard University Press.

Massy, William. 2003. *Honoring the Trust.* Bolton, MA: Anker Press.

McCormick, Richard P. 1966. *Rutgers: A Bicentennial History.* New Brunswick, NJ: Rutgers University Press.

McCormick, Richard P. 1990. *The Black Student Protest Movement at Rutgers.* New Brunswick, NJ: Rutgers University Press.

McIntosh, Peggy. 1992. "White Privilege and Male Privilege: A Personal Account of Coming to See Correspondences Through Work in Women's Studies." In *Race, Class and Gender: An Anthology,* ed. Margaret Andersen and Patricia Hill Collins. Belmont, CA: Wadsworth.

"Memorandum on the Status of Faculty Women at Rutgers University, Newark." 1971. November. Courtesy of Lillian Robbins.

"Men of the Year." 1961. *Time,* January 2, 40–46.

Message from the LSA Dean. http://www.lsa.umich.edu/lsa-about/dean.

Messer-Davidow, Ellen. 2002. *Disciplining Feminism: From Social Activism to Academic Discourse.* Durham, NC: Duke University Press.

The Michigan Agenda for Women: Leadership for a New Century. 1995. July.

Mooney, Carolyn. 1988. "Sweeping Curricular Change Is Under Way at Stanford as University Phases Out Its 'Western Culture' Program." *Chronicle of Higher Education,* December 14, A12.

Moya, Paula M. L. 2002. *Learning From Experience.* Berkeley: University of California Press.

National Science Foundation. http://www.nsf.gov/statistics/infbrief/nsf05322/.

Newman, Frank, Lara Couturier, and Jamie Scurry. 2004. *The Future of Higher Education.* San Francisco: Jossey-Bass.

"Norman Samuels in His Own Words." 2002. *Commemoration Booklet: Norman Samuels, Celebrating 20 Years of Vision and Leadership.* Rutgers University–Newark, June 12.

"NSF–ADVANCE at the University of Michigan." 2001. Proposal submitted to the National Science Foundation.

Okihiro, Gary Y. 1999. *Storied Lives: Japanese American Students and World War II.* Seattle and London: University of Washington Press.

O'Mara, Margaret Pugh. 2005. *Cities of Knowledge: Cold War Science and the Search for the Next Silicon Valley.* Princeton, NJ: Princeton University Press.

Ortner, Sherry B. 2003. *New Jersey Dreaming: Capital, Culture and the Class of '58.* Durham, NC, and London: Duke University Press.

Owen, Mary. 2005. "Study: Ballot Proposition Bad for Women in Michigan." *University Record,* March 14, 1–10.

Pearson, Willie, Jr., and H. Kenneth Bechtel, eds. 1989. *Blacks, Science, and American Education.* New Brunswick, NJ: Rutgers University Press.

Peckham, Howard H. 1994. *The Making of the University of Michigan: 1817–1992.* Ed. Margaret L. Steneck and Nicholas H. Steneck. Ann Arbor, MI: Bentley Historical Library.

Powell, Walter W., and Jason Owen-Smith. 2002. "The New World of Knowledge Production in the Life Sciences." In *The Future of the City of Intellect: The Changing American University,* ed. Steven Brint, 107–130. Stanford, CA: Stanford University Press.

Pratt, Mary Louise. 1990. "Humanities for the Future: Reflections on the Western Culture Debate at Stanford." *South Atlantic Quarterly* 89 (Winter): 7–25.

Rabow, Jerome. 2006. *Excellent Teaching in the Excellent University.* New York: Academic Press.

Readings, Bill. 1996. *The University in Ruins.* Cambridge, MA: Harvard University Press.

Reich, Robert B. 2000. "How Selective Colleges Heighten Inequality." *Chronicle of Higher Education,* September 15, B7.

Report of the Commission on Undergraduate Education. 1994. Stanford, CA: Stanford University Press.

"Report of the Provost's Advisory Committee on the Status of Women Faculty." 2005. September. In *Building on Excellence Executive Summary.*

"Report of the Provost's Committee on the Recruitment and Retention of Women Faculty." 1993. Stanford University. Unpublished document.

Research Institute of Comparative Studies in Race and Ethnicity. 2006. http://ccsre.stanford.edu/RI_resInst.htm.

"The Right Person for the Right Time." 2000. *Stanford Report,* April 5. http://news-service. stanford.edu/news/2000/april5/announce-45.html.

Rimer, Sara. 2005. "For Women in Sciences, Slow Progress in Academia." *New York Times,* April 15. http://topics.nytimes.com/top/reference/timestopics/people/r/sara_rimer/index.html.

Rimer, Sara, and Karen Arenson. 2004. "Top Colleges Take More Blacks, but Which Ones?" *New York Times,* June 24, A1, A18.

Roediger, David. 1991. *The Wages of Whiteness: Race and the Making of the American Working Class.* New York: Verso.

Roediger, David. 1994. *Toward the Abolition of Whiteness: Essays on Race, Politics and the Working Class.* New York: Verso.

Rogers, Everett M., and Judith K. Larsen. 1984. *Silicon Valley Fever.* New York: Basic Books.

Rooks, Noliwe M. 2006. "The Beginnings of Black Studies." *Chronicle of Higher Education,* February 10, B8–B9.

Rosser, Sue. 2000. *Women, Science and Society.* New York: Teachers College Press.

Rossiter, Margaret W. 1995. *Women Scientists in America: Before Affirmative Action 1940–1972.* Baltimore: Johns Hopkins University Press.

Rudolph, Frederick. 1962. *The American College and University: A History.* New York: Knopf.

Rutgers University Factbook. 2005–2006. Office of Institutional Research and Academic Planning, Rutgers, the State University of New Jersey, Geology Hall, 85 Somerset St., New Brunswick, NJ 08901.

Rutgers University Libraries, Department of Special Collections and University Archives. *Records of the University of Newark, 1934–1946: Administrative History,* 1, 2. Records of the University of Newark, 1934–1946; Trustee and Presidential Papers, 8.74 in 21 boxes. RG N2/NO/1.

Rutgers University–Newark Provost's Annual Report, 2002–2003. http://www.newark.rutgers. edu/provost/index.php?sId=reports.

Rutgers University–Newark Provost's Annual Report, 2003–2004. http://www.newark.rutgers. edu/provost/index.php?sId=reports.

Sanford, John. "Race, Ethnicity Research Institute Gets $5 Million Boost." http://www.stanford. edu/dept/news/pr/01/raceethnicity/031.html.

Saxenian, Anna Lee. 1994. *Regional Advantage: Culture and Competition in Silicon Valley and Route 128.* Cambridge, MA: Harvard University Press.

Schiebinger, Londa. 1999. *Has Feminism Changed Science?* Cambridge, MA: Harvard University Press.

Schiebinger, Londa. 2005. "Remarks for Summers Forum: Gender in Science." February 9. http:// www.stanford.edu/group/IRWG/NewsAndEvents/SchiebingerForumTalk.pdf.

Schiffrin, Andre, ed. 1997. *The Cold War and the University.* New York: New Press.

Schmidt, Peter. 2003. "Affirmative Action Survives, and So Does the Debate." *Chronicle of Higher Education,* July 4, S1–S4.

Schmitz, Betty, Johnnella Butler, Beverly Guy-Sheftall, and Deborah Rosenfelt. 2004. "Women's Studies and Curriculum Transformation in the United States." In *Handbook of Research on Multicultural Education,* 2nd ed., ed. James A. Banks and Cherry A. McGee Banks, 882–905. San Francisco: Jossey-Bass.

Schrecker, Ellen. 2006. "Worse Than McCarthy." *Chronicle of Higher Education,* February 10, B20.

Schuster, Marilyn, and Susan Van Dyne. 1984. "Placing Women in the Liberal Arts: Stages of Curriculum Transformation." *Harvard Educational Review* 54 (4): 413–428.

Segal, Daniel A., and Sylvia J. Yanagisako, eds. 2005. *Unwrapping the Sacred Bundle: Reflections on the Disciplining of Anthropology.* Durham, NC, and London: Duke University Press.

Selingo, Jeffrey. 2005. "Michigan: Who Really Won?" *Chronicle of Higher Education,* January 14, A21.

Shweder, Richard A., Martha Minow, and Hazel Rose Markus, eds. 2002. *Engaging Cultural Differences.* New York: Russell Sage Foundation.

Sklar, Kathryn Kish. 2000. "The Women's Studies Moment: 1972." In *The Politics of Women's Studies: Testimony From Thirty Founding Mothers,* ed. Florence Howe, 130–141. New York: Feminist Press.

Slaughter, Sheila. 2002. "The Political Economy of Curriculum Making in American Universities." In *The Future of the City of Intellect: The Changing American University,* ed. Steven Brint, 260–289. Stanford, CA: Stanford University Press.

Slaughter, Sheila, and Larry K. Leslie. 1997. *Academic Capitalism: Politics, Policies, and the Entrepreneurial University*. Baltimore: Johns Hopkins University Press.

Smith, Daryl G., et al. 2004. "Interrupting the Usual: Successful Strategies for Hiring Diverse Faculty." *Journal of Higher Education* 75 (2): 133–160.

Smith, Dorothy E. 1999. *Writing the Social: Critique, Theory, and Investigations*. Toronto, Canada: University of Toronto Press.

Smith, William, Philip G. Altbach, and Kofi Lomotey, eds. 2002. *The Racial Crisis in American Higher Education*. Albany: State University of New York Press.

Solmon, Lewis C., Matthew S. Solmon, and Tamara Schiff. 2002. "The Changing Demographics: Problems and Opportunities." In *The Racial Crisis in American Higher Education*, ed. William Smith, Philip G. Altbach, and Kofi Lomotey, 43–75. Albany: State University of New York Press.

"Stanford Anthropology Department Will Split." 1998. *Chronicle of Higher Education*, May 29.

Stanford Facts 2005. Office of University Communications, Stanford University. Unpublished report. http://www.stanford.edu/home/stanford/facts/.

Stanford Facts 2006. Office of University Communications, Stanford University. Unpublished report. http://www.stanford.edu/home/stanford/facts/.

Stanford Humanities Center. http://shc.stanford.edu/center/about.htm.

Stanford Humanities Lab. http://shl.stanford.edu/.

Stanford University. 1987. "Proposed Legislation, Area One Requirement: Cultures, Ideas and Values (CIV)." November 16.

Steele, Claude. 1999. "Thin Ice: Stereotype Threat and Black College Students." *Atlantic Monthly* (August), 44–54.

Steering Committee of the Study of Education at Stanford. 1968. *The Study of Education at Stanford*.

"A Study on the Status of Women Faculty in Science at MIT." 1999. *MIT Faculty Newsletter* II (4). March. http://web.mit.edu/fnl/women/women.html.

Sugrue, Thomas J. 1996. *The Origins of the Urban Crisis: Race and Inequality in Postwar Detroit*. Princeton, NJ: Princeton University Press.

Sutton, Mike. 2004. "Coming Home: Ex N. J. Legislator, Governor's Cabinet Member to Head Cornwall Center." *Rutgers–Newark Connections* (Winter), 1, 6.

Tetreault, Mary Kay. 1985. "Feminist Phase Theory: An Experience-Derived Evaluation Model." *Journal of Higher Education* 56 (4): 363–384.

Thelin, John R. 2004. *A History of American Higher Education*. Baltimore: Johns Hopkins University Press.

Trei, Lisa. 2004. "IRWG Director Hopes to Create 'Go To' Center for Gender Studies." *Stanford Report*, October 13, 2.

Turner, Caroline Sotello Viernes. 2002. "Women of Color in Academe: Living With Multiple Marginality." *Journal of Higher Education* 73 (1): 74–93.

University of Michigan. 2005. "Report of the Committee to Consider a More Flexible Tenure Probationary Period." http://www.provost.umich.edu/reports/flexible_tenure/contents.html.

University of Michigan Admissions Lawsuits. "The Compelling Need for Diversity in Higher Education." http://www.umich.edu/%7Eurel/admissions/legal/expert/toc.html.

University of Michigan, Ann Arbor. "Fall 2005 Enrollment." http://www.umich.edu/news/BG/FA05_Total_Enrollment.pdf.

University of Michigan, Ann Arbor. "Graduation Rates of Freshmen Cohorts." http://sitemaker.umich.edu/obpinfo.

University of Michigan Electronic Fact Pages: Faculty Headcount (Based on Primary Job) by Rank, Gender, Race and Full-Time/Part Time. 2004. http://www.umich.edu/~oapainfo/contents.html.

Valian, Virginia. 1999. *Why So Slow? The Advancement of Women*. Cambridge, MA: MIT Press.

Villalpando, Octavio, and Dolores Delgado Bernal. 2002. "A Critical Race Theory Analysis of Barriers That Impede the Success of Faculty of Color." In *The Racial Crisis in American Higher Education: Continuing Challenges for the Twenty-First Century*, ed. William Smith, et al., 243–269. Albany: State University of New York Press.

Volume of Research Expenditures by Sponsor, University of Michigan. http://www.research.umich.edu/research_guide/annual_reports/FY04/FY04ExpendBySponsor.pdf.

Wadley, Jared. 2004. "ADVANCE Findings Spur U–M to Improve Work Environment." *University Record*, March 8.

Washburn, Jennifer. 2005. *University, Inc: The Corporate Corruption of American Higher Education.* New York: Basic Books.

Weber, David S. 1986. *Academic Quality Rankings of American Colleges and Universities.* Springfield, IL: Charles C. Thomas.

Wechsler, Harold. 2005. "Brewing Bachelors: The History of the University of Newark." http://www.newark.rutgers.edu/history/history-wechsler.pdf.

Wilson, Robin. 2004. "Where the Elite Teach, It's Still a Man's World." *Chronicle of Higher Education,* December 3, A8.

Wilson, Robin. 2006. "Off the Clock." *Chronicle of Higher Education,* July 21, A8-A11.

"Work Force Analysis From the Director of Affirmative Action and Employment Research; Newark Campus." 1983. January 17. Document provided by Lillian Robbins.

Wyden, Ron. 2006. "Using Title IX to Ensure Equal Opportunity for Women in Math and Science." http://wiseli.engr.wisc.edu/news/Wyden.pdf.

Yangisako, Sylvia. 1998. "Department of Cultural and Social Anthropology—Vision Statement." *Anthropological Newsletter* (October), 21, 23.

Yoshino, Kenji. 2006. *Covering: The Hidden Assault on Our Civil Rights.* New York: Random House.

Yoshino, Kenji. 2006. "The Myth of the Mainstream." *Chronicle of Higher Education,* February 17, B11–B12.

Notes

Chapter 1

1. Interview with Terrence (Terry) McDonald, March 24, 2005. McDonald has a PhD in history from Stanford (1979) and was professor and chair of the History Department before becoming the dean of the College of Literature, Science, and Arts. We will introduce each new informant we quote for the first time; other references to or quotes from their interview will not be noted.
2. Interview with Hazel Rose Markus, May 9, 2005. Markus has been a professor of psychology at Stanford since 1994 and before that at Michigan. She has a PhD in psychology from Michigan (1975).
3. Moving beyond essentialized identities of race, class, and gender, Linda Alcoff and other feminist scholars of the 1980s argued that seeing gender and race as societal positions, rather than as fixed identities, historicized and contextualized the experiences of women and minorities, granting them both the authority of their experiences of oppression and the possibility of making change. Linda Alcoff, "Cultural Feminism Versus Post-Structuralism: The Identity Crisis in Feminist Theory," *Signs* 13 (March 1988): 405–436.
4. Frances Maher and Mary Kay Tetreault, *The Feminist Classroom* (New York: Basic Books, 1994; 2nd ed., Lanham, MD: Rowman and Littlefield, 2001).
5. See, for example, Michael Berube and Cary Nelson, eds., *Higher Education Under Fire: Politics, Economics, and the Crisis of the Humanities* (New York: Routledge, 1995); Patricia Gumport, "Academic Restructuring: Organizational Change and Institutional Imperatives," *Higher Education* 39 (2000): 67–91; David Kirp, *Shakespeare, Einstein, and the Bottom Line* (Cambridge, MA: Harvard University Press, 2003); Frank Newman, Lara Couturier, and Jamie Scurry, *The Future of Higher Education* (San Francisco: Jossey-Bass, 2004); Sheila Slaughter and Larry K. Leslie, *Academic Capitalism: Politics, Policies, and the Entrepreneurial University* (Baltimore: Johns Hopkins University Press, 1997); and Jennifer Washburn, *University, Inc.: The Corporate Corruption of American Higher Education* (New York: Basic Books, 2005).
6. Special thanks to Nancy Porter for bringing the Latin roots of *privilege* to our attention. Personal conversation with Porter, December 12, 2004.
7. White privilege was one of the "silent laws" we uncovered in the process of writing *The Feminist Classroom*. In the first edition, as White feminists, we had failed to examine what it means to be "White." In the course of writing the second edition, informed by the literature on Whiteness, we revisited our data with these issues in mind. Examples of this recent literature include the following: Ruth Frankenberg, *White Women, Race Matters: The Social Construction of Whiteness* (Minneapolis: University of Minnesota Press, 1993); Peggy McIntosh, "White Privilege and Male Privilege: A Personal Account of Coming to See Correspondences Through Work in Women's Studies," in *Race, Class and Gender: An Anthology*, ed. Margaret Andersen and Patricia Hill Collins (Belmont, CA: Wadsworth, 1992); David Roediger, *The Wages of Whiteness: Race and the Making of the American Working Class* (New York: Verso, 1991) and *Toward the Abolition of Whiteness: Essays on Race, Politics and the Working Class* (New York: Verso, 1994); and Andrew Hacker, *Two Nations, Black and White, Separate, Hostile, Unequal* (New York: Ballantine Books, 1995). See also Frances Maher and Mary Kay Tetreault, "Learning in the Dark: How Assumptions of Whiteness Shape Classroom Knowledge," *Harvard Education Review* 67, no. 2 (1997): 321–349, for a fuller discussion of White privilege in the classroom.
8. S. Griffiths, "A Class Sister Act," *Times Higher Education Supplement,* 1197 (1995): 20. Quoted in Caroline Sotello Viernes Turner, "Women of Color in Academe: Living With Multiple Marginality," *Journal of Higher Education* 73, no. 1 (2002), 88.

9. Jane Roland Martin, *Coming of Age in Academe: Rekindling Women's Hopes and Transforming the Academy* (New York: Routledge, 2000), 118.

10. Kenji Yoshino, "The Myth of the Mainstream," *Chronicle of Higher Education,* February 17, 2006, B11. His book is titled *Covering: The Hidden Assault on Our Civil Rights* (New York: Random House, 2006).

11. We first read of this particular construction of institutional ethnography in Marjorie DeVault and Liza McCoy, "Institutional Ethnography: Using Interviews to Investigate Ruling Relations," in *Handbook of Interview Research: Context and Method,* ed. J. F. Gubrium and J. A. Holstein (Thousand Oaks, CA: Sage, 2002), 751–776.

12. Dorothy E. Smith, *Writing the Social: Critique, Theory, and Investigations* (Toronto Canada: University of Toronto Press, 1999), 74, 76.

13. Ibid., 200–202. We spent the equivalent of four weeks on each campus interviewing an average of 30 faculty and administrators in each setting.

14. Conversations with Carolyn Lougee and Sylvia Yanagisako, January 21, 2000.

15. Karen Brodkin, *How Jews Became White Folks and What That Says About Race in America* (New Brunswick, NJ: Rutgers University Press, 1998), 89.

16. "Intent" is the title of part 1 of Margaret Pugh O'Mara's book, *Cities of Knowledge: Cold War Science and the Search for the Next Silicon Valley* (Princeton, NJ: Princeton University Press, 2005). We have borrowed this title for our purposes because we think it is so apt for our analysis.

17. Ibid., 45–47.

18. Ibid., 48. For instance, the Health Professions Education Act replicated the National Defense Education Act and provided funds for medical and dental schools. See also pp. 49–51, 69.

19. E-mail from James (Dick) Pratt, March 4, 2006.

20. O'Mara, *Cities of Knowledge,* 53.

21. Roger L. Geiger, *Research and Relevant Knowledge: American Research Universities Since World War II* (New York: Oxford University Press, 1993), 60–61.

22. Ibid., 61.

23. Until the early 1970s, the Santa Clara Valley was known for its fruit orchards; a reporter at the *San Jose Mercury News* renamed it Silicon Valley after the main ingredient in the semiconductor.

24. O'Mara, *Cities of Knowledge,* 27–28.

25. Ibid., 54.

26. Geiger, *Research and Relevant Knowledge,* 106.

27. Ibid., 125.

28. Ibid., 127, 128. Several major cases of academic freedom occurred at Michigan during the height of McCarthyism. The apolitical behaviorist turn in social science research might be partly explained not only by the threats of McCarthyism but also by a widespread distrust of ideologically inflected research in the wake of Nazism. See David A. Hollinger, "Intellectual Culture at the University of Michigan, 1938–1998," in *Science, Jews and Secular Culture: Studies in Mid-Twentieth Century Intellectual History* (Princeton, NJ: Princeton University Press, 1996).

29. Ira Katznelson, *When Affirmative Action Was White: An Untold History of Racial Inequality in Twentieth-Century America* (New York: Norton, 2005), 113, 114, 104.

30. For a discussion of racial discrimination in housing previous to 1950, see Kenneth T. Jackson, *Crabgrass Frontier: The Suburbanization of the United States* (New York: Oxford University Press, 1985).

31. Brodkin, *How Jews Became White Folks,* 50.

32. Katznelson, *When Affirmative Action Was White,* 121–125.

33. See Rosalyn Baxandall and Elizabeth Ewen, *Picture Windows: How the Suburbs Happened* (New York: Basic Books, 2000). Their account of the building of Levittown and other new suburbs shows how they were racially segregated and also contributed to the relegation of women to the domestic sphere after the war.

34. Katznelson, *When Affirmative Action Was White,* 116.

35. Brodkin, *How Jews Became White Folks,* 35. Federal, state, and local subsidies built roads, public services, schools, and shopping centers for these new communities, as well as other industrial and commercial developments. Title VI of the FHA, passed in the late 1940s, allowed up to 90% of housing loans to go directly to the builder, thus enabling builders such as William Levitt of Levittown, the "Henry Ford of housing," to build their vast, prefabricated, single-home communities in advance. Lower-middle-class families with mortgages funded by the GI Bill could afford to move in right away. See also Baxandall and Ewen, *Picture Windows.*

36. Brodkin, *How Jews Became White Folks,* 174–175.

37. Redlining, a practice devised in the 1930s, rated neighborhoods by placing the highest value (green) on all-White, middle-class neighborhoods and the lowest value (red) on racially non-White or mixed and working-class neighborhoods.

38. Brodkin, *How Jews Became White Folks,* 49–50. As Brodkin indicates, other work on the persistent segregation of American society suggests that, although FHA policies have officially changed to outlaw protective covenants, enforcement of fair housing still leaves much to be desired. It leaves prosecution up to individual victims, "to combat a social problem that [is] systemic and institutional in nature."

39. Katznelson, *When Affirmative Action Was White,* 14.

40. Baxandall and Ewen, *Picture Windows,* 148–149.

41. O'Mara, *Cities of Knowledge,* 17–18.

42. Ibid., 115.

43. Besides O'Mara, see Anna Lee Saxenian, *Regional Advantage: Culture and Competition in Silicon Valley and Route 128* (Cambridge, MA: Harvard University Press, 1994). Income from the Stanford Industrial Park was unrestricted and paid for faculty recruitment. See also Everett M. Rogers and Judith K. Larsen, *Silicon Valley Fever* (New York: Basic Books, 1984), 36; and James F. Gibbons, "The Role of Stanford University: A Dean's Reflections," in *The Silicon Valley Edge,* ed. Chong-Moon Lee, William F. Miller, Marguerite Gong Hancock, and Henry S. Rowen (Stanford, CA: Stanford University Press, 2000), 200–217.

44. O'Mara, *Cities of Knowledge,* 130–131. A West Coast builder, Joe Eichler, had a policy of selling to African Americans who could afford to buy. But there was little chance of many Blacks moving to Palo Alto because of the few African Americans in the Bay area and the fewer still who could afford Palo Alto prices. See Brodkin, *How Jews Became White Folks,* 47.

45. See Jean Anyon, *Ghetto Schooling: A Political Economy of Urban Education Reform* (New York: Teachers College Press, 1997), which is an extensive analysis of how Newark declined during this period.

46. Ibid., 38–49.

47. Ibid., 77–79.

48. Ibid, 156.

49. See Sherry B. Ortner, *New Jersey Dreaming: Capital, Culture and the Class of '58* (Durham, NC, and London: Duke University Press, 2003), 154.

50. For a postwar history of Detroit, see Thomas J. Sugrue, *The Origins of the Urban Crisis: Race and Inequality in Postwar Detroit* (Princeton, NJ: Princeton University Press, 1996).

51. John R. Thelin, *A History of American Higher Education* (Baltimore: Johns Hopkins University Press, 2004), 263. Thelin pointed out that Rutgers went from 7,000 to 16,000 students by 1948 (a figure not divided by campuses and maybe referring to RU–New Brunswick only) and that Stanford enrollments increased from 3,000 to 7,000.

52. Katznelson, *When Affirmative Action Was White,* 129–131. Japanese American college students wishing to continue their education during World War II were helped by the Student Relocation Committee to attend colleges primarily east of the exclusion zone. See Gary Y. Okihiro, *Storied Lives: Japanese American Students and World War II* (Seattle and London: University of Washington Press, 1999). We were unable to locate information on how Japanese American GIs fared with the GI Bill.

53. This group included Mexican Americans in the Southwest and Midwest and Puerto Ricans in Chicago and New York. Hispanic veterans in Colorado were responsible for creating the San Luis Institute, a public 2-year college. The creation of the American GI Forum in Texas in 1948, an activist group designed to protect the civil rights of returning Mexican American GIs, suggested that veterans were not uniformly interested in individual success. Victoria-Maria MacDonald and Teresa Garcia, "Historical Perspectives on Latino Access to Higher Education 1848-1990," in *The Majority in the Minority: Expanding the Representation of Latina/o Faculty, Administrators and Students in Higher Education,* ed. Jeanette Castellanos and Lee Jones (Sterling, VA: Stylus, 2003), 25–26.

54. Thelin, *A History of American Higher Education,* 267.

55. Nicholas Lemann, *The Big Test: The Secret History of the American Meritocracy* (New York: Farrar, Straus, and Giroux, 1999). See especially 58–69.

56. Joseph Alsop and Stewart Alsop, *We Accuse! The Story of the Miscarriage of American Justice in the Case of J. Robert Oppenheimer* (New York: Simon and Schuster, 1954), 6. Cited in O'Mara, *Cities of Knowledge,* 20.

57. Ibid., 17, 12.

58. Ibid., 28.

59. Margaret W. Rossiter, *Women Scientists in America: Before Affirmative Action 1940-1972* (Baltimore: Johns Hopkins University Press, 1995), 123, xvi.

60. H. Kenneth Bechtel, "Introduction," in Willie Pearson, Jr., and H. Kenneth Bechtel, eds. *Blacks, Science, and American Education.* New Brunswick, Rutgers University Press, 1989, 1-20. 17, 18.

61. Steven Diner, "Remarks at the Commemoration of Conklin Hall Takeover," February 24, 2004, http://www.newark.rutgers.edu/provostoffice/index.php?sId=022404. We interviewed Steve Diner on October 14, 2003, and January 30, 2006. He came to RU–N in 1998 as dean of the Faculty of Arts and Sciences–Newark and has been RU–N provost since 2002. He has a PhD in history from the University of Chicago (1972).

62. Sara Rimer and Karen Arenson, "Top Colleges Take More Blacks, but Which Ones?" *New York Times,* June 24, 2004, A1, A18.

63. Interview with James Jackson, October 14, 2005. Jackson is the former director (1991–1998) of the Center for Afroamerican and African Studies and the director of the Research Center for Group Dynamics. He came to Michigan in 1971 and has a PhD in social psychology from Wayne State University (1972).

64. Hazel Rose Markus, Claude M. Steele, and Dorothy M. Steele, "Color Blindness as a Barrier to Inclusion: Assimilation and Nonimmigrant Minorities," in *Engaging Cultural Differences,* ed. Richard A. Shweder, Martha Minow, and Hazel Rose Markus (New York: Russell Sage Foundation, 2002), 453–454.

65. Ellen Messer-Davidow, *Disciplining Feminism: From Social Activism to Academic Discourse* (Durham, NC: Duke University Press, 2002), 52.

66. Virginia Valian, *Why So Slow? The Advancement of Women* (Cambridge, MA: MIT Press, 1998), 15.

67. See, for example, Anthony Lising Antonio, "Faculty of Color Reconsidered: Reassessing Contributions to Scholarship," *Journal of Higher Education* 73, no. 5 (2002): 582–602; and Daryl G. Smith, et al., "Interrupting the Usual: Successful Strategies for Hiring Diverse Faculty," *Journal of Higher Education* 75, no. 2 (2004): 133–160.

68. Octavio Villalpando and Dolores Delgado Bernal, "A Critical Race Theory Analysis of Barriers That Impede the Success of Faculty of Color," in *The Racial Crisis in American Higher Education: Continuing Challenges for the Twenty-First Century,* ed. William Smith, et al. (Albany, NY: SUNY Press, 2002), 253.

69. Ibid., 256–259.

70. Turner, "Women of Color in Academe," 83-84.

71. Thelin, *History of American Higher Education,* 260–261.

72. Ibid, 357.

73. See William Massy, *Honoring the Trust* (Bolton, MA: Anker Press, 2003). We thank Dick Pratt for this brief summary of federal funding for research here and on the following page (e-mail March 4, 2006).

74. National Science Foundation Web page. http://www.nsf.gov/statistics/infbrief/nsf05322/.

75. R. C. Lewontin, "The Cold War and the Transformation of the Academy," in *The Cold War and the University,* ed. Andre Schiffrin (New York: New Press, 1997), 8–10.

76. Walter W. Powell and Jason Owen-Smith, "The New World of Knowledge Production in the Life Sciences," in *The Future of the City of Intellect: The Changing American University,* ed. Steven Brint (Stanford, CA: Stanford University Press, 2002), 115.

77. Ibid., 107, 109, 117.

78. Washburn, *University, Inc.,* 183.

79. For a discussion of the competitive nature of American higher education see John V. Lombardi and Elizabeth D. Capaldi, *The Top American Research Universities* (Gainesville: University of Florida, 2001), 38. Data from 2005 are also available at the same Web page. http://thecenter.ufl.edu.research.html.

80. Interview with David Hosford, February 25, 2004. Now professor of history, he was the dean of the Faculty of Arts and Sciences–Newark from 1982–1998. He has a PhD from the University of Wisconsin (1970).

81. Interview with Mark Chesler, May 18, 2005. Chesler came to Michigan for a PhD in social psychology (1967) and has been there ever since. Today Chesler is professor emeritus of sociology.

82. Howard H. Peckham, *The Making of the University of Michigan: 1817–1992,* edited and updated by Margaret L. Steneck and Nicholas H. Steneck (Ann Arbor, MI: Bentley Historical Library, 1994), 261.

83. Interview with Patricia (Pat) Gurin, October 12, 2004. Gurin is the Nancy Cantor Distinguished Professor Emerita of psychology and women's studies, having been former chair of psychology (1991–1998) and interim dean of the College of Literature, Science, and Arts. Gurin got her PhD at Michigan in 1964 and began teaching on the nontenure track, moving to the tenure track in 1966.

84. Clara Lovett, "The Perils of Pursuing Prestige," *Chronicle of Higher Education,* January 21, 2005. http://chronicle.com/weekly/vol51/i20/20b02001.htm.

85. James Duderstadt and Farris W. Womack, *The Future of the Public University in America: Beyond the Crossroads* (Baltimore: Johns Hopkins University Press, 2003), 49.

86. Interview with James (Jim) Duderstadt, October 13, 2004. Duderstadt was president of the University of Michigan (1988–1996) and currently directs the university's program in Science, Technology, and Public Policy and the Center for a New World Order Millennium Project. He has a PhD in engineering science and physics from the California Institute of Technology (1967). He was the dean of the College of Engineering and provost before assuming the presidency.

87. Roger L. Geiger, "The Competition for High Ability Students: Universities in a Key Marketplace," in *The Future of the City of Intellect,* 89.

88. Robert B. Reich, "How Selective Colleges Heighten Inequality," *Chronicle of Higher Education,* September 15, 2000, B7.

89. Interview with President John Pope Hennessy, February 16, 2005. Hennessy has been president since 2000; before that he was dean of the School of Engineering and provost. He received his PhD from SUNY Stony Brook in computer science in 1977 and came to Stanford that year.

90. James Duderstadt, *A University for the 21st Century* (Ann Arbor: University of Michigan Press, 2000), 214.

91. Ibid., 43.

92. Lombardi and Capaldi, *The Top American Research Universities,* 2005, 82–89. This category includes memberships in the National Academy of Sciences, National Academy of Engineering, and the Institute of Medicine.

93. Thelin, *A History of American Higher Education,* 356–357.

94. Randall Collins, "Credential Inflation and the Future of Universities," in *The Future of the City of Intellect,* 38.

95. Marilyn Boxer, *When Women Ask the Questions: Creating Women's Studies in America* (Baltimore: Johns Hopkins University Press, 1998), 1.

96. Betty Schmitz, et al., "Women's Studies and Curriculum Transformation in the United States," in *Handbook of Research on Multicultural Education,* ed. James A. Banks and Cherry A. McGee Banks, 2nd ed. (San Francisco: Jossey-Bass, 2004), 882.

97. The first Black studies department was founded at San Francisco State in 1968, which also has the oldest Asian American studies program in the country, founded in 1969. The Chicana and Chicano studies began at UC–Santa Barbara in 1968; in 1969 Berkeley founded an ethnic studies program that had four programs—Black studies, Chicano studies, Asian American studies, and Native American studies. See Evelyn Hu-DeHart, "Ethnic Studies in U.S. Higher Education," in *Handbook of Research on Multicultural Education,* 869-871.

98. Noliwe M. Rooks, "The Beginnings of Black Studies," *Chronicle of Higher Education,* February 10, 2006, B8–B9.

99. Ibid., B8.

100. Hu-DeHart, "Ethnic Studies," 873–876.

101. Philip Altbach, et al., "Race in Higher Education: The Continuing Crisis," in *The Racial Crisis in American Higher Education,* 33.

102. Boxer, *When Women Ask the Questions,* 243.

103. Hu-DeHart, "Ethnic Studies," 877.

104. Messer-Davidow, *Disciplining Feminism,* 165.

105. Referenced in Hu-DeHart, "Ethnic Studies," 877.

106. Rooks, "The Beginnings of Black Studies," B9.

107. Messer-Davidow, *Disciplining Feminism,* 154.

108. Patricia Gumport, "Graduate Education and Research: Interdependence and Strain," in *American Higher Education in the Twenty-First Century: Social, Political and Economic Challenges,* ed. Philip Altbach, et al. (Baltimore: Johns Hopkins University Press, 1999), 413.

109. Sheila Slaughter, "The Political Economy of Curriculum Making in American Universities," in *The Future of the City of Intellect,* 271, 280–281.

110. Interview with Carolyn Lougee, January 30, 2004. Lougee received a PhD in history from Michigan in 1972 and has been at Stanford since 1973.

111. Interview with Sherri-Ann Butterfield, February 25, 2004. Butterfield is an assistant professor of sociology, having received her PhD in sociology from Michigan in 2001.

Chapter 2

1. Burton Clark, ed., *The Academic Profession: National, Disciplinary, and Institutional Settings* (Berkeley: University of California Press, 1987). Cited in Hollinger, *Science, Jews and Secular Culture,* 123.

2. Harold Wechsler, "Brewing Bachelors: The History of the University of Newark," 48. http://www.newark.rutgers.edu/history/history-wechsler.pdf.

3. Rutgers University Libraries, Department of Special Collections and University Archives, *Records of the University of Newark, 1934–1946: Administrative History,* 1, 2; Harold Wechsler, personal communication.

4. "Norman Samuels in His Own Words," *Commemoration Booklet: Norman Samuels, Celebrating 20 Years of Vision and Leadership.* Rutgers University–Newark, June 12, 2002, 16, 17. Norman Samuels came to RU–N in 1967; after 1-1/2 years at Medgar Evers College, he returned to RU–N in 1971 as associate dean. He received his PhD in political science at Duke University in 1967. We interviewed Samuels on October 14, 2003, and January 19, 2006.

5. Robeson was a Rutgers University–New Brunswick graduate.

6. A new dormitory broke ground on November 30, 2004, the first new residence hall on campus in 14 years. Carla Capizzi, "New Era for Rutgers–Newark," *Rutgers Focus,* December 6, 2004, 2.

7. "Norman Samuels in His Own Words," 20.

8. *Rutgers University–Newark Provost's Annual Report, 2003–2004,* 24. http://www.newark.rutgers.edu/provost/index.php?sId=report. Figures for African Americans do not distinguish between nonimmigrants and immigrants from the Caribbean; similarly, no distinctions are made between American-born and immigrant Puerto Ricans.

9. Ibid.

10. Interview with Maggie Shiffrar, February 23, 2005. Shiffrar is currently chair of the Psychology Department, having been there since 1991. She has a PhD in psychology from Stanford (1990).

11. Interview with President Richard L. McCormick, New Brunswick, February 21, 2003. McCormick came to the university from the presidency of the University of Washington in 2002. He received his PhD in history from Yale in 1976.
12. Interview with Jean Anyon, October 25, 2004. Anyon, who is currently a professor of education at the Graduate School at City College of New York, was on RU–N's faculty from 1981 to 2001. She received her PhD in education and psycholinguistics from New York University in 1980.
13. Wechsler, "Brewing Bachelors," 24.
14. Richard P. McCormick, *The Black Student Protest Movement at Rutgers* (New Brunswick, NJ: Rutgers University Press, 1990), 34, 35.
15. Ibid., 37. The university had long had intermittent ties to the city, including a "city-oriented research center in the 1930s." See also Wechsler, "Brewing Bachelors," 35.
16. Ibid., 87–88. According to President McCormick this financial support for students continues today. The Tuition Aid Grant program, which helps fund needy students, has kept New Jersey higher education within reach of many students not otherwise able to enroll. New Jersey has the best record in the country in this regard. "Access to Rutgers by disadvantaged students, which, of course, includes kids of color, has not gone down despite the tuition increases."
17. Ibid., 89, 99.
18. Interview with Acela Laguna Diaz. Diaz has a PhD in comparative literature from the University of Illinois–Urbana (1973) and has been at RU–N since then.
19. Interviews with Charles Russell, May 19, 2004, and January 18, 2006. Russell has a PhD in comparative literature from Cornell (1972) and has been at RU–N since 1977. Over the past 20 years, Russell has been vice provost for research and chair of the English Department; he is currently director of a new American Studies PhD program.
20. Interview with Gary Roth, April 18, 2005. Roth received a Doctor of Politics degree from the Freie Universität, Berlin (1982). He has worked at RU–N for 16 years.
21. Interview with Belinda Edmondson, May 17, 2004. She has a PhD in English from Northwestern (1993) and has been at RU–N since 1992.
22. Interview with Clement (Clem) Price, May 19, 2004. Price has a PhD in history from Rutgers (1975) and has been at RU–N since 1969. He is known as "Mr. Newark" for his involvements with the city.
23. Interview with Jamie Lew, February 25, 2004. Lew has a PhD in comparative education and sociology from Teachers College, Columbia (2001) and has been at RU–N since then.
24. Faculty in business at RU–N have not been as successful, which Diner attributes to the school's not being competitive nationally because of its lower starting salaries.
25. Steven Diner, "Goals for Rutgers–Newark," April 2004, 2. http://www.newark.rutgers.edu/provostoffice/index.php?sId=goals.
26. John Hennessy, "Stanford in the 21st Century." Inaugural speech as president of Stanford University, October 25, 2000. http://news-service.stanford.edu/news/2000/october25/inaug_speech-1025.html.
27. Ray Delgado, "New Science and Engineering Quad Planned for Campus Core," *Stanford Report,* February 9, 2005, 1.
28. History of Stanford Web page, http://www.stanford.edu/home/stanford/history/.
29. Larry Cuban, *How Scholars Trumped Teachers: Change Without Reform in University Curriculum, Teaching and Research, 1890–1990* (New York: Teachers College Press, 1999), 28.
30. Interview with Stanford President Emeritus Richard Lyman, January 30, 2004. Lyman was president of Stanford from 1970 to 1980; before that he was associate dean of the School of Humanities and Sciences, vice president and provost. He has a PhD in history from Harvard (1954).
31. Cuban, *How Scholars Trumped Teachers,* 6. See also Rebecca Lowen, *Creating the Cold War University: The Transformation of Stanford* (Berkeley: University of California Press, 1997), 7.
32. Cuban, *How Scholars Trumped Teachers,* 45, 29.
33. Lowen, *Creating the Cold War University,* 89.
34. Rossiter, *Women Scientists in America:* 132–133, 135.
35. Lowen, *Creating the Cold War University,* 156.

36. Ibid., 15.
37. Interview with Stanford President Emeritus Donald Kennedy, May 9, 2005. Kennedy went from being chair of the Biological Sciences Department to being U.S. FDA commissioner (1977–1979) to being Stanford president in the 1980s. He has a PhD from Harvard (1956). James Gibbs also emphasized the importance of the Medical School in Stanford's growth since the 1950s (e-mail from James Gibbs, March 2, 2006).
38. Saxenian, *Regional Advantage,* 23.
39. Interview with James (Jim) Plummer, June 16, 2004. Plummer came to Stanford as a graduate student in 1966. He received his PhD in electrical engineering in 1971 and was appointed an associate professor in 1978.
40. Sue Rosser, *Women, Science and Society* (New York: Teachers College Press, 2000), 4, 11.
41. Interview with Pamela (Pam) Matson, January 29, 2004. Matson received her PhD in Forest Science from Oregon State University in 1983. She joined the faculty at Stanford as the Goldman Professor of Environmental Studies in 1997.
42. These words of President Sterling are often invoked at Stanford, especially during Gerhard Casper's presidency (1992–2000). See for example his speech, "Cares of the University," 1992. http://www.stanford.edu/home/stanford/cares/frames/crystal.html.
43. Today 37.5% of students are from California. See http://www.stanford.edu/home/stanford/facts/undergraduate.html.
44. Faculty Senate Report, May 1, 2003, *Stanford Report,* May 7, 2003, 10–11.
45. E-mail from James Gibbs, March 2, 2006.
46. Steering Committee of the Study of Education at Stanford, *The Study of Education at Stanford,* 1968. Many other universities instituted a similar policy.
47. Interview with Albert (Al) Camarillo, January 22, 2003. Camarillo received his PhD from UCLA in 1975 and was appointed an assistant professor at Stanford the same year.
48. Interviews with Renato Rosaldo, October 15, 2001, January 22, 2003, and June 18, 2003. Rosaldo joined the Stanford faculty in 1970, from which he retired in 2004. He presently is a faculty member in anthropology at New York University. He received a PhD from Harvard in 1971.
49. *Stanford Facts 2006* (Office of University Communications), 18–19. http://www.stanford.edu/home/stanford/facts.html.
50. Jean H. Fetter, *Questions and Admission: Reflections on 100,000 Admissions Decisions at Stanford* (Stanford, CA: Stanford University Press, 1995), 97.
51. Interview with Maria Cotera, October 13, 2005. She is currently an assistant professor in American Culture and Latina/o Studies and Women's Studies at Michigan.
52. Interview with Claude Steele, February 16, 2005. At Stanford since 1991, he was formerly at Michigan; his research on "stereotype threat" is widely known and led to his contribution to the Michigan affirmative action case briefings organized by Patricia Gurin. He has a PhD in psychology from Ohio State (1971).
53. Interview with John Bravman, January 23, 2003. Bravman has a PhD from Stanford in materials science and engineering and has been on the faculty since 1985 the year he received his doctorate. He has spent his whole academic career, beginning as an undergraduate, at Stanford.
54. *Stanford Facts 2006,* 31.
55. *Building a Multiracial, Multicultural University Community.* Final Report of the University Committee on Minority Issues, Stanford University, 1989. Al Camarillo chaired the committee.
56. Interview with Mary Sue Coleman, May 17, 2005. Coleman is a biochemist who received her PhD from North Carolina in 1970. She served as vice chancellor at the University of North Carolina from 1992 to 1993, as provost at the University of New Mexico, and seven years as president of the University of Iowa before going to Michigan in 2002.
57. The Ann Arbor campus is one of three campuses that comprise the University of Michigan, all of which are governed by a single publicly elected Board of Regents. Regional campuses in Dearborn and Flint were opened in the 1960s to relieve baby boom enrollment pressures on the Ann Arbor campus.

58. Interview with Nancy Cantor, June 17, 2005. Cantor received her PhD in psychology from Stanford in 1978. She became provost under President Lee Bollinger in 1997. She is largely credited with leading the university through the defense of the Supreme Court cases over the years of her tenure as provost. She left the university in 2001 and is currently president of Syracuse University.
59. Remark made at the Futuring Diversity Conference, University of Michigan, May 17, 2005.
60. Message from the LSA Dean: http://www.lsa.umich.edu/lsa/about.dean.
61. Lombardi and Capaldi, *The Top American Research Universities,* 2001, 38.
62. Volume of Research Expenditures by Sponsor, University of Michigan. http://www.research.umich.edu/research_guide/annual_reports/FY04/FY04ExpendBySponsor.pdf.
63. Duderstadt and Womack, *The Future of the Public University,* 215–216.
64. Tappan's speech is quoted in Frederick Rudolph, *The American College and University: A History* (New York, Knopf, 1962), 234.
65. Ruth Bordin, *Women at Michigan* (Ann Arbor: University of Michigan Press 1999), 7.
66. Rudolph, *The American College and University,* 233–234.
67. Bordin, *Women at Michigan,* 8.
68. Duderstadt and Womack, *The Future of the Public University,* 49.
69. Duderstadt, *A University for the 21st Century,* 201.
70. Bordin, *Women at Michigan,* 8.
71. Rossiter, *Women Scientists in America.* By the 1950s applications for a room in the dormitories, including those from African American students, were accepted in the order of receipt.
72. Interview with Philip Deloria, March 23, 2005. Deloria got his PhD in American Studies at Yale in 1994. He is professor of history and director of the Program in American Culture. His work is on Native American cultures and their interactions with American culture.
73. Peckham, *The Making of the University of Michigan,* 278, 294, 295.
74. Ibid., 349.
75. Earl Lewis, "Why History Remains a Factor in the Search for Racial Equality," in *Defending Diversity: Affirmative Action at the University of Michigan,* ed. Patricia Gurin, et al. (Ann Arbor: University of Michigan Press, 2004), 50–51.
76. Peter Schmidt, "Affirmative Action Survives, and So Does the Debate," *Chronicle of Higher Education,* July 4, 2003, S1–S4.
77. Ibid., S3, S4.
78. Patricia Gurin, "The Educational Value of Diversity," in *Defending Diversity,* 115.
79. Ibid., 133–134.
80. Nancy Cantor, "Introduction," in *Defending Diversity,* 3, 4.
81. Nancy Cantor, "A Victory for Justice, and a Vindication," *Chronicle of Higher Education,* July 4, 2003, B12.
82. Interview with Lester Monts, October 11, 2004. Monts came to Michigan in 1993; he received a PhD in musicology from the University of Minnesota (1980).
83. University of Michigan, Ann Arbor, "Fall 2005 Enrollment." http://www.umich.edu/news/BG/FA05_Total-Enrollment.pdf.
84. University of Michigan, Ann Arbor, "Graduation Rates of Freshmen Cohorts." http://sitemaker.umich.edu/obpinfo.
85. Message from the LSA Dean. It is noteworthy that Michigan has been included in and takes pride in a new category at *U.S. News and World Report,* Programs that Work, which ranks programs that focus on student learning.
86. Hollinger, *Science, Jews, and Secular Culture,* 125.
87. Jean O'Barr is quoted in an interview with Abigail Stewart, October 13, 2004.
88. Duderstadt, *A University for the 21st Century,* 49–52.
89. Interview with Abigail (Abby) Stewart, October 10, 2004. Stewart is a professor of psychology and the former director of the Women's Studies program; she was also the founding director of the Institute for Research on Women and Gender and the founder and first director of the ADVANCE Program for women in the sciences. She came to Michigan in 1987 from Boston University and has a PhD in psychology and social relations from Harvard University (1975).

90. Anne Frantilla, *Social Science in the Public Interest: A Fiftieth-Year History of the Institute for Social Research* (Ann Arbor: Bentley Historical Library of the University of Michigan, 1998), 11, 15.
91. One example is Jewel Plummer Cobb's candidacy for the dean of LSA in 1975. When President Fleming offered her the position without tenure and a two year contract, rather than the standard five, she demanded a reconvening of the Regents to revise the offer. The position went to an inside candidate. Recalling her exclusion from the dorms as an undergraduate in the 1940s because of her race, she recalls telling Fleming that she found it ironic that her treatment as a dean's candidate bore the same marks of racism and sexism she had experienced as a student more than thirty years earlier.
92. Rudolph, *The American College and University*, 234.

Chapter 3

1. Interview with James Gibbs, May 9, 2005. Gibbs, who had tenure at the University of Minnesota before coming to Stanford, was appointed Stanford's first dean of undergraduate studies in 1970. He has a PhD in anthropology from Harvard (1961).
2. Letter to Elliott Richardson, secretary of the U.S. Department of Health, Education, and Welfare (HEW), May 3, 1971.
3. We studied only tenured and tenure-track faculty because it is to tenured faculty that institutions make a long-term commitment and devote a major portion of their resources. Tenure-related faculty members, in turn, have an investment in the institution and are in large part responsible for its identity.
4. E-mail from Al Camarillo, September 22, 2005. Camarillo chaired the University Committee on Minority Issues.
5. For a discussion of feminist phase theory, see Mary Kay Tetreault, "Feminist Phase Theory: An Experience-Derived Evaluation Model," *Journal of Higher Education* 56, no. 4 (1985, 363–384). See also Marilyn Schuster and Susan Van Dyne, "Placing Women in the Liberal Arts: Stages of Curriculum Transformation," *Harvard Educational Review* 54, no. 4 (1984, 413–428).
6. Our thanks to Barrie Thorne for bringing to our attention the phrase "critical incidents" and the book that describes it. See Veena Das, *Critical Events* (Delhi, India: Oxford University Press, 1995), 2, 198.
7. Patricia Albjerg Graham, "Expansion and Exclusion: A History of Women in Higher Education," *Signs,* 3 (1978) 759–773.
8. Gerald Warner Brace, *The Department* (New York: W. W. Norton, 1968), 33, 280.
9. John Hope Franklin, *Mirror to America* (New York: Farrar, Straus and Giroux, 2005), 167.
10. George Palmer, in honor of his wife, Alice Freeman Palmer, established a chair in history to be held by a woman. A year later, the regents tried unsuccessfully to persuade Palmer to let them appoint a man to the chair. It was not filled until the 1957–1958 academic year, and then by a nonpermanent nontenurable woman.
11. Bordin, *Women at Michigan,* 78.
12. Personal communication with Robert Textor, April 2005.
13. Tom Hayden, *Reunion: A Memoir* (New York: Random House, 1988), 93, 97, 101.
14. Title VII of the Civil Rights Act prohibited discrimination in employment and was extended in 1972 to include all educational institutions. Presidential Executive Order 11246 prohibited discrimination by all federal contractors. Miriam K. Chamberlain, ed., *Women in Academe* (New York: Russell Sage Foundation, 1988), 172.
15. "Memorandum on the Status of Faculty Women at Rutgers University, Newark," November 1971.
16. Dinnerstein's letter was addressed to Elliott Richardson, secretary of HEW, May 13, 1971. Documents for this section can be found in the University Archives, Alexander Library, RU–New Brunswick. They include letters to HEW and Rutgers president Edward Bloustein, affirmative action materials, statistics, and so on. Supplemental materials came to us courtesy of Lillian Robbins, a member of the Psychology Department since 1971. Interview with Lillian Robbins, February 24, 2005. Robbins received her PhD in social psychology in 1967 from CUNY.

17. Interview with Myra Strober, January 30, 2004. Strober received a PhD in economics from MIT in 1969. Strober found men in the School of Education, and particularly David Tyack, the historian of education whom she had begun doing research with, to be "welcoming in a way that men at the Business School had never been." In 1979 she moved to the School of Education with tenure.

18. "Affirmative Action Work Force Analysis of Full-Time Faculty and Non-Instructional Staff Personnel, Rutgers University, 1971–1975," February 1976, 4.

19. Bordin, *Women at Michigan*, 83.

20. According to Robbins there were two tenured White women in the Academic Foundations Department, who were only assistant professors; they resented that Arthur B. Powell had associate rank. One filed an unsuccessful grievance, and both retired early.

21. Interview with Arthur B. Powell, May 18, 2004. He has been at RU–N since 1981.

22. Peckham, *The Making of the University of Michigan*, 349–350.

23. Interview with Estelle B. Freedman, January 22, 2003. She has a PhD in history (1976) from Columbia and came to Stanford in 1976 to teach social history.

24. Estelle B. Freedman, "Women's Networks and Women's Loyalties: Reflections on a Tenure Case," *Frontiers* 8, no. 3 (1986), 52.

25. Stanford's involvement with these issues was long-standing. Although there was a Western civilization requirement beginning in the 1930s, a 1960s self-study concluded that the core requirement be abolished. A small elective freshman seminar program followed. In efforts to restore a core, senior faculty gained approval in 1978 to offer a pilot program that was adopted in 1980 as the "Western Culture" program. *The Study of Education at Stanford*, 10 vols., vol. 1 (Stanford, 1968), 14. Referenced in Gilbert Allardyce, "The Rise and Fall of the Western Civilization Course," *American Historical Review* 87 (1982) 720.

26. *Campus Report*, June 16, 1986, 26–34, 36. The Faculty Senate debated the issues surrounding the proposal from January until March 1988. The Western Culture Program, a requirement since 1980, was a yearlong course taken by all first-year students. It offered freshman a choice of eight different yearlong course sequences emphasizing great works, philosophy, and other distinct themes. It was one part of a nine-part system of introductory and distribution requirements that composed the core curriculum.

27. "Lougee: Core List Impedes Other Lines of Scholarly Inquiry," *Campus Report*, January 27, 1988, 10–11.

28. Ibid.

29. "Retain Current Western Culture With Some Amendments, Professors Urge," *Campus Report*, January 20, 1988, 1.

30. *Campus Report*, January 27, 1988, 1.

31. Degler felt that a strengthened non-Western requirement was the answer. "Historian Degler: No Direct Connection to American Ideas From East Asia, Africa," *Campus Report*, February 10, 1988, 22.

32. "Rosaldo, Stanford Should Develop Models for the 21 Century," *Campus Report*, February 10, 1988, 23.

33. "African Study Would Enhance Freshman Course, Profs Say," *Campus Report*, February 3, 1988, 4.

34. One day following the official release of the report by the Committee on Undergraduate Studies on January 19, 1988, U.S. Secretary of Education William Bennett delivered a speech featured in the *New York Times*, which generated national attention. "This kind of debate has gone on before, and since it's going on at Stanford, it may have a ripple effect. … It looks to me as though policy by intimidation is at work. Unfortunately, a lot of academic leadership is readily intimidated by the noisiest of its students and faculty." This response, which President Kennedy noted happened before the Faculty Senate debated the issues, showed that the Secretary of Education "has chosen to declare his view on an issue about which he is uninformed … and on the basis of an outcome that is unreached. It is reprehensible to assert that intimidation has occurred before the fact." See Richard Bernstein, "In Dispute on Bias, Stanford Is Likely to Alter Western Culture Program," *New York Times*, January 19, 1988, A12.

35. John Guillory, *Cultural Capital: The Problem of Literary Canon Formation* (Chicago: University of Chicago Press, 1993), 30–31.

36. "Royden: Review the Core List to Ensure That Unconscious Bias Has Not Crept In," *Campus Report*, February 24, 1988, 14.

37. "70 Scholars Endorse Task Force Proposal for Culture Course," *Campus Report,* February 3, 1988, 4.
38. "Retain Current Western Culture Program With Some Amendments, Professors Urge," *Campus Report,* January 20, 1988, 13.
39. Bob Beyers, "Faculty Senate Agrees All Freshmen Should Study Ancient, Medieval Culture," *Campus Report,* February 24, 1988, 1, 13.
40. "Davis: Eurocentrism 'Pernicious' Influence Among Western Academics," *Campus Report,* February 24, 1988, 15.
41. "Perry Responds to Major Questions About Proposed Change," *Campus Report,* January 27, 1988, 7–8.
42. Carolyn Mooney, "Sweeping Curricular Change Is Under Way at Stanford as University Phases Out Its 'Western Culture' Program," *Chronicle of Higher Education,* December 14, 1988, A12.
43. Mary Louise Pratt, "Humanities for the Future: Reflections on the Western Culture Debate at Stanford," *Southern Atlantic Quarterly* 89 (1990, Winter), 17–18, 21–22.
44. See, for example, Mary M. Ash, "Do Most Women Believe Changes Are Warranted?" *Campus Report,* March 2, 1988, 10.
45. The "indirect costs controversy" involved costs associated with research such as use of the library and utilities that could not be charged to particular projects. An investigation by the Office of Naval Research led to a Congressional hearing in March 1991 and extensive negotiations with the government in 1991–1992. Admitting some shortcomings, the administration altered some accounting practices and acknowledged a failure to examine the appropriateness of costs that were technically "allowable." Even though Stanford was vindicated and received a Congressional apology, Kennedy concluded that the institution's reputation had been damaged and resigned at the end of the 1991–1992 academic year. See Donald Kennedy, *The Last of Your Springs* (Stanford, CA: Stanford Historical Society, 1998), 188–197, 204–206. Casper was only the third president appointed from outside Stanford. He served as dean of the Law School from 1979 to 1987 and provost from 1989 to 1992 at the University of Chicago before assuming the Stanford presidency.
46. For the 2002–2003 academic year, courses emphasizing science, engineering, and technology predominated, roughly representing 40% of the offerings, whereas those with multicultural content represent about 12%. There were originally 170 seminars in 1997–1998 and are more than 200 today.
47. Interview with Gerhard Casper, January 22, 2003.
48. Gerhard Casper, "Concerning Culture and Cultures: Welcome to Freshmen and Their Parents," Stanford University, September 23, 1993, 8, 9. http://www.stanford.edu/dept/pres-provost/president/speeches/930923culture.html.
49. See Gerhard Casper, "On the Synthesis of Teachers and Students: Remarks to the Meeting of the Senate of the Academic Council," May 9, 1996, 7–8. http://www.stanford.edu/dept/pres-provost/president/speeches/960509synthesis.html. See also "Concerning Culture and Cultures," 8.
50. Gerhard Casper, "Transitions and Endurances," speech delivered on March 2, 2000, 10–11. http://news-service.stanford.edu/news/2000/march8/stateutext-38.html.
51. "Report of the Provost's Committee on the Recruitment and Retention of Women Faculty," Stanford University, November 1993.
52. Interview with David Halperin, March 23, 2005. Halperin went to Michigan in 1999. He has a PhD in classics and humanities from Stanford (1980).
53. E-mail from Judith Ramaley, August 17, 2002. Ramaley is president of Winona State University and former president of Portland State University, where she successfully oversaw the implementation of a nationally recognized general education program.
54. Stanford University, "Proposed Legislation, Area One Requirement: Cultures, Ideas and Values (CIV)," November 16, 1987, 2, unpublished report. The student body at Stanford changed from being 12% minority in 1970 to 32% in 1988. Tenured women were only 4% of the faculty when Lougee arrived in 1973. At the time of the great debate in 1988 women were 8% of the tenured faculty and 11% of the total faculty. People of color were 8%.

Chapter 4

1. Duderstadt and Womack, *Future of the Public University,* 49, 50.

2. Faculty Senate report, May 1, 2003, *Stanford Report,* May 7, 2003, 11.
3. Interview with Elizabeth Cole, October 13, 2005. Cole received her PhD in psychology from Michigan in 1993. She returned to Michigan in 1999 (from Northeastern) as the first joint appointment in Women's Studies and the Center for African and African-American Studies (CAAS).
4. Duderstadt and Womack, *Future of the Public University,* 204, 205, 51.
5. Gurin said there were about 139 faculty in psychology, totaling 89 to 90 Full-Time Equivalents (FTEs)because of all the joint appointments held in psychology.
6. Bordin, *Women at Michigan,* 98.
7. Interview with Julie Ellison, October 13, 2004. Ellison received her PhD from Yale in 1980 and was hired at Michigan the same year. She is director of the national program Imagining America: Artists and Scholars in Public Life. Henceforth, we use the term English Department when referring to the Department of English Language and Literature.
8. The university established the Center for the Education of Women (1964), the Commission for Women (1971), the Women's Studies Program (1972), the Women of Color Task Force (1979), and the Women in Science Program (1980). Women were 17% of the faculty at Michigan in 1980. In LSA they were 11% of the faculty, whereas in the College of Engineering, they were 2%. Predominently in the humanities, there were very few women in the sciences—none in astronomy, geological sciences, mathematics, physics, and statistics.
9. Interview with Edie Goldenberg, May 18, 2005. Goldenberg is professor of political science and professor of public policy at the Gerald R. Ford School of Public Policy. She was dean of LSA from 1990 to 1998. She received a PhD in political science from Stanford (1974).
10. They include Sonya Rose, recruited from Bates College as a tenured professor in sociology and history in 1993. Sidonie Smith, the current chair of English, was hired from SUNY Binghamton in 1996 in English and Women's Studies and also was director in the latter.
11. Interview with Conrad Kottak, March 23, 2005. Kottak has been at Michigan since 1968. He has a PhD in anthropology from Columbia University (1966).
12. Interview with Valerie Traub, October 12, 2004. Traub has a PhD in English from the University of Massachusetts–Amherst (1990). In 1994 Traub was hired with tenure jointly in English and Women's Studies to work on gender and sexuality in Renaissance literature and culture. Other appointments include the historian Carroll Smith Rosenberg, the musicologist Nadine Hubbs, the anthropologist Esther Newton, and Anna Kirkland to teach, among other things, courses on sexuality and the law. Other units hired faculty who subsequently became unbudgeted affiliates of the Women's Studies Program, including David Halperin in 1999 as an endowed chair in English and the anthropologist Gayle Rubin in 2002.
13. Interview with Nadine Hubbs, March 22, 2005. She has been at Michigan since 1997 and has a PhD in music theory, also from Michigan (1990).
14. "Diversity Now a Matter of Daily Routine for English Department," *University Record,* November 23, 1992, http://www.umich.edu/~urecord/9293/Nov23_92/7.htm.
15. Interview with Homer Neal, October 14, 2005. Neal received a PhD from Michigan in physics in 1966. He returned to the university as chair of physics in 1987 after having served as dean of research at Indiana University and provost at SUNY Stony Brook.
16. Duderstadt, *A University for the 21st Century,* 207. In 1995 female faculty throughout the university remained at 20%. Their proportion decreased steadily up the academic ladder: they were 34% of assistant professors, 23% of associates, and only 9% of full professors.
17. Ronald J. Lomax, Thomas E. Moore, and Charles B. Smith, "The Michigan Mandate: Promise and Progress," *University Record,* April 17, 1995. Of the 544 full-time, tenure-track faculty, 200 responded.
18. "Diversity Now a Matter of Daily Routine for English Department."
19. Diner, "Goals for Rutgers–Newark," 5.
20. Philip Furmanski, "Memorandum to the Committee on Educational Policy and Planning: Faculty Diversity Initiatives," November 18, 2004, 1, 2. Furmanski is the executive vice president for academic affairs.
21. Turner, "Women of Color in Academe," 82.
22. "Hennessy, Panelists Outline University's Successes, Future Challenges," *Stanford Report,* March 14, 2001. http://www.stanford.edu/dept/news/report/news/march14/takingstock-314.html.

23. Interview with Paula Moya, February 16, 2005. Moya has been at Stanford since 1996 and has recently gained tenure in the English Department; she has a PhD in English from Cornell (1998).

24. Interview with Claudine Gay, February 14, 2006. Gay has a PhD in government from Harvard (1997).

25. Faculty Senate report, May 1, 2003, 11.

26. Ibid.

27. Interview with Ramon Saldivar, January 23, 2003. Saldivar is the current chair of English and has been at Stanford since 1991. He was formerly the dean of undergraduate studies in the School of Humanities and Sciences. He has a PhD in comparative literature from Yale (1977).

28. "Report of the Provost's Advisory Committee on the Status of Women Faculty." May 2004. http://www.stanford.edu/dept/provost/womenfacultyreport. See also Kate Chesley, "Stanford Releases Findings of Three-Year Study on Status of Women Faculty," Stanford News Service, May 27, 2004. http://www.stanford.edu/dept/news/pr/2004/womenrelease-527.html.

29. All findings on these pages are taken from "Report of the Provost's Advisory Committee on the Status of Women Faculty."

30. See also Turner, "Women of Color in Academe."

31. Interview with Milbrey McLaughlin, January 29, 2002. Professor of education and public policy, she has been at Stanford since 1980. She has a PhD in education and social policy from Harvard (1973).

32. Interview with John Etchemendy, May 9, 2005. He received his PhD in philosophy from Stanford in 1982 and joined the faculty in 1983.

33. There have been a larger number of senior male new hires in engineering, the humanities, social sciences, and medicine.

34. Faculty Senate report, May 15, 2003, Stanford Report, May 21, 2003, 12. The report found that the Medical School has a reputation for being the most intractable on unequal gender relations.

35. Faculty Senate report, October 12, 2004. Stanford Report, October 20, 2004, 12. See also Ray Delgado, "Faculty Women's Forum to Be Created, Childcare Center Expedited," Stanford Report, October 6, 2004, 4. The university has since helped renovate one child care center, opened one more, and promised a third.

36. Chesley, "Stanford Releases Findings."

37. "Report of the Provost's Advisory Committee on the Status of Women Faculty," in Building on Excellence: Guide to Recruiting and Retaining an Excellent and Diverse Faculty at Stanford University. Executive Summary, September 2005, vi–x. http://www.stanford.edu/dept/provost/diversity.pdf. See also Family Matters @ Stanford for Faculty, Stanford University, September 2005. http://www.stanford.edu/dept/provost/family.pdf.

38. "Stanford University Campus Diversity Initiatives," prepared for James W. Irvine Foundation, no date. The Irvine Foundation has funded the Stanford University Campus Diversity Initiatives to increase faculty and graduate student diversity.

39. Interview with Sally Dickson, February 14, 2006. Dickson has a law degree from Rutgers (1975). She held numerous positions at Stanford, including director of campus relations.

40. Interview with Sharon Long, June 16, 2004. Long has been at Stanford since 1982. She received her PhD in biology from Yale (1979).

41. Interview with Michele Elam, February 15, 2006. Elam received a PhD in English from the University of Washington in 1992. She joined the faculty at Stanford in 2003 after teaching at several institutions, including Pacific Lutheran University.

42. Two other faculty, Michael Awkward and Sharon Patton, were directors in the mid-1990s, but Lewis and Jackson are the ones most credited with building the program. Center Directors, CAAS Web site. http://www.umich.edu/~iinet/caas/TheCenter/directors.htm.

43. Interview with Kevin Gaines, October 12, 2005. Gaines came to Michigan in 1999 and has a PhD in American studies from Brown (1991).

44. University of Michigan, "Report of the Committee to Consider a More Flexible Tenure Probationary Period," June 30, 2005, 7 (1–27). http://www.provost.umich.edu/reports/ flexible_tenure/contents.html. While many support these changes, they are also controversial in some quarters, according to a recent piece in the *Chronicle of Higher Education*. Some see them as fostering mediocrity, as keeping junior scholars in limbo for too long, and as potentially threatening to the whole tenure system. Robin Wilson, "Off the Clock," *Chronicle of Higher Education*, July 21, 2006, A8-A11.

45. Interview with Alford (Al) Young, October 12, 2005. Young, who came to Michigan in 1996, received his PhD in sociology from the University of Chicago in the same year.

46. Interview with Carla O'Connor, October 13, 2005. O'Connor received her PhD in education from the University of Chicago (1996).

47. Jared Wadley, "ADVANCE Findings Spur U–M to Improve Work Environment," *University Record*, March 8, 2004.

48. bell hooks, *Teaching to Transgress: Education as the Practice of Freedom* (New York: Routledge, 1994), 182.

49. Londa Schiebinger, *Has Feminism Changed Science?* (Cambridge, MA: Harvard University Press, 1999), 140, 160.

50. Sandra Harding, *Is Science Multicultural? Postcolonialism, Feminisms, and Epistemologies.* (Bloomington: Indiana University Press, 1998), 2. Here Harding is quoting Richard Rorty.

51. Many of the same challenges that apply to women and science also apply to people of color. Homer Neal of Michigan told us that efforts to hire people of color into the Physics Department cannot be regarded as successful because of the paucity of minority candidates for faculty positions in such departments. This paucity is one of the reasons he and others explicitly strengthened the department's minority graduate student recruitment and enrollment (e-mail from Homer Neal, April 2, 2006).

52. Interview with Judith Weis, October 22, 2004. Weis received a PhD from New York University in biology in 1967.

53. Interview with Robert Simoni, January 30, 2004. He came to Stanford in 1972 after receiving his PhD from UC–Davis (1966) in biochemistry followed by a postdoctorate from Johns Hopkins.

54. Interview with Patricia Pat Jones, October 16, 2002. Jones has a PhD in biology from Johns Hopkins University (1974) and was appointed a professor of biological sciences at Stanford in 1978.

55. Stanford has yet to apply for an NSF–ADVANCE grant; their major institutional energy toward diversifying the faculty has been devoted to managing the Irvine Foundation grant.

56. Interview with Paula Tallal, November 22, 2004. Both Tallal and Crees received PhDs at Cambridge University in 1973 in experimental psychology. They then went to San Diego together after postdoctoral fellowships at Johns Hopkins.

57. "A Study on the Status of Women Faculty in Science at MIT," *MIT Faculty Newsletter* II, no. 4, March 1999. http://MIT.edu/fnl/women/women.html. The first committee at MIT was established in 1995.

58. "NSF–ADVANCE at the University of Michigan." Proposal submitted to the National Science Foundation, 2001. The description of the program that follows is taken from the proposal.

59. Sara Rimer, "For Women in Sciences, Slow Progress in Academia," *New York Times*, April 15, 2005. http://topics.nytimes.com/top/reference/timestopics/people/r/sara-rimer/index.html.

60. Lotte Bailyn, et al., *Site Visit Report, U-M NSF ADVANCE Program*, September 19–21, 2004.

61. Londa Schiebinger, "Remarks for Summers Forum: Gender in Science," February 9, 2005. http://www.stanford.edu/group/IRWG/NewsAndEvents/SchiebingerForumTalk.pdf. See also Theresa Johnston, "No Evidence of Innate Gender Differences in Math and Science, Scholars Assert," *Stanford Report*, February 9, 2005, 3.

62. "Dual-Career Couples in the Academy," Stanford University. http://www.stanford.edu/ group/IRWG/Research Programs/Dual Career/index.html.

63. All of this good news, however, does not explain why the School of Engineering still hires more men than women at senior levels. Plummer takes issue with us on this point, noting that women represent less that 10% of the available pool and that universities "steal" senior women at a rate greater than 10%. He believes this does nothing to improve the national picture and that the emphasis should be put on hiring women and minorities at the entry level as well (e-mail from James Plummer, January 7, 2006).

64. Interview with Londa Schiebinger, February 15, 2006. Schiebinger has a PhD from Harvard in the history of science (1984).

65. Harding, *Is Science Multicultural?* 153, 155.

66. See *University of Michigan Electronic Fact Pages: Faculty Headcount (Based on Primary Job) by Rank, Gender, Race and Full-Time/Part-Time, 2004.* http://www.umich.edu/~oapainfo/contents.html. The race/ethnicity percentages for tenure-track faculty at Stanford are African American/Black 3%, Hispanic 3%, and Native Americans less than 1% (see *Stanford Facts 2006*). Of the men, 38.8% were full professors, and only 12.7% of the women were full professors (see *Stanford Facts 2005*, http://www.stanford.edu/home/stanford/facts/faculty.html). At RU–N African Americans are 7% and Hispanics are 2% (e-mail from Carol Martancik, March 27, 2006).

67. Mark Chesler, "Improving the Organizational and Classroom Climate for Multicultural Teaching," in *Excellent Teaching in the Excellent University*, ed. Jerome Rabinow (New York: Academic Press, 2006), 79.

Chapter 5

1. Andrew Abbot, "The Disciplines and the Future," in Brint, ed., *The Future of the City of Intellect,* 210.

2. Interview with Sidonie Smith, March 24, 2005. Smith received her PhD at Case Western Reserve in 1971 and has been at Michigan since 1996, when she was recruited from SUNY Binghamton to direct the Women's Studies Program.

3. Deborah A. Burghardt and Carol L. Colbeck, "Women's Studies Faculty at the Intersection of Institutional Power and Feminist Values," *Journal of Higher Education* 76, no. 3 (2005), 306.

4. Randall Collins, "Credential Inflation and the Future of Universities," in Brint, ed., *The Future of the City of Intellect,* 44–45.

5. Biological sciences, mathematics, neuroscience, physics, chemistry, and environmental sciences all have doctoral programs, many in conjunction with the New Jersey Institute of Technology (NJIT).

6. Grants were made mainly in the sciences but also for business, criminal justice, and public school initiatives. Our thanks to Jacqueline Corneli for this data and that regarding the Center for Molecular and Behavioral Neuroscience's (CMBN's) research grants (e-mail, March 27, 2006).

7. Bill Glovin, "Can You Help My Child?" *Rutgers Magazine*, Winter 1998, 22.

8. According to Barry Komisaruk, in 1984 the state of New Jersey offered the university system funding for six "Centers of Excellence," research centers in a variety of fields. He suggested that the Institute of Animal Behavior (IAB) apply to be such a center, and Norman Samuels enthusiastically took up the idea. Interview with Barry Komisaruk, February 2, 2005. At RU–N since 1961, he received the university's first doctorate in psychobiology in 1965.

9. CMBN is housed in the Aidekman Center, a huge facility in a prime spot in the RU–N quadrangle.

10. Interview with Edward Bonder, March 22, 2005. Bonder went to RU–N in 1987. He received his PhD in cell biology from the University of Pennsylvania (1983).

11. Interview with Edward Kirby, October 22, 2004. Kirby is a former chair of Biological Sciences and has been dean of Faculty of Arts and Sciences-Newark since 2002. He received his PhD in botany from the University of Florida in 1977 and has been at RU–N since 1978.

12. Diner, "Remarks at the Commemoration of Conklin Hall Takeover," 3.

13. Mike Sutton, "Coming Home: Ex N. J. Legislator, Governor's Cabinet Member to Head Cornwall Center," *Rutgers–Newark Connections,* Winter 2004, 1, 6.
14. Ashanti Alvarez, "Growing the Grass Roots," *Rutgers Focus,* November 15, 2004, 3.
15. *Cornwall Center Urban Research Inventory 2000–2002.* Examples of urban research projects in the Faculty of Arts and Sciences not mentioned in the body of the text are the Ironbound Oral History Project (Kimberly DeCosta Holton), Urban School Improvement (Alan Sadovnik), and Reinventing Downtown (Elizabeth Strom).
16. Ibid., 34–57.
17. The Wright Lecture Series is much older than the Institute.
18. Rooks, "The Beginnings of Black Studies," B8.
19. The New Jersey Project, directed by Paula Rothenberg from Paterson State College, offered workshops for faculty across the state to infuse the study of women into their courses. It became a national model of curriculum transformation. Interview with Fran Bartkowski, September 20, 2004. Bartkowski has a PhD in comparative literature from the University of Iowa (1982) and has been at RU–N since 1989.
20. Interview with Jyl Josephson, May 18, 2004. Josephson came to RU–N via Texas Tech and Illinois State University. She received her PhD in political science from the University of Maryland, College Park (1994).
21. Joint PhD Program in Urban Systems. http://www.umdnj.edu/urbsyweb.
22. "The Right Person for the Right Time," *Stanford Report,* April 5, 2000. http://news-service. stanford.edu/news/2000/april5/announce-45.html. At Stanford since 1977, Hennessy, by 1981, had initiated a simpler computer architecture known as RISC (Reduced Instruction Set Computer), revolutionizing the computer industry. In 1984–1985 he cofounded MIPS Computer Systems and credits his time at MIPS for giving him an appreciation for the world of business. As dean of the School of Engineering from 1996 to 1999, he oversaw a 5-year plan for a major new thrust in bioengineering and biomedical engineering. The Silicon Graphics and Netscape cofounder James Clark, Hennessy's former colleague in the Department of Electrical Engineering, also funded the Clark Center for Biomedical Engineering and Sciences.
23. Hennessey's quotes in this section were taken from his remarks in the videotape *Research Universities 101,* unless otherwise noted. In his presentation during a session of *Research Universities 101,* he chose the topic of "Stanford and Society: Where Do We Go From Here?" as the focus of his remarks.
24. Tim Lenoir, "A History of Stanford and Silicon Valley," videotape of *Research Universities 101, Stanford: A Case History.* Between 1977 and 1999, 379 patents were issued to the School of Engineering, 232 to the Medical School, and 228 to humanities and sciences. Stanford ranks in the top three universities nationally in this area, taking equity with licenses granted to start-up companies. For example, it has held 7% of Google from the start.
25. Kennedy, *The Last of Your Springs,* 22–23; Casper, "Transitions and Endurances," 19–20.
26. John Hennessy "Stanford in the 21st Century," October 25, 2000. http://news-service. stanford.edu/news/2000/october25/inaug_speech-1025.html.
27. Stanford Humanities Lab. http://shl.stanford.edu.
28. Interview with Cecilia Ridgeway, October 10, 2002. Ridgeway came to Stanford from the University of Iowa. She has a PhD in sociology from Cornell (1972).
29. See Burghardt and Colbeck, "Women's Studies Faculty," 306. Economics is similar to Biological Sciences in that both rank tops in the country and are among the most popular majors among undergraduates. However, these similarities do not extend to diversity among the faculty. Economics has only one senior woman and two junior women. There are a number of Asians but no Blacks. Americans are barely represented in the department. According to the chair, John Pencavel, the department tenures only about 20% of their junior faculty members.
30. Interview with John Pencavel, January 29, 2003. Pencavel came to Stanford in 1969 and has a PhD in economics from Princeton (1969).
31. Institute for Research in the Social Sciences at Stanford University. http://www.stanford. edu/group/iriss.
32. "Faculty Senate Disrupted by Students Seeking Asian American Studies," Stanford News Service, May 18, 1994. http://www.stanford.edu/dept/news/pr/94/940518Arc4256.html.

33. The Research Institute of Comparative Studies in Race and Ethnicity. http://ccsre.stanford.edu/RI_resInst.htm.
34. IRWG also "puts research into action by working with the media, policy makers, industry, and other leading community and national opinion-formers." The Institute aims to be the nation's primary institution-of-record for data-driven research on gender; see the IRWG Web site at http://www.stanford.edu/group/IRWG/.
35. See Susan Christopher, "Required Knowledge: Incorporating Gender Into a Core Curriculum" (PhD dissertation, Stanford University, 1995), 52–68.
36. Ibid., 65.
37. Personal communication with Jane Atkinson, 1982.
38. Christopher, "Required Knowledge," 67.
39. Ibid.
40. Interview with Penny Eckert, October 16, 2002. Eckert came to Stanford in 1994 and is a professor of linguistics. She has a PhD in linguistics from Columbia (1978).
41. Interview with Barbara Gelpi, October 16 and 17, 2002. Gelpi received her PhD from Radcliffe in English in 1962 and followed her husband, Albert, to Stanford. It was not until she became editor of Signs (1980–1985) that she was put on the tenure track. That and the publication of a second book enabled her to achieve tenure in 1992, at 59 years old.
42. The departments in humanities and sciences are English, Linguistics, Biological Sciences, Chemistry, Statistics, Economics, Political Science, and Psychology (Stanford School of Humanities and Sciences,) http://www.stanford.edu/dept/humsci/humsci/about/national_rankings.html. (In the School of Engineering the departments are Computer Science, Electrical Engineering, Mechanical Engineering, Civil & Environmental Engineering, and Aeronautics and Astronautics) http://soe.stanford.edu/about/facts.html.
43. Ray Delgado, "Five Years of the 10th President: Hennessy Reflects on Past, Thinks About Future," Stanford Report, December 7, 2005. http://news-service.stanford.edu/news/2005/december7/hennessy-120705.html.
44. Frantilla, Social Science in the Public Interest, 9.
45. Interview with Steve Raudenbush, March 23, 2005. Raudenbush has an EdD from Harvard University (1984). Raudenbush left Michigan in 2005 for the University of Chicago.
46. They include Psychology, Sociology, Anthropology, Political Sciences and Women's History. Those in the sciences are Behavioral Neuroscience and Geological Sciences http://www.lsa.umich.edu/UofM/Content/lsa/documents/LSAprofile2006.pdf. In Engineering those in the top five include Aerospace/Aeronautical, Environmental, Industrial Manufacturing, and Mechanical http://www.umich.edu/urecord/0304/Apro5_04/07.shtml.
47. Interview with Jacque Eccles, March 22, 2005. Eccles has also been affiliated with the Center for Group Dynamics at the Institute for Social Research. She has a PhD from UCLA (1974) and has been at Michigan since 1977.
48. Interview with Howard Kimeldorf, October 13, 2005. Kimeldorf was hired at Michigan in 1985, the year he received his doctorate from UCLA.
49. Interview with Deborah Goldberg, March 23, 2005. Goldberg is professor and chair of the Department of Ecology and Evolutionary Biology. She has been at Michigan since 1983 and has a PhD in biology from the University of Arizona (1980).
50. Interview with Martha Pollack, March 21, 2005. Pollack has been at Michigan since 2001, being one of the senior women hired, in her case, from the University of Pittsburgh. She has a PhD in computer and information science from the University of Pennsylvania (1986).
51. Interview with Marvin Parnes, March 23, 2005. Parnes is the associate vice president for research and executive director of research administration. He has a Michigan MSW and has been on the professional staff at the university since 1974, working with successive administrations on a variety of projects.
52. Interview with Richard Gonzalez, March 24, 2005. Gonzalez received his PhD in psychology in 1990 from Stanford University. He was hired the University of Michigan in 1997, after receiving tenure at the University of Washington.
53. Interview with Sonya Rose, March 24, 2005. Rose has been at Michigan since 1993 and has a PhD from Northwestern in sociology (1974).
54. Except for lecturers, all CAAS faculty are joint appointments—there are about 15 to 20 FTEs, according to Gaines.
55. American Culture Web site. http://www.lsa.umich.edu/ac.

56. Bordin, *Women at Michigan*, 91. An undergraduate major in women's studies was approved in 1975, and graduate courses were added in 1984.
57. Kathryn Kish Sklar, "The Women's Studies Moment: 1972," in *The Politics of Women's Studies: Testimony From Thirty Founding Mothers*, ed. Florence Howe (New York: Feminist Press, 2000), 137.
58. Because of particular hires that became possible two years ago, women's studies now has three 100% appointments.
59. Bordin, *Women at Michigan*, 99.
60. A visible manifestation of the university's commitment to the Women's Studies Program and IRWG is the newly renovated building, Lane Hall. Situated at the edge of the main campus, the building houses administrative offices, faculty offices, a classroom, a library with thousands of volumes of feminist scholarship, and seminar and meeting rooms.
61. Boxer, *When Women Ask the Questions*, 190, 192.

Chapter 6

1. Faculty Senate report, May 1, 2003, 11.
2. Ibid.
3. For example, see Eleanor Flexner, *A Century of Struggle: The Women's Rights Movement in the United States* (Cambridge, MA: Harvard University Press, 1959), and John Hope Franklin, *From Slavery to Freedom: A History of American Negroes* (New York: Knopf, 1947).
4. Paula M. L. Moya, *Learning From Experience* (Berkeley: University of California Press, 2002), 90 and note 35.
5. James Gibbs, "Stanford Anthropology Department Splits," *Anthropology Newsletter*, October 1998, 21.
6. Mitchell Leslie, in an article in the *Stanford Magazine*, characterized anthropology in this way: "Franz Boas, considered the founder of American anthropology, believed that no single perspective could encompass multifarious man. He envisioned the discipline as an ensemble of four subfields: cultural and social anthropology, physical and biological anthropology, archeology, and linguistics. ... Many of the earliest anthropology departments, including those at Harvard and Michigan, started out with Boas's four-field approach as their organizing principle." "Divided They Stand," *Stanford Magazine*, 2000. http://www.stanfordalumni.org/news/magazine/2000/janfeb/articles/anthro.html.
7. Interview with William Durham, February 16, 2005. Durham received his PhD in ecology and evolutionary biology from Michigan (1977).
8. The archaeologist Bert Gerow and the linguist Joseph Greenberg were already in the department. The new hires did not change the department's emphasis on cultural anthropology.
9. Leslie, "Divided They Stand," 3.
10. Gibbs, who registered surprise that some of his colleagues thought he could have held the department together, was skeptical that any person could have done it because of departmental politics. In that vein, he thought it was significant that it was the acting chair (a professor from the Law School), not departmental colleagues, who asked him to consider postponing retirement to become chair. It is ironic that it was liberal White men who brought in faculty of color and White women. They proudly emphasized a diverse faculty and student body but controlled departmental leadership for nearly 20 years. Although James Gibbs was hired in 1966, it was not until 1984 that a person of color was chair (Harumi Befu).
11. E-mails from James Gibbs, May 13, 2005, and January 19, 2006.
12. Gibbs, "Stanford Anthropology Department Splits," 23.
13. Leslie, "Divided They Stand," 1.
14. "Stanford Anthropology Department Will Split," *Chronicle of Higher Education*, May 29, 1998. http://chronicle.com/che-data/articles.dir/art-44.dir/issue=38.dir/38a05101.htm.
15. Leslie, "Divided They Stand," 3.
16. Interview with Sylvia Yanagisako, January 30, 2004. She received her PhD in anthropology from the University of Washington in 1975 and came to Stanford in that year.

17. Two of the senior cultural anthropologists went to Anthropological Sciences, although they are cultural anthropologists "with an evolutionary approach." Also, the Cultural and Social Anthropology Department now has a few archaeologists as well who do contextual and situated archaeology.
18. William Durham, "Department of Anthropological Sciences—Vision Statement," *Anthropology Newsletter,* October 1998, 21, 23.
19. Sylvia Yanagisako, "Department of Cultural and Social Anthropology—Vision Statement," *Anthropology Newsletter,* October 1998, 21, 23.
20. Yanagisako's recently published book takes up the debates about the configuration of the discipline of anthropology. She, along with others, revisits the standard definition of the discipline as a "holistic" study of humanity based on the integration of the four fields. See Daniel A. Segal and Sylvia J. Yanagisako, eds., *Unwrapping the Sacred Bundle: Reflections on the Disciplining of Anthropology* (Durham, NC and London: Duke University Press, 2005).
21. Ian Hodder, "An Archaeology of the Four-Field Approach in Anthropology in the United States," in Segal and Yanagisako, *Unwrapping the Sacred Bundle,* 130, 134, 139.
22. Daniel A. Segal and Sylvia Yanagisako, "Introduction", in Seagal and Yanagisako, *Unwrapping the Sacred Bundle,* 12.
23. Gibbs felt another issue of privilege working here was the attention and resources available to the scientific anthropologists because of the appeal to their research to wealthy alumni, who signed up for tours they were leading and would then provide money for endowed chairs and research support.
24. Moya, *Learning From Experience,* 67.
25. John Sanford, "Race, Ethnicity Research Institute Gets $5 Million Boost." http://www.stanford.edu/dept/news/pr/01/raceethnicity1031.html. Until the endowment is raised, the president's office is providing $250,000 a year.
26. Cornwall Center for Metropolitan Studies, *Urban Research Inventory,* 2000–2002, 10, 11.
27. Ibid., 24, 25.
28. Ibid., 5–7.
29. Glovin, "Can You Help My Child?" 18, 19. Fast ForWord, a series of software products that address language and reading from preschool through high school, is the result of Tallal's investigations. According to the *Rutgers Focus,* 450,000 children are now using this software in 2,700 school districts in 25 states. See *Rutgers Focus,* March 21, 2005, 5.
30. Today the program has 28 budgeted faculty lines and 39 unbudgeted faculty members, but because of joint appointments, their total FTE is 12.15. The program offers four joint doctoral degrees with English, psychology, history, and sociology. At the undergraduate level, the emphasis is on providing courses to undergraduate students (between 3,100 and 3,750 students take their courses annually), and an average of 40 students graduate each year with a women's studies concentration.
31. Information here is drawn from the *Long-Range Plan, Program in Women's Studies, 2003-2004,* 5–6.
32. "Global Feminisms Project" from the IRWG Web page http://www.umich.edu/%irwg/research/current/glblfem.html.
33. Interview with Vicente Diaz, October 14, 2005. Diaz received his PhD in the History of Consciousness program at UC–Santa Cruz in 1991 and taught at the University of Guam before coming to Michigan in 2001.
34. Nancy Cantor and Steven T. Levine, "Taking Public Scholarship Seriously," *Chronicle of Higher Education,* June 9, 2006 B20.
35. We thank Denise Taylor in the RU–N provost's office for providing us with this figure.
36. See *Stanford Facts 2006,* 50. see also http://www.umich.edu/news/?BG/endowment_Profile.pdf and http://www.umich.edu.UofM/Content/lsa/document/LSA profile2006.pdf.
37. Duderstadt and Womack, *The Future of the Public University,* 214.

Chapter 7

1. Harding. *Is Science Multicultural?,* x.
2. Smith. *Writing the Social,* 217.

3. Paul Lauter and Jeffrey Herf, cited in "Money, Merit and Democracy: An Exchange," in *Higher Education Under Fire: Politics, Economics, and the Crisis of the Humanities,* ed. Michael Berube and Cary Nelson (New York: Routledge, 1995), 164, 171.

4. Research Institute of Comparative Studies in Race and Ethnicity, Stanford University, 2006. http://ccsre.stanford.edu/RI_resInst.htm.

5. Smith, *Writing the Social*, 74, 76.

6. Information here is drawn from the *Long-Range Plan, Program in Women's Studies, 2003–2004,* 5–6.

7. Ray Delgado. "Five Years of the 10th President: Hennessy Reflects on Past, Thinks About Future," *Stanford Report,* December 7, 2005, http://news-service.stanford.edu/news/2005/december7/hennessy-120705.html.

8. Smith, *Writing the Social*, 202.

9. Audre Lorde, *Sister Outsider: Essays and Speeches*, Freedom, CA, Crossing Press, 1984. 110, 113.

10. *Long Range Plan, Program in Women's Studies, 2003-2004,* 5, 6.

11. Mary Sue Coleman, "Remarks Upon Release of the 2003 'Women at the University of Michigan' Report," *University Record,* October 21, 2003, and Laurel Thomas Gnagey and Jared Wadley, "Cracks in the Glass Ceiling," *University Record,* October 6, 2003.

12. E-mail from Mark Chesler, January 11, 2006.

13. The sex discrimination suits of the 1970s showed the power of federal legislation in beginning female faculty members' march toward equality. An initiative of Senators Ron Wyden of Oregon and Barbara Boxer of California has countered the common misconception that Title IX applies only to sports. The law says, "No person ... shall on the basis of sex, be excluded from participation in, be denied the benefits of, or be subjected to discrimination under any educational program or activity receiving Federal financial assistance." The two senators have requested that the Government Accounting Office monitor compliance with Title IX in the sciences. According to Wyden, "Using Title IX to Ensure Equal Opportunity for Women in Math and Science," before Title IX, one in 17 girls (or 0.06%) played sports, whereas today it is 40%. "Imagine if those same changes could be seen in math, science, and engineering ... from the six percent of engineering professors who are women today, to 40 percent" (see http://wiseli.engr.wisc.edu/news/Wyden.pdf). We thank Londa Schiebinger for telling us of this initiative.

14. Ellen Schrecker, "Worse Than McCarthy," *Chronicle of Higher Education,* February 10, 2006, B20. According to Schrecker, as of early 2006, 17 state legislatures have considered some version of the bill and Congress may incorporate it into the Higher Education Reauthorization Act.

15. Jennifer Gratz, one of the plaintiffs in the Supreme Court case, is the director of the group.

16. Mary Owen, "Study: Ballot Proposition Bad for Women in Michigan." *University Record,* March 14, 2005, 1, 10.

17. Susan W. Kaufmann and Anne K. Davis, *The Gender Impact of the Proposed Michigan Civil Rights Initiative* (Ann Arbor, MI: Center for the Education of Women, 2005).

18. Interview with Patricia Gumport, January 28, 2004. Gumport received her PhD in higher education from Stanford in 1987.

19. Letters to the Editor, *Social Education* 46, no. 6 (1982), 378–380.

Index